The Tyranny of Time

of Time

When 24 Hours Is Not Enough

Robert Banks

INTERVARSITY PRESS
DOWNERS GROVE, ILLINOIS 60515

To Julie who,
most of the time,
was ahead
in dealing with
the problem
of time

Published in the United States of America by InterVarsity Press, Downers Grove, Illinois,
with permission from Lancer Books, Australia.

InterVarsity Press is the book-publishing division of Inter-Varsity Christian Fellowship,
a student movement active on campus at hundreds of universities, colleges
and schools of nursing. For information about local and regional activities, write
IVCF, 233 Langdon St., Madison, WI 53703.

Distributed in Canada through InterVarsity Press, 860 Denison St., Unit 3, Markham, Ontario
L3R 4H1, Canada.

Cover photograph: Michael Goss

ISBN 0-87784-338-4
Printed in the United States of America

Library of Congress Cataloging in Publication Data

Banks, Robert J.
    The tyranny of time.

    Includes bibliographies.
    1. Time management.   2. Time management—Religious
aspects—Christianity.   I. Title.
HF5549.5.T5B36   1983   640'.43   84-28855
ISBN 0-87784-338-4

| 17 | 16 | 15 | 14 | 13 | 12 | 11 | 10 | 9 | 8 | 7 | 6 | 5 | 4 | 3 | 2 | 1 |
| 97 | 96 | 95 | 94 | 93 | 92 | 91 | 90 | 89 | 88 | 87 | 86 | 85 | | | | |

Prologue   11

The Problem: Time Lost   **15**

Part 1   The Pressure of Time Today   *17*

  1   The Scarcity of Time in Everyday Life   *18*

  2   The Victims of Time in the Wristwatch Society   *27*

Part 2   The Oppressive Effects of Time   *39*

  3   The Threat to Physical and Psychological Health   *40*

  4   The Decline in Social and Political Life   *48*

  5   The Erosion of Thought and Leisure   *57*

  6   The Undermining of Religion and Spirituality   *65*

Part 3   Dreams of an Age of Leisure   *75*

  7   The Myth of Increased Free Time   *76*

  8   The Illusion of a Timeful Society   *86*

Part 4   The Emergence of Clockwork Man   *97*

  9   Advances in the Measurement of Time   *98*

 10   Changing Attitudes to Time and Reality   *107*

11 The Industrialisation of Work and Leisure *116*

12 The Deifying and Impoverishing of Time *126*

The Solution: Time Regained **135**

Part 5 Breaking Out of the Time Prison *137*

13 The Legacy of Pre-industrial Attitudes *138*

14 The Protest of the Counter Culture *146*

15 The Limits of Time Management Principles *157*

Part 6 Toward an Ecology of Time *167*

16 Time in Judaeo-Christian Perspective *168*

17 The Outlook of the Biblical Writings *179*

18 The Contours of a Christian Attitude *190*

Part 7 Putting Time in Its Proper Place *203*

19 The Primacy of Becoming over Doing *204*

20 A Singleminded Approach to Life *213*

21 A Developing Sense of Personal and Social Rhythms *222*

Part 8 There Is a Time for Everything *231*

22 A New Quality of Family Life and Friendship *232*

23 A Revised Shape for the Church and Christian
    Organisations *242*

24 A More Relaxed Attitude to Work and Leisure *252*

Epilogue *263*

Acknowledgments

Over the three years it took me to research and write this book, many people drew my attention to ideas or materials relevant to it. I would therefore like to thank Stephen Barton, John Buchner, Daphne Campbell, David Farmer, Robert Forsyth, Chris Gardiner, Doug Hynd, David Kendall, Kim Read, Ger Reesink, as well as Dr David Millikan, Dr Bill Woolcock and Bishop Cecil Warren. Others whom I approached for help also generously gave it, especially Mal Anderson, Anthony Ashbolt, Prof. Frank Lancaster Jones, Nick Gruen and Prof. C.M. Williams.

Special assistance was given by a number of people who read and commented on individual chapters of the book, viz., Richard Begbie, Vaughan Bowie, Spencer Colliver, Dr Graham Hughes, Dr John Kleinig, Ken Rolph, Senator Baden Teague, Rev. Colin Tunbridge, Rev. Bruce Wilson. A number of these also supplied me with references to discussions on time.

At various points along the way, I was able to test out some of my findings on groups interested in the subject. Their reactions invariably caused me to think again about aspects of the problem of time or provided me with additional material on it. In this connection I want to thank those involved in several monthly Open House Discussions in our home in 1980, participants in an A.F.E.S. Graduates' Conference Seminar in Canberra, January, 1981, attenders at the Annual N.S.W. Baptist Ministers' Fraternal Conference in July, 1980, members of a cell group of O'Connor Uniting Church in July, 1981, the audience of the Forum series of talks at the Australian National University over five weeks in July/August, 1982 and the group at the Summer Institute of Linguistics Biennial Conference, Ukarumpa, Papua New Guinea in November, 1982.

I gained even more stimulus from groups meeting under the auspices of various theological institutions who gave sufficiently substantial periods of time to cover most or all of the material on time. I have in mind here the staff and students of the United Theological College, Sydney, and members of the Annual Clergy School there in August, 1980, students of Vision College, Sydney, and of the Bible College of South Australia in October, 1981 and June, 1982 respectively but most of all clergy members of the Canberra Collegium of the San Francisco Theological Seminary D.Min. programme who, between February and April, 1982 read, and in turn critiqued, each chapter of an earlier draft of the book.

I also wish to thank those individuals who responded creatively to the presentation of the material and sent me cartoons, poems, songs, hymns, etc, which crystallised their feelings, especially Freda Banks, Shirley Mitchell, Wayne and Jinnie Vincent, and the Rt. Rev. Owen Dowling. My mother, Chris Banks, did much of the typing and re-typing and Bill Woolcock, Elizabeth and Peter Yuile, Clive Monty, Charles and Doris Rowland kindly read the proofs. Jeff Blair, of Anzea Publishers, encouraged the project throughout. To all these I owe a great deal.

Finally, however, my deepest gratitude goes to Patricia Woolcock, who read the first complete draft of the MS, suggested many important stylistic changes, pointed out a number of weaknesses in argument and encouraged me to re-arrange the order. Also to Robyn Walton, then editor at Anzea Publishers, who worked painstakingly through the revised draft and managed to turn some of my stumbling English into flowing prose. She also assisted in a further re-ordering of the material. The help of both these people was invaluable at crucial stages in the book's development.

Prologue

'A person's sense of time is a way of discerning his personality. We may almost say: Tell me what you think of time and I will know what to think of you.'[1] This is quite true. Your view of time and use of it will tell me more about you, and you more about yourself, than almost anything else. Our attitude towards time is not something we take on as an extra in life, like so many other ideas or commitments. It is the framework within which our ideas and commitments come to expression. Time is the medium in which all that we see, hear, feel, imagine, think, judge and do takes place. This is why our attitude towards time will leave its imprint upon every aspect of our lives. So it is important for us to know exactly how we perceive time and whether this is a hindrance or a help to us. If our attitude is flawed, then all that we are and hope to become, along with everyone and everything we touch, will be flawed also.

There is something radically astray with our view and use of time in the West, particularly among those who are its more affluent, middle-class, urban citizens. We need to dispel various illusions we entertain about reduced working hours and the coming leisure society. And we have to face the facts about the damage we are inflicting upon ourselves by living at the pace we do. There is an alternative to our present busy lifestyle, and we do not have to drop out of society to find it. It is neither hectic nor procrastinating; neither regulated nor unorganised; neither planned nor impulsive. It does not swing between an active attitude to work and a passive approach to leisure but has a dynamic approach to both. It does not admit the gap between work and leisure as we understand them but possesses a unified conception of life. Unfortunately, the terms used in this discussion suffer from either too wide or too planned a range of meaning. Let it be clear at the outset, however, that the kind of 'time' I am interested in is not primarily the more abstract notion which scientists and philosophers, historians and theologians favour. I am concerned about the kind of time that we experience as we go about our ordinary affairs. Sadly, very few scholars ever help us to understand what is happening at this level.

When I use words like 'work' I am not only talking about what people do when they have a job. Housework, schoolwork, homework, as these words suggest, are every bit as much work as the tasks people undertake in paid employment. So are other things like shopping, mowing the lawn or running a youth club. It should be clear from the context whether I am using the word in its narrower or wider sense. I would prefer to reserve the word 'leisure' for things which contain a genuine element of fulfilment. But the term is used today as a description of anything people do in their free time. So I have had to content myself with placing it in inverted commas, or qualifying it in some way at points, rather than restricting its application.

In writing this book I have drawn upon a wide range of sources. Alongside empirical data supplied by the social sciences and historical judgments offered by historians, I have utilised the artistic impressions of writers and poets and the personal observations of ordinary people. Interwoven with these are my own intuitive perceptions and personal experiences. In some places I move from one of these to the other in fairly rapid sequence. But the transition will be either well-signalled or obvious and the reader can make up his own mind about how much weight to give to various statements. I make no apology for approaching the problem in this way. All these sources are valid ways of learning. If we have tended to disparage some at the expense of others in the modern period, that has only been to our loss. Similarly, I make no apology for borrowing insights from so-called high and low culture or for placing them side by side in the text.

I begin with a short parable and a brief anecdote. They will set the scene for all that follows. If they do this in a somewhat extreme form, let us remember Kierkegaard's insight that only if truth is cast in partially exaggerated form will it have any chance of cutting through the fog of commonplaces that assail us.

In his book *Earth Abides* George Stewart tells the following story

> 'When once they stalked the deer, or crouched shivering in the mud for the flight of ducks to alight, or risked their lives on the crags after goats, or closed in with shouts upon a wild boar at bay—that was not work, though often the breath came hard and the limbs were heavy. When the women bore and nursed children, or wandered in the woods for berries and mushrooms, or tended the fire at the entrance to the rock-shelter—that was not work either.
>
> So also, when they sang and danced and made love, that was not play. By the singing and dancing the spirits of forest and water might be placated—a serious matter, though still one might enjoy the song and the dance. And as for the making of love, by that—and by the favour of the gods—the tribe was maintained.
>
> So in the first years work and play mingled always, and there were not even the words for one against the other.
>
> But centuries flowed by and then more of them, and many things changed. Man invented civilization, and was inordinately proud of it. But in no way did civilization change life more than by sharpening the line between work and play, and at last that division came to be more important than the old one between sleeping and waking. Sleep came to be thought a kind of relaxation, and 'sleeping on the job' a heinous sin. The turning out of the light and the ringing of the alarm-clock were not so much the symbols of man's dual life as were the punching of the time-clock and the blowing of the whistle. Men marched on picket-lines and threw bricks and exploded dynamite to shift an hour from one classification to the other, and other men fought equally hard to prevent them. And always work became more laborious and odious, and play grew more artificial and febrile.'[2]

In a newspaper column I also came across a report of the following incident

Horace Whittell, a dockworker of Gillingham, England, hated his alarm clock.

Every workday for 47 years, its bell had jarred him awake. For 47 years, he had longed to ignore it. For 47 years, he had felt the pressure of time. Then he got his revenge.

On the day he retired, Mr. Whittell flattened the clock under an 80-ton hydraulic press.

"It was a lovely feeling", he said.

Footnotes

1. J.T. Fraser, *The Voices of Time* (New York: Braziller) 1966, xix.
2. George R. Stewart, *Earth Abides* (London: Gollancz, 1977) p. 190.

The Problem: Time Lost

Part 1
The Pressure of Time Today

Nothing is more characteristic of modern man than the complaint, 'If only I had time'.

R. E. Neale, **In Praise of Play: Toward a Psychology of Religion**

1

The Scarcity of Time in Everyday Life

According to one survey, almost four out of every five people in societies like our own feel continuously or regularly rushed for time.[1] In another survey, conducted in Australia recently, the main reason given by more than one-third of the respondents for not filling out a 24-hour diary of their activities was 'too busy, not enough time'.[2]

But we do not need statistics to tell us we have time problems. In homes today husbands and wives frequently pass like ships in the night as they pursue their separate interests. Parents and children rarely talk to each other in depth for more than a few minutes a day. Friends cannot always stop to chat when they meet by chance and colleagues do not often have time for more than the customary greetings, banter and farewells.

A humorous look at the problem turned up in an Australian newspaper on June 22nd. The significance of the date should not escape you.

> Look, if the Government doesn't do something about it soon, someone's going to die of a heart attack.
> I mean, I woke yesterday at the normal hour and rushed out to get the paper as usual. I don't know why I bothered; there wasn't even time to get past page three.
> I dressed like a fury and rushed into the kitchen, only to find that the kettle hadn't even boiled.

'Can't wait', I said. 'What about your toast and Vegemite?' said my wife. 'Can't wait', I said. 'You'll never get through the day without your Vegemite', she said. 'Have to go', I said.

I raced to the bus stop, but there was no bus in sight and I had no time to wait. I walked to the office, moving like the wind. I collapsed at my desk and threw myself into my work, but there just wasn't time to finish any job properly. I leapt from one thing to another, completing none of them.

I had to skip lunch because there wasn't time to queue in the sandwich shop. And I had to race up the street to the hardware store to get four of those spear things to stick on the ends of the curtain rods I'd put up in the rumpus room at the weekend. They had only three on display because the shop hadn't been restocked after the weekend rush. But I didn't have time to wait while they got another from the storeroom.

Back at work it was all go, go, go again, rushing from one task to the next and no time to finish any properly. The boss went crook, but I explained that I had no time to explain. Later, I said. Tomorrow, sir, I said, when there's more time.

After work I barely had time to finish a beer at the pub, and I certainly couldn't wait to buy my round.

I couldn't waste time queueing for the bus, so I grabbed a passing taxi, blowing my budget for the week. Still, time and tide wait for no man, let alone his money.

There wasn't time to take the dog for a walk and it seemed grossly unfair that he, poor innocent creature, should suffer from this madness, too.

I had intended to put up the spear-ends on the curtain rods when I got home, but there wasn't time. I couldn't even finish my dinner because I had to rush in and watch the telly.

And still there wasn't time to see how Sara Dane ended up because I had to race off to bed. I tossed and turned so much I began to wonder if I even had time to sleep.

'What on earth is the matter with you today?' my wife said, brushing her hair ritually as though she had all the time in the world.

'I'm utterly exhausted', I said. 'It's ridiculous. There just weren't enough hours in the day.'

'But why?' she said.

'God, you must know', I said. 'It was June 21, the shortest day of the year.'[3]

While many of us are reasonably well off financially, with respect to time almost all of us are paupers. Everywhere you look, time is

in increasingly short supply. We all feel the pinch in this area and
spend a good deal of our time complaining about it. How often
have you heard yourself, or others, saying one of the following? If
only I had the time ... There's never enough time, is there? ... I
don't know where the time goes ... But how do you find the time?
... I'm hardpressed for time at present ... The time gets away from
you, doesn't it? ... I'll try to find time ... Is that the time already?
... My, how the time flies! ... Could you fit in time? ... I don't
even get time to think! ... Mustn't waste time, must we? ... I just
ran out of time.

We have a wide range of other expressions as well: I haven't
got a moment to spare ... There are never enough hours in the day
... We always seem to be 'on the go' ... There's always so much to
do ... I never seem to stop! ... We're flat out at the moment ... I've
just got to rush ... The week's simply flown! ... Back to the
treadmill ... On with the rat-race ... No rest for the wicked ... and
the revealing invitation: You must come around *some time*.

Jim Croce lamented in one of his songs: 'there never seems
enough time for all the things you want to do'. And according to
Kenneth Slessor:

> There's not a moment I can call my own—
> My clocks, my keys, my wheels and instruments
> And that fierce Ethiop, the telephone.
> No doubt it's very charming out in the sun,
> But there are other things you know. In any case,
> I've got no time, no time. There's much to be done ...[4]

Less poetically, a character in *Airport 77* exclaims: 'A week behind
schedule? So what! The whole world's a week behind schedule.'
For time, as the urban poet Bruce Dawe more soberly puts it, 'is
the one thing fearfully dwindling'.[5]

The pace of life

There seems to be general agreement that life is more hectic than it
once was. Our conversation is laced with phrases which convey
the haste endemic in modern society. Along with the expressions
mentioned earlier, note the way we talk of the 'peak' or 'rush'
hour, the way we are always telling our children to 'hurry up' or

'get a move on', and the way words like 'urgent' and 'priority' recur in business and even family life. There was a time when telegrams were considered adequate for sending sudden news, but now they are frequently considered too slow and so we have 'urgent' as well as 'ordinary' telegrams. There is also a fascination with speed in our society. We are constantly being reminded how much faster a car can accelerate to a given number of kph, how much more quickly one can travel between two points, how often records are being broken. We are always trying to find the shortest way of going somewhere, the fastest way of doing something, the quickest way of contacting someone. Speed is considered one of the chief virtues in our society. As the title song in *Thoroughly Modern Millie* runs: 'Everything today is thoroughly modern ... Everything today makes yesterday slow'.

Alvin Toffler pointed out in his bestseller *Future Shock* that many social processes are speeding up,[6] and it is easy to understand why so many conventions, conferences, seminars and meetings choose as their theme 'The Challenge of Change'. It is no wonder either that politicians, executives, academics, doctors and others find they cannot keep up with developments taking place in their fields. To take just one illustration of rapid change: the range of available goods and services doubles every 15 or so years. Daniel Bell, one of the foremost social thinkers today, comments:

> Today, not only are we aware of trying to identify processes of change ... but there has been a speeding up of the 'time machine', so that the intervals between the initial forces of change and their application have been radically reduced. Perhaps the most important social change of our time is a process of direct and deliberate contrivance. Men now seek to anticipate change, measure the course of its direction and its impact, control it, and even shape it for predetermined ends.[7]

The feeling that things are moving faster is combined at times with a strong suspicion that change is out of control. According to one historian, 'Nothing defines our age more than the furious and relentless increase in the rate of change ... [This] has been the

primary shaping force in the development of the modern consciousness.'[8] A theologian recognises that 'today, in a century of
technology and speed, the problem of time has become particularly acute'.[9] A cultural critic muses on how odd it is 'that a
century which should, by all rights, be the most leisurely in all
history is also known to be, and condemned for being, the
fastest'.[10] A philosopher comments: 'In the past the time-span of
important change was considerably longer than that of a single
human life … Today this time-span is considerably shorter … and
accordingly our training must prepare individuals to face a novelty
of situations'.[11] Finally, a poet portrays the inner turmoil created
by rapid change when he says:

> My heart beating, my heart running,
> The light brimming,
> My mind moving, the ground turning,
> My eyes blinking, the air flowing,
> The clock's quick-ticking,
> Time moving, time dying,
> Time perpetually perishing …[12]

The regulation of society

In his short story *Chronopolis*, J.G. Ballard postulates a society
excessively concerned with the effects of traffic accidents. In order
to prevent injuries and fatalities taking place, the whole society
becomes governed by a detailed timetable. The hope is that by
regulating every detail of every person's life the problem will be
overcome. In another novel, *We* by Y. Zamiatin, the narrator lives
in a world in which everything is dominated by time. So
scheduled are his activities that he looks back on our society as a
relatively casual one in which ordinary people could decide to go
for a walk or make love almost whenever they liked.

Yet in some areas of life we are already well on the way to the
conditions these writers depict. Many workers are virtually
strait-jacketed by the clock. An airline reservations clerk inter-
viewed by Studs Terkel recounted the differences made by the
coming of the computer:

> You were allowed no more than three minutes on the tele-
> phone. You had twenty seconds, 'busy-out' time it was called,

to put the information in. Then you had to be available for another phone call. It was almost like a production line. We adjusted to the machine. The casualness, the informality that had been there previously were no longer there. They monitored you and listened to your conversations. If you were a minute late for work it went on your file. You took thirty minutes for lunch, not thirty-one! If you got a break you took ten minutes, not eleven! I was on eight tranquillisers a day. With the airline I had no free will. I was just part of that stupid computer.[13]

But the problem already begins at school. The newsletter of an independent school in a large Australian city describes the average day of a primary school child. I have italicised those references that reflect the undue concern with time that so characterises modern life. The majority of these have to do with regulation by the clock.

For the third morning *in succession* Peter rose *early*. He had the best part of *an hour's travel* ahead of him and he had arranged to meet several of his classmates on the school court for a *7.30* game of tennis. Competition to be first on the court was keen so he knew he had *little time to waste*. When he arrived at school he heard some of his friends *already* on the court so he *ran* through the undercover area of the ... wing and was *soon* involved in the game.

Today, however, he had to leave the tennis *early* to attend an *8.15* choir practice. Peter was a member of the 'Selected Voices' choir which was being prepared for entry with the City of Sydney Eisteddfod held early in Third Term. This *tight and demanding* rehearsal ended at *8.45* and Peter *ran* to take his books to his classroom, change into school shoes and collect his hymn book for Assembly. The bell rang at *8.50* and the school of 440 boys gathered in class groups on the Quadrangle before moving into the Assembly Hall ...

Peter's classes started at *9.40*. He had a Maths test first period and as the end-of-term tests were *not far off* he was anxious to do well. He completed the test by *10.30* and was satisfied that he had done his best. *Period 3* saw Peter's class leave their classroom for Science and this took him through until Morning Break, which allowed for *twenty minutes* of 'British Bulldog'.

Immediately after Break, Peter had Music and he joined his class in the Music Room and *Period 4*, the last before Lunch, saw him back in his 'home room' for English — the end-of-week Spelling and Dictation test. The Lunch bell rang at *12.20* and Peter joined his friends on the Quadrangle.

As soon as the ice-block bell sounded, Peter knew that he had *15 minutes* to return an *overdue* library book and to check out another from his reading list before Orchestra rehearsal. He had been learning the violin at school since Third Class and had been a member of the School Orchestra *since the beginning* of this year. The concentration required of him during Orchestra was *as intense, if not more intense,* as that expected of him during classes. The end-of-lunch bell did not affect the rehearsal which continued until *2 pm,* the end of *Period 5.* The last two periods went *quickly:* Craft classes held in the Art Room in this period were a particular favourite with Peter—and the final period of the day (of the week, he reminded himself) was spent in his classroom on reading skills. The bell rang at *3 pm.*

Amid the loud good wishes for tomorrow's game and for a pleasant weekend, the noisy, *rapid* movement of small boys leaving the school, Peter knew he had *fifteen minutes* in which to change and be on the field ready for Rugby practice.

His goodbyes and packing-up were *swift* and he headed for the ... House changing room. By *3.30* he was *fully involved* in Rugby. It was to be an important game tomorrow, played against traditionally strong opponents. The practice was hard with the coach drilling skills and new moves for set play. It ended by *4.30* but, *by the time* the coach had finished speaking to his team, it was closer to *a quarter to five.* Peter changed and walked to the station with a few team members. He caught the *5.30* train.

He arrived home at *6.30.* He showered, changed and began his homework. Among other things, he had his History project to finish—he was *not up to date* with this work and he had to find *extra time* to catch up. He was soon called for the evening meal, during which his father asked him, *'What did you do at school today, son?'*

'Nothing much.'

Considering that we are looking here at only one day in the life of a young person, it is apparent how early some children's activities are regulated by the clock. The example I have cited is mild compared to life in an institution such as St Paul's Cathedral School in London. As a recent BBC TV documentary showed, even at weekends there were programmed and daily schedules dominated by the clock to an even greater degree. Most of us may not feel the intrusion of the clock to anything like the same extent as in these examples. Watches, clocks and other measuring devices do pervade our lives, however, to an alarming degree. Symptomatically the watch stays on our wrists both at work and away from it. It is there for reference during holidays as much as the rest of the year. In fact, all year round: 'we get up, work, eat, sleep, play, visit and, in short, live by what time the clock tells us. We are encased by the time and tempo demands of our mechanical creation.'[14]

Conclusion

It is the combination of this regulation by the clock and our corresponding pace of life that gives rise to our sense of the scarcity of time. It is because our days are too full and because they move too fast that we seem never quite to catch up with ourselves. Not everyone experiences this to the same degree. Some are better off than others. Much depends on where you live, who you are and what you do. In the following chapter we shall go on to identify those who are worst hit by the time problem.

Footnotes

1. This 1965–66 American study is cited in J.P. Robinson, *How Americans Use Time: A Social-Psychological Analysis of Everyday Behaviour* (New York: Praeger, 1977) p. 133.

2. *Australians' Use of Time: A Contribution to Social Planning and Urban Use Design* (Canberra: Cities Commission, 1975) p. 7.

3. Des Colquhoun, *Adelaide Advertiser* (June 22nd, 1982). He was, of course, a day out in his reckoning, as his wife went on to point out in the column.

4. See K. Slessor, 'Crustacean's Rejoinder', *Selected Poems* (Sydney: Angus and Robertson, 1977) p. 103.

5. B. Dawe, 'The Family Man', *Selected Poems* (Sydney: Angus and Robertson, 1971) p. 47.

6. Cf. A. Toffler, *Future Shock* (London: Pan, 1970) p. 29.

7. D. Bell, *The Coming of Post-Industrial Society: An Essay in Social Forecasting* (New York: Basic Books, 1973) p. 345.

8. A. Schlesinger Jnr, 'The Modern Consciousness and the Winged Chariot', in S. Gorman and A.E. Wessmann (eds.), *The Personal Experience of Time* (New York: Plenum, 1977) p. 269.

9. N. Berdyaev, *Solitude and Society* (London: Bles, 1938) p. 109.

10. W. Kerr, *The Decline of Pleasure* (New York: Simon and Schuster, 1965) p. 39. See also P. Valèry, *The Outlook for Intelligence* (New York: Harper, 1963) p. 167.
11. A.N. Whitehead, *Adventures of Ideas* (Harmondsworth: Pelican, 1933) p. 94.
12. D. Schwartz, 'Time's Dedication', *What Is to be Given: Selected Poems* (Manchester: Carcanet, 1976) p. 38.
13. S. Terkel, *Working: People Talk About What They Do All Day and How They Feel About What They Do* (London: Wildwood House, 1975) pp. 76, 77.
14. P. Lee, *Religion and Leisure in America: A Study in Four Dimensions* (Nashville: Abingdon, 1964) p. 209.

2

The Victims of Time
in the Wristwatch Society

Not all people are equally caught up by today's hectic pace of life. Those most severely affected belong to the newer Western societies, live in urban areas and come from the middle-class white collar bracket. Professional groups, working women with children and clergy are particularly badly off.

The new Western societies

People in young Western societies such as Canada, the United States and Australia have felt the impact of time pressures more than those in the older civilizations of Europe. Initially the one thing in abundant supply in the new lands was space. In the established societies cramped physical conditions prevented people from enjoying much freedom of movement and as an alternative they sought to keep free time relatively unpressured. In places like North America, this position was reversed. There, possession of land gave settlers room for personal expression. Time tended to be absorbed, channelled, exploited in the pursuit of space.[1]

This is why the American, in particular, 'has always been short of time! And not time only in the sense of hours to do things in'.[2] In this connection it is interesting to note that 'time-budget' studies in Europe have tended to classify activities differently to those conducted in America. The latter work on a clocktime

reckoning system, the former on the recurrence of cycles with
common elements, eg, eating and sleeping.[3] This reflects the
differing value still placed on time in the Old World and the New,
despite the increasing blurring of divergences between the two.
Australians have mostly clustered in coastal enclaves, despite
all the wide-open spaces at their back door. Yet the desire for
more space still exercises a strong appeal and, in some measure,
time seems to have been sacrificed to the need for space. A
preference for the quarter-acre suburban block, despite the
increased time travelling to and from work, is one example of this.
Australians' desire for space helps explain the continuing
popularity of caravanning, the lure of the 'weekender' somewhere
in the mountains or on the coast, the phenomenon of the
get-away-from-it-all long weekend. In differing degrees all these
require a fairly intensive use of time, especially in travelling, when
people could be taking it easy and relaxing. Australia may be 'the
Timeless Land', as novelist Eleanor Dark calls it, but only for its
Aboriginal, rarely for its White, inhabitants.

The urban areas
In his great autobiographical poem 'The Prelude', William Words
worth writes of the impression made upon him by the turbulent
atmosphere of London after the peace and solitude of the Lake
District. The great metropolis is like:

> [a] monstrous ant-hill on the plain
> Of a too busy world. Before me flow,
> Thou endless stream of living things!
> Thy every-day appearance, as it strikes—
> With wonder heightened, or sublimed by awe—
> On strangers, of all ages; the quick dance,
> Of colours, lights and forms; the deafening din;
> The comers and the goers face to face,
> Face after face; the string of dazzling wares,
> Shop after shop, with symbols, blazoned names ...[4]

A century later the Australian 'bush' poet A. 'Banjo' Paterson, in
his ballad 'Clancy of the Overflow', commented wryly and more
colloquially on the difference between these two worlds, this time
with the young but bustling city of Sydney in mind:

And in place of lowing cattle, the fiendish rattle
Of the tramways and the buses making hurry down the street;
And the language uninviting of the gutter children fighting
Comes fitfully and faintly through the ceaseless tramp of feet.
And the people hurrying daunt me, and their pallid faces haunt me
As they shoulder one another in their rush and nervous haste,
With their eager eyes and greedy, and their stunted forms and weedy,
For *townsfolk have no time to grow, they have no time to waste.*[5]

Surveys of time use in city and rural areas bear out the truth of these impressions. Country people in larger Australian towns devote one hour less a day to working and travelling to work than residents of the big cities. They also have more time for social and recreational activities.[6] Between five and six of every ten city dwellers would prefer to live in a smaller city or town because of the friendlier relationships and less hectic life they think exist there.[7] Such surveys apart, anyone who has had much to do with country folks knows that their commonest complaint on visiting or moving to the city is that city people don't have time to stop and talk. Even visitors from a small city often comment on the fact that people in large cities or metropolises walk faster, so accustomed have the latter become to a busier manner of life.

The middle-class

In the cities it is those who belong to the middle-classes who are most caught up in the time vortex. Since the interests of this upwardly mobile group are linked to the social and economic changes taking place in society, these people tend more than others to co-operate with the forces of change or move along almost insensibly in their wake. They are future-oriented and tend to have many plans, expectations and goals for themselves and their children. Sociologist George Gurvitch remarks: 'the middle-classes are harassed by the chaos of social times in which they live. They are prey to the perpetual fear of the social times confronting them. There are no other collectivities which are less able to master their time ... than the groups which are designated as "middle-classes".'[8]

Upper income groups have a more past-dominated outlook, while the lower classes are more present-oriented; neither group is so likely to be carried along by the accelerating forces of change. One has an anchor which enables it to partially hold against the tide; the other dips in and out of it, enjoying what it offers but little interested in its ultimate destination.

Among those exhibiting middle-class attitudes, some groups suffer more than others from the modern scarcity of time and velocity of change: people in managerial or senior positions in the private and public spheres, and members of the professions. De Grazia estimated that two-thirds of all business executives he studied brought work home at night or over the weekend. In addition they spent considerable amounts of time entertaining at home and travelling on business. He concluded that this kind of person 'has little free time, perhaps the least of all'.[9]

The high-level technocrat or bureaucrat is no better off. Every public servant knows that the higher levels of the Service bring not only increased financial rewards and status but also interrupted lunch-times, longer hours at work, invasion of privacy at home and more trips away from the family. Gurvitch claims the techno-bureaucratic groupings, among which he includes economic planners, industrial engineers and technical experts as well as public servants, 'are victims of an illusion: they imagine themselves living in a time ahead of itself or even in an explosive time of creation which they think they alone know how to dominate'.[10] In reality, he says, they frequently fail to understand the significance of the times they live in and are simply carried along in the wake of the forces of change about them.

Well-established members of the professions often experience a serious shortage of time and have an inadequate grasp of the times in which they live. Quite apart from any extra official or public responsibilities they might have, medical practitioners in Australia work almost half as long again as the average person.[11] Lawyers are probably in much the same position.

In universities and colleges, academic staff participate in administration, run courses, undertake specialised research and cope with heavier teaching workloads because of staff reductions;

all these factors mean longer hours, especially at the professorial and sub-professorial level. A 1978 survey showed that two-thirds of the 2,000 academics sampled felt they were busier than two years previously; more than one-third said they worked over 41 hours per week; almost one-sixth worked more than 60 hours per week; and about 1 in 10 worked up to 100 hours per week.[12] There is, in fact, an 'academic rat-race which is every bit as vicious as the commercial kind'.[13]

Then there are politicians, some of whom rank among the most over-worked members of our society. Moving hurriedly from city to city, meeting to meeting, or crisis to crisis, they have few pauses for rest, privacy and reflection. This is particularly true at the Cabinet level, as a recent book, Can Ministers Cope?, forcefully brings out.[14]

Working women with children to look after and/or marriage partners work long hours. While on average they work about 2 hours less a week than men in paid employment, and travel about 1 hour less per week to and from work, they still bear the brunt of household responsibilities and children's upbringing.[15] Most manage by devoting much less time to housework,[16] and by asking their husbands to help out a little more around the home. Even the few top-level working women manage, fairly successfully it seems, to fulfil their household responsibilities.[17] Working women have less free time at night than either working men or full-time housewives, while at weekends they expend more energy in supporting charitable organisations, worthy causes and the like. So both during the week and at weekends they tend to be more involved outside the home and to have less time just for themselves. No wonder a report on Australians' use of time spoke of 'the harried existence of the working wife'.[18] An earlier cross-cultural study of time expenditure in 12 countries concluded that 'the plight of the employed woman pervades all of our time-budget records'.[19] In concentrating on the plight of working women, however, we should not overlook the fact that women at home who have several children under pre-school age, particularly if their husbands work long hours or have a second job and their wider family is no longer close enough to give assistance, are also in a high pressured situation with respect to their time.

How vulnerable are Christians?

With respect to time, Christians are a good deal worse off than many. This is especially the case if they live in a large city, belong to the middle-classes, have managerial or professional positions, or combine outside employment with substantial household responsibilities.

Christians and people raised in a Christian setting tend to take their work more seriously than others.[20] They also place a high value on family obligations. And they are often in the forefront of community and charitable associations. The upshot of this commitment to work, community and family is, as my eldest son commented: 'Christians are like trains—always on the move, always in a rush, and always *late!*'

Over and above their obligations at work, home and in the community, Christians have heavy demands placed upon them by their local churches and Christian organisations. There are Sunday schools to be staffed, youth fellowships to be run, sidesmen's and flower rosters to be filled. There are Bible studies, prayer meetings and charismatic fellowships to attend, men's and women's societies to join, the parish council and other committees on which to serve. Not to speak of houseparties, conferences, theological and Christian education courses, scripture and missionary meetings, evangelistic rallies and ecumenical get-togethers, visitation programs and social action groups. It is not uncommon to find three or four evenings a week taken up with such activities, and most of Sunday as well. Some local churches even boast that every night of the week they have something to which their members can come! In such cases the church announcements take nearly as much time as the sermon. As Mr. Bundle, the 'Christian gentleman' in the 1940s Australian radio serial *Mrs 'Obbs*, used to lament, there is always 'so much to do and so little time to do it in'.

Without doubt it is the clergy—and their spouses—who are most seriously affected. Indeed one of the main reasons for clergy busyness is the multi-faceted character of their role. Probably no other person in our society is the focus of as many expectations from as many people as the local minister. Torn between conflicting obligations and moving in several directions at once, subject to conflicting demands from parishioners, superiors and his or her own conscience, doubting whether his achievements amount to very much at all, the pastor of the typical church is often the most harried of people. It is not surprising that in a recent survey of ministers one of the commonest complaints was lack of time: 'Many said there was insufficient time to do everything they felt should be done or, in fact, to do anything properly'.[21] The hours most clergy work and the pressures associated with their work are abnormally high. In a city church to which I was attached some years ago, the three clergymen on the staff each worked over 80 hours per week. Similar hours are worked by many theological students. The startling increase in divorce rates, nervous breakdowns and premature deaths within the clergy group, and the growth in the number of men leaving the ministry, in large part stem from these strains.[22] It would probably be true to say that the clergyman or clergywoman is the busy person *par excellence* of our times; his or her life more than anyone else's exhibits the desperate shortage of time and accelerating pace of life that have become characteristic of our age.

It is not surprising then that Australian poet Douglas Stewart should deduce, as the title of one of his poems runs, that 'Heaven is a busy place':

> Heaven is a busy place.
> Those in a state of grace
> Continually twanging the harp.
> And Court at eight-thirty sharp.
> Did he do ill or well,
> Shall he be sent to hell
> That scoundrel in the dock?
> The great black Judgment Book
> Says nothing good of him;
> Weeping of seraphim.
>
> Twanging the harp and mourning.
> Three more, a score for burning,

And always, if not the best,
Those of most interest.
And then the deputations—
Bishops for their congregations,
Relations and friends of cherubs,
Mahomet and all those Arabs ...
Arrival with knocking knees
Of sixty thousand Chinese.

Incessant tinkle of strings.
And rain for Alice Springs
Now seven years in arrears.
Such multifarious cares,
Sparrows to be watched as they fall,
Elephants, ants and all,
To the egg of the frog in the slime.
Then wind up the clock of time,
Douse the red sun in the deep,
Put the cat on the moon, and sleep.

Sir, I would make my petitions:
Love and fulfilled ambition;
Some friends to be partly protected,
Some enemies grossly afflicted,
And, if I rise no higher,
A place at least by the fire.
But earth is a busy planet
And, failing the timely minute,
I found it best to postpone,
Do as well as I could on my own.

Now I have found a place
Where in their twisted grace
Soft-footed mangroves glide,
Fishing the green of the tide
With net and club and spear:
And all is so silent here
Lying by the gum-tree's root
I listen to a beetle's foot
Loud as a midnight thief
Crash on a fallen leaf.

If in the heavenly clime
They share such gaps in time,
Here if ever is the place
And the chance to state one's case.

> But I must return a favour:
> Life has a lovely flavour
> And now there is time to waste
> Now there is time to taste
> (I think I shall not intrude)
> Heaven is finding it good.[23]

Conclusion

We have seen that it is certain groups amongst the middle-class urban members of highly industrialised countries who are hardest hit by the time problem. It is pre-eminently those people whom I am addressing in this book. I am aware that there are others within Western societies who do not have this problem at all, or at least do not appear to do so. I am thinking of the unemployed, the disadvantaged and the prematurely retired. Their problem is that they have too much time on their hands. They feel they do not have enough to do. I am concerned about such people. In my own way I am attempting to do something to alleviate and alter their situation. Fortunately, a reasonable amount of attention is being directed to their predicament, among Christian thinkers, groups and activists as well as among others. But very little attention is being directed to those who have too little time. Yet the problems are related. The internal drives and external mechanisms that produce the time-scarce condition are the selfsame ones that produce its opposite. Overemployment of some people's time and underemployment of others' are inextricably linked. In coming to terms with the causes of the one, therefore, we also begin to understand better the causes of the other.

Footnotes

1. See further S. Mead, 'The American People: Their Space, Time and Religion', *Journal of Religion* (34, 1954) pp. 244–245.
2. J. Sittler, 'Space and Time in American Religious Experience', *Interpretation* (30, 1, 1976) p. 48. The full article is worth reading for the light it throws on this phenomenon. See too A.J. Heschel, *The Sabbath: Its Meaning for Modern Man* (New York: Farrar, Straus and Co., 1951) p. 5.

3. Cf. R.L. Rotenberg, *The Social Organisation of Time in Complex Societies: A Case Study from Vienna, Austria* (Ph.D., University of Massachusetts, 1978) p. 45.

4. W. Wordsworth, *The Prelude*, Book VII, 149–158 in the Harmondsworth (Penguin, 1971) edition, pp. 259–261.

5. In D. Stewart (ed.), *The Wide Brown Land and Other Verse* (Sydney: Angus and Robertson, 1971) pp. 14–15 (italics mine).

6. See *Australians' Use of Time* p. 14, quoted earlier. For American figures, in which the difference is less marked, see J.P. Robinson, *op.cit.*, pp. 91–96.

7. The figures come from a Saulwick Poll conducted on behalf of *The Sydney Morning Herald* and associate papers in July and August 1978, and the reasons for the earlier report quoted in the previous footnote.

8. G. Gurvitch, *The Spectrum of Social Time* (Dordrecht: Reidel, 1964) p. 100.

9. S. de Grazia, *Of Time, Work and Leisure* (New York: Doubleday, 1964) p. 130. A survey of businessmen in the late 'sixties showed that the average American executive worked 67 hours per week. See 'Executive Workloads: The Triumph of Trivia', *The Wall Street Journal* (13th August, 1968).

10. G. Gurvitch, *op.cit.*, p. 102.

11. In 1979, fifty-six hours a week according to figures cited in *The Canberra Times* (26th February, 1980).

12. See the report in *The National Times* (20th–25th January, 1980).

13. M. Thornton, *The Future of Theology* (London: Hodder and Stoughton, 1969) p. 49.

14. P. Weller and M. Grattan, *Can Ministers Cope?* (Sydney: Hutchinson, 1981).

15. On travelling time see the report *Australians' Use of Time* p. 67. Other figures come from the *Official Year Book of Australia* (Canberra: A.B.S., Vol. 63, 1979).

16. *Australians' Use of Time* p. 34.

17. See (ed.) D. Weir, *Men and Work in Modern Britain: An Introductory Reader* (London: Collins, 1973) p. 46.

18. See p. 33 and figures listed on pp. 17, 34.

19. J.P. Robinson, P.E. Converse and A. Szalai, 'Everyday Life in Twelve Cities' in A. Szalai, *The Use of Time* (The Hague: Mouton, 1972) p. 119. Employed women themselves are 'most likely to complain about always being rushed'. Cf. J.P. Robinson, *op.cit.*, p. 133.

20. For example, university students with religious affiliations generally score better than their peers who in every other respect are identical with them, at least according to an unpublished survey I carried out at Macquarie University, Sydney, during the late 'seventies.

21. See N. Blaikie, *The Plight of the Australian Clergy* (St. Lucia: University of Queensland Press, 1979) p. 161. On the connection between this and the reasons clergy give for abandoning the ministry see further comments on p. 219.

22. See D. and V. Mace, *What's Happening to Clergy Marriages?* (New York: Abingdon, 1980) pp. 61–71.

23. D. Stewart, 'Heaven is a Busy Place', *The Penguin Book of Modern Australian Verse*, J. Thompson, K. Slessor and R.G. Howarth (eds.) (Harmondsworth: Penguin, 1961) pp. 178–179.

OUR LAND Metre 76.76.D
(Tune: King's Lynn)

'The timeless land' we call it:
beyond the scraggy back
of town and holding paddock,
hoarding and railway track;
beleaguered time still holds us
impatient in its grasp;
the timeless one eludes us,
we're blinded by our task.

'The heathen in his blindness
bows down to wood and stone';
the modern Christian worker
is slave to door and' phone;
the diary his bible
to guide the daily plan,
dispensing or refusing
the love of God for man.

The land can still enchant us
and open out our mind;
there's room for harried spirits
by time and space confined.
Spirit of God disturb us,
our fettered order sure,
teach us the love that covers
the universe, and more.

Our lives are all time-shackled,
programmed and set in place,
and scarcely ever able
to apprehend your grace;
our spirits want the freedom
the risen Christ can give:
a space for timeless praying,
a land of spacious praise.

Owen Dowling

Part 2
The Oppressive Effects of Time

The clock represents an element of mechanical tyranny in the lives of modern man more potent than any individual exploiter or any other machine.
G. A. Woodcock, 'The Tyranny of the Clock', An Introduction to Social Science

3

The Threat to Physical
and Psychological Health

Our modern hustle and bustle places us in the grip of what Swiss psychologist Paul Tournier calls 'universal fatigue'. This fatigue has reached epidemic proportions in the West. People are constantly complaining about how tired they feel. They feel tired when they get up in the morning, tired at the office or around the house during the day, tired at home in the evenings, tired at times on weekends or even during holidays. You see this tiredness in children at school, or in students at university and college, as much as in their elders.

Where does this 'universal fatigue' come from? It has many sources, among them the tension created by the shifting values in modern society, the frustration that arises from industrial and bureaucratic regulation, and the loneliness that exists in our great urban conurbations. But in the first instance it stems from the compulsive drive of modern life.[1] The sheer pace at which we live and work, and the rate of change taking place around us, result in a growing weariness on all sides. This has an effect upon both our bodies and our nerves. Its consequences in these areas arise not only from our haste and regulation by the clock but also indirectly from the impact these have upon other aspects of our lives that we shall now go on to examine.

Effects upon our bodies
We have less time for meals than we once did, and we do not always have them when we should. We cook the wrong foods, or

the right foods in the wrong way, to save time. We fail to give ourselves time to properly digest what we have eaten. Meals are sandwiched between other activities or, as with the 'business lunch', become the means to some end. We fit eating in when there is a gap, or when our work schedule insists we stop to eat, not when we feel hungry. Meals are all too often 'grabbed' or 'snatched', drinks are 'downed' and food 'bolted'. We no longer 'partake' of meals but abruptly 'have' them, and there are always 'fast-food' stores to help us along. Artificial products and artificially preserved foods take over our cupboards and refrigerators. Harmful additives are mixed into natural foods to extend their supermarket 'shelf life'. All this impairs our health and capacity to cope.

There is also less time for exercise. In suburbia almost everything is done by car—even minor trips like going to the corner shop. It never occurs to some people to walk when they can drive. And since in parts of suburbia there are no footpaths anyway, this possibility does not appear to have occurred to urban planners either! Bicycle riding is happily on the increase, but only a small minority are involved. Despite widespread community agreement that in view of the growing energy problem private car use should fall, it is clear that most Australians do not practise what they preach. Where exercise is undertaken, time-intensive forms are most popular. Participants try to extract the maximum benefit in the shortest period of time. Exercise classes, jogging, squash and the 'exercise bicycle' come into their own here. It is certainly better to engage in these than to get no exercise at all. For sedentary professionals such as managers, judges, lawyers and doctors the premature death rate is nearly six times higher than for people in physically active jobs such as farming and mining.[2] We should recognise, however, that too great a dependence on intensive exercise tends to produce as much time pressure as the work it is designed to balance.

Relaxation also suffers in modern society. Not only do many have less time for relaxing but some find themselves incapable of it. Studies suggest that people returning from work need up to an hour to unwind before they can genuinely relax. At weekends many find it difficult to slow down for any period of time at all. They simply cannot sit still. Unable to break the work cycle, they find one thing after another to do. When holidays come they spend up to half their time 'winding down' into a more normal state, and much of the remainder winding up again for the job. (Note how much clock language has affected our way of speaking here!) Once upon a time people could play, read and drive for enjoyment, appreciating those things for themselves. Now such activities are a kind of work. All too frequently we read only for profit, play only for exercise, and drive only to see how many kilometres we can clock up.[3] 'Relaxation' has become almost entirely a means to some end.

Sleep is also affected. As the rising use of sleeping pills indicates, insomnia is one of the commonest problems of our age. People allow less time for sleep and are less able to sleep when they try to settle down. 'It seems as if our hectic daylight hours make it increasingly difficult to utilize the hours set aside for rest. The same hectic pressure of life then cruelly squeezes the sufferer from bed in the morning'.[4] Full, uninterrupted dreaming is crucial for our psychological well-being, and lack of sleep contains more dangers than are immediately noticeable.[5] Once again general health and ability to cope suffer. Attempts to gain time by neglecting the maintenance of our bodies yield only short-term advantages.

Further problems arise from disregard of our biological rhythms and the natural rhythms of our environment. While within limits we can carry on our lives independently of these rhythms, we do not have a great deal of room for manoeuvre unless we are willing to risk serious impairment of health.[6] There are daily, monthly, seasonal and annual rhythms which we should be aware of and attuned to. There are also smaller rhythms which should guide the way we structure our activities. For example, we work best if our time is divided into units of about three hours and we take a break every hour-and-a-half or so. Circadian or twenty-four-hour rhythms are important. People who choose or are forced to ignore these inevitably suffer. Shift workers, for instance, are more vulnerable to physical and marital breakdowns than other groups in society.[7] Jet travellers who fail to ease, over several days, into or out of the time changes they undergo are more likely to catch colds and infections.[8] Students who disrupt their meal and sleep patterns around exam times run a greater risk of falling ill. So far as monthly rhythms are concerned, we are all aware how the menstrual cycle affects women, emotionally as well as physically, but few realise that to a lesser extent men are similarly affected. While as yet there is little proof that humans undergo seasonal changes as other animals do—though note associations between spring and romance, and observations that mental breakdowns increase during the winter months—many inexplicable changes in our moods, emotions and attitudes may stem from seasonal fluctuations. We tend to mark out annual patterns for ourselves, instinctively sensing their appropriateness. All this goes to show that our health depends upon integrating our personal time structures with those in the world about us.

Effects on our nerves
The speed at which we operate threatens our psychological equilibrium as well as our physical health. Many psychological problems arise because we live at a pace dissonant with our inner needs. For example, aspiring to undeviating performance at work, and expecting consistent behaviour in the people around us, we ignore the ups and downs of our psychological make-up in favour of measuring ourselves and others against some unrealistic norm. Also, coveting the affluence which machines can bring, we conform to social scheduling which is economically efficient but not humanly beneficial. When we become distressed and unhappy at the pace of urban life, we think it is our own fault. City life has created a new kind of patient, the person who cannot identify one single event as a source of their psychological problems. As G.G. Luce says:

> Stress may not be an event. Illness may result from the cumulative impact of the environment rather than from a specific factor. Today the signs of stress are everywhere, in the polluted air, the din of cities, the crowding, pressure, violence and economic insecurity. But for most individuals the [most] difficult aspect of life is probably the rate of change.[9]

There are many ways in which the speed of life places us under stress. Take the many machines which demand rapid responses. When driving a car in a metropolitan area we face a proliferation of signs, lights and special lanes as well as a large number of other vehicles. The driver has more and more information to process in less and less time. Not only does this lead to a higher accident rate but few drivers appear to realise that this over-stimulus, particularly when it involves a close call, takes its toll upon the nervous system. It is not surprising that many people returning by car from work find they cannot sit down to a meal immediately upon arriving home—they 'don't feel like eating yet'. There is such a thing as 'car-lag', too! Studies show the degree of stress felt at work is related to the amount of time spent travelling to and from work. Although the problems of travel may become so familiar that the individual eventually ceases to notice them, a psychic cost is involved: the ability to cope with other problems during the day is reduced.[10]

All of us these days, from housewives to executives, are forced to multiply the number of roles we play and increase the number of decisions we make. Think, for example, of 'managers plagued by demands for rapid, incessant and complex decisions; pupils deluged with facts and hit with repeated tests; housewives confronted with squalling children, jangling telephones, broken washing machines, the wail of rock and roll from the teenager's living-room and the whine of the television set … It is more than possible that some of the symptoms noted among battle-stressed soldiers, disaster victims, and culture-shocked travellers are related to this kind of information overload'.[11] To some extent all of us carry the psychological scars that such increased demands leave.

The difficulty is exacerbated by the fact that more people than ever before are switching jobs, moving house and changing partners. Increasing mobility enlarges the number of major situations which we have to deal with and hastens the speed with which we have to come to terms with them. The rate of change in a person's life is generally predictive of future health.[12] Serious illness and psychological instability frequently follow within a year of major change.

Conclusion

The message in all this is clear: change carries with it a heavy physical and psychological price tag, one that increases along with the modern pace of life. Matthew Arnold foresaw all this a century ago:

> For what wears out the life of mortal man?
> 'Tis that from change to change, their being rolls;
> 'Tis that repeated shocks, again, again,
> Exhaust the energy of the strongest souls
> And numb the elastic powers.[13]

Our bodies and feelings know this, even if our minds and imaginations do not. They have their own solution to the problem, independently of whether we think we can survive or even control what is happening around us. They force us to stop, right here in the present, by refusing to function any further. When they can't cope any longer with the demands made upon them, when the overload becomes too great, their only course of action is to shut everything down. For many people, physical or nervous breakdown is the only way out of the impasse. Paradoxically, it is actually a healthy response to the problem, for it springs from a deep-seated cry that 'enough is enough'. It has its basis in a well-based intuition that the present state of affairs is too absurd to be allowed to continue. In fact it is a last-ditch way of gaining time so that there is some hope of finding a way around it. But it is an extreme solution. While it gives the person a breathing-space, it does not necessarily alter any of the circumstances which brought on the reaction in the first place. After the sufferers have regained their equilibrium, many just return to their original situation like a lamb to the slaughter.

This opens the way to an even more drastic solution to the problem: premature death. The lives of too many people in our society are cut short because of the unrealistic pressures they place upon themselves. The most common way in which this happens is through a heart-attack. Men in their late thirties, forties and fifties are particularly vulnerable here, especially if they hold down very responsible or highly competitive positions. Medical researchers have now investigated in some detail the kind of person who is

most susceptible to heart seizure. Among the various characteristics of people who exhibit what is called a 'type A behaviour
pattern', high on the list are such things as a compulsive drive to
work, extreme busyness and an inability to relax when the
occasion demands.[14] Even the experience of a heart-attack is not
always sufficient to prevent such people from scaling down their
activities to a more natural level.

Premature death also strikes a large number of men in the
period immediately following upon their retirement. Stood down
from the work that has sustained them all their lives, they are
often at a loss to know what to do. This is difficult enough in
itself. But what makes the transition from employment to retirement particularly hard is the change in pace involved. Many men
have worked at too pressured a rate through their lives and find
the sedate rhythm of life in retirement too much a shock to their
system. They are unable to switch down from overdrive into first
gear. Their bodies and their psyches have become addicted to a
different speed and cannot take the change. Instead they just seize
up and stop. This is one of the reasons why men commonly have a
shorter lifespan than women.

All in all, then, our bodies, nerves and even lives pay a
frighteningly high price for the haste-ridden, clock-dominated,
booked-up way of life that we have chosen for ourselves.

Footnotes

1. Cf. M. Hilliard, *Women and Fatigue* (Family Life Movement of Australia, 1975) p. 118.
2. W. Daume, 'Challenges in Sport', *Leisure: A New Perspective. Papers presented at a National Seminar in Canberra, 22nd–24th April, 1974* (Canberra: Dept. of Tourism and Recreation, 1975) p. 10.
3. W. Kerr, *op.cit.*, pp. 30–38.
4. S.B. Linder, *The Harried Leisure Class* (New York: Columbia University, 1970) p. 48. More generally see J. Dumazedier, *Toward a Sociology of Leisure* (New York: Free Press, 1967) p. 15.
5. The literature of this is growing all the time. Among others see W. Dement, 'The Effect of Dream Deprivation', *Science* (131, 1960) pp. 1705–1707 and R.T. Burger and

T. Oswald, 'Effects of Sleep Deprivation on Behaviour, Subsequent Sleep, and Dreaming', *Journal of Mental Science* (108, 1962) pp. 455–462.

6. On most of what follows I am indebted to G.G. Luce, *Body Time: The Natural Rhythms of the Body* (St. Albans: Paladin, 1973).

7. See also the searingly graphic representation of this in David Ireland's novel, *The Unknown Industrial Prisoner* (Sydney: Angus and Robertson, 1971) p. 2. Many studies substantiate this. The most thorough is M. Maurice, *Shift Work: Economic Advantages and Social Cost* (Geneva: International Labour Office, 1975) pp. 36–59.

8. K. Lynch, *What Time is This Place?* (Cambridge, Mass.: MIT Press, 1972) p. 119. Cf. R.R. Ward, *The Living Clocks* (London: Collins, 1972) p. 268.

9. G.G. Luce, *op.cit.*, p. 194.

10. I.G. Cullen, 'The Treatment of Time in the Explanation of Spatial Behaviour', in *Timing Space and Spacing Time, Vol. 2: Human Activity and Time Geography*, T. Carlstein, D. Parkes and N. Thrift (eds.) (London: Edward Arnold, 1978) p. 37. See also R.W. Cumming and P.G. Croft, 'Human Information Processing under Varying Time Demands', *Man Under Stress*, ed. A.T. Welford (London: Taylor and Francis, 1974) p. 19.

11. Cf. A Toffler, p. 321. On the link between time and other demands on executives and stress illnesses, see the report on the study carried out by the Administrative Staff College, London, and the Department of Management Sciences, University of Manchester, in *The Canberra Times* (31st May, 1981).

12. These studies were initially carried out at the Cornell Medical Center in New York and at the Washington School of Medicine, but have now been corroborated elsewhere. See further G.G. Luce, *op.cit.*, pp. 194–196. The breakthrough in this area began with the medical work and technical writings of Hans Selye. A more popular account of his approach may be found in H. Selye, *The Stress of Life* (London: Longmans, Green and Co., 1956) and in his more recent book *Stress Without Distress* (London: Hodder and Stoughton, 1974). For further refinements see L. Levi, *Stress-Sources, Management and Prediction* (New York: Liveright, 1967), M. Friedman and R.H. Rosenman, 'The Key Cause—Type A Behaviour Pattern', *Stress and Coping: An Anthology*, A. Monat and R. Lazarus (eds.), (New York: Columbia, 1977) pp. 203–212 and R.L. Woolfolk and F.C. Richardson, *Stress: Sanity and Survival* (London: Futura, 1979) pp. 143–154, who do give more attention to the time factor.

13. 'The Scholar Gypsy', lines 142–146, *Matthew Arnold: A Selection of His Poems* (Harmondsworth: Penguin, 1954) p. 211.

14. See further M. Friedman and R.H. Rosenman, *Type A Behaviour and Your Heart* (New York: Knopf, 1974).

4

The Decline in Social
and Political Life

It is commonplace that the quality of interpersonal relationships
and the strength of political life is in decline today. Many reasons
are advanced for this state of affairs, viz, the growing anonymity
of large cities and countries, high mobility both within and
between nations, consumerism and the intrusion of multi-national
conglomerates, the commercialisation of leisure and increasing
bureaucratisation of the world. Occasionally someone will point
to the impact on personal and civic life of the increasing pace of life
and rate of change. Only rarely is mention made of our regulation
by the clock. Yet the time pressures we experience do adversely
affect our social life and our political stability to a quite marked
degree.

The weakening of interpersonal relations
The increased regulation and pace of modern living weaken
interpersonal relationships. Since families spend less time together
over meals, there is less opportunity to enter into each other's
concerns and develop a fully rounded common life. Breakfast has
largely become a self-serve affair, taken by different members of
the family at times which suit their personal schedules. Unlike the
custom in some European countries, lunch is characteristically an
away-from-home meal. With the advent of television, the
increased amount of time spent travelling from work to home,

and the proliferation of evening activities, even dinner is under serious threat.[1]

The move to time-intensive sports such as squash and jogging has also led to a decrease in sociability and interaction with others. Though some people make deliberate efforts to round off such occasions with relaxed conversation, generally speaking there is not much time for chit-chat on the squash court or while you are huffing or puffing along the footpath. Both pastimes also tend to operate under the constraint of the clock.

Since the coming of the telephone, television and car we rarely write long letters or pay protracted visits. Indeed few people manage to keep up even a minimal correspondence. In particular we seem to have lost the art of writing long letters to those who live far away. Even if we still have the ability, how many of us have the time? As George Eliot remarks in *Middlemarch*, 'The bias of human nature to be slow in correspondence triumphs even over the present quickening in the general pace of things'. So while the telephone has undoubtedly improved the range and quality of close contacts, friends at a distance suffer. While the car enables us to visit people easily, and to see them more often, several visits frequently get packed into one day; the time needed to genuinely deepen relationships, rather than to simply catch up with others, is not allowed. As well, the coming of television has markedly curtailed the amount of time spent in entertaining and visiting.[2]

Modern pressures also show up in tensions between husbands and wives over their differing attitudes to time itself. Working men, whose schedules lead them to become geared to the clock, often complain that their non-working wives (who generally feel under less constraint about time) take too long to get ready, keep them waiting or turn up late for appointments.[3] Strained family relationships are common at the end of the normal day. A survey conducted by the Leisure Research Institute in West Germany concluded that the typical after-work mood was negative and irritable. Family disputes—for instance, wars of nerves with the children—topped the list of problems.[4] In this country the number

DOONESBURY   by Garry Trudeau

one difficulty in married life is reported to be 'communication'.[5] Time pressures, the small amount of time people actually spend together, play a part in this, as well as our lack of skills for dealing with communication problems.

So constant is the rate of change about us that we develop an increasingly transitory, provisional and therefore superficial attitude towards others. This even affects our most significant personal relationships—close friendships and marriage. For these are based on the assumption that people have intrinsic worth and are capable of entering into commitments with a sense of continuity and identity. Seizing on the image of a familiar children's toy, Don McLean compares the average person to a spinning top:

> Round and round this world you go,
> Spinning through the lives of the people you know ...
> How you gonna keep on turning from day to day?
> How you gonna keep from turning your life away?

Consequently our encounters with others are becoming more and more limited and instrumental. We associate rather than interrelate, hold ourselves back rather than open ourselves up, pass on or steal by one another rather than pause and linger awhile. The number of our close friends drops and the quality of our married life diminishes.

There is another reason why we devote less time to being friendly, neighbourly or just plain sociable. As Fred Hirsch notes:

> Friendliness is time consuming and therefore liable to be economized because of its extravagant absorption of this increasingly scarce input. The casual nature of such contacts means that they rarely 'pay' as piecemeal individual transactions.[6]

This explains why we are not inclined to put ourselves out for others or to aid them in any significant way. Like the priest and the Levite in the parable of the Good Samaritan, we pass by on the other side. At a time when more people are in need of personal attention and help, and desire to be in closer contact with others, the number of people willing to provide such assistance is falling and the quality of personal relationships is depreciating.

Church life is also affected by time pressures. Too much of it—meetings, organisations, services—lies under the shadow of the clock. In worship even God is expected to operate according to the dictates of our schedules. In many places he can gather with the people for only an hour once a week, and this time limit has to be strictly observed. When he speaks he must do so for only twenty minutes, not a minute more. A minister once told me that he never preached for longer than nineteen minutes, since that way no one could accuse him of going on for too long! Time constraints of this kind scarcely allow worship or genuine fellowship between people to occur at all.

Some people give far too much time to various church organisations and spend too little time with their families and friends. They lock themselves into an almost purely religious world and have little contact with people or responsibilities outside it. But others find they cannot apportion very much time to such activities at all. Even where there is a real desire to deepen relationships in the church and to develop small concerned groups within it, one of the main problems that arises is lack of time. The difficulty people have in giving extended, quality time to each other in churches these days is as great a barrier to genuine change taking place as the churches' out-dated and intrusive structures.

Other voluntary organisations suffer as well. Anyone acquainted with the academic world knows how little is left of the numerous, and healthy, student societies that once vied for people's attention during lunch hours on campuses. The heavier workloads that students have to bear and the spread of lectures, tutorials and demonstrations into lunchtime periods has made it extremely difficult for these societies to continue. Some tertiary institutions no longer have a single common lunch hour during the week. This means that two people wishing simply to have a meal together may no longer be able to arrange this on campus.

The fragility of political processes
The adverse effects of time pressures at the national and international levels could be illustrated in any number of ways, but I

will concentrate here on several examples which have received news coverage lately.

The application of computer technology to management makes data on the outcome of given actions quickly available to decision-makers. However, improved access can be an inhibiting factor. For investors, the government and, through the media, the public as well also receive information about a firm's operations much more quickly than previously. Every quarter financial analysts register the slightest difference in a firm's performance and tell others how well it is doing. As a result, businessmen are forced to keep a closer and closer eye on the day-to-day details of management, for fear of losing their reputation on the market ... This fear magnifies the relative influence of short-term, quantitative management, as against the necessarily qualitative decisions of the long term. More generally speaking, the closer the state of the game among competitors, the less will they take the risk of making uncertain innovations.[7]

Management experts are now beginning to be disturbed by this turn of events. They are realising that the rationalisation of management is having a suffocating effect. Much criticism is made of the business sector these days for its failure to develop creatively and flexibly. But the contribution of time pressures to this rarely comes in for mention. The very speed of the latest information technology is paradoxically slowing up or even retarding industrial advance. This in turn contributes to the growing uncertainty and unemployment that has become part of life today.

Another problem was highlighted by a US computer expert speaking at a meeting of the European Management Forum in 1981.[8] Systems analysts, he claimed, are obliged to produce solutions to ill-defined problems as quickly as possible. Development of the system takes place through a series of random mutations, the original team generally disbanding before everything is fully functional or properly comprehended. The speed of technological innovation requires the team members elsewhere, and the users of the system lack the expertise and time to control it. This situation can cause 'information catastrophes' like the November 1979 incident when the US air defence's computer system indicated for six minutes that a Soviet submarine had launched nuclear weapons towards the US mainland. Computer-system failures of a similar kind are said to occur regularly in many organisations throughout the world, and they possess an appalling potential for creating industrial, financial and political havoc.

A third illustration comes from the area of humanitarian relief. There are many Western organisations giving aid to disadvantaged parts of the Third World. Africa alone has 400 such agencies. Though many agencies aim to supply help on a short-term basis only, the sheer constancy of the need tends to perpetuate their work. For instance, an aid project was established in Kurtenwaare, Somalia, in 1975 to deal with the short-term consequences of a drought; almost a decade later, with that drought well behind them, the outpost is still there. Is there any way in which this cycle can be broken? Explaining how virtually every moment of every day is taken up with getting food delivered, an agency representative confessed: 'Look, we haven't had time to think it through'.[9] Humanitarian efforts consume so much time at so fast a rate that the people involved cannot control the situation and aid recipients become permanently dependent on welfare.

In the political area, so much has to be done at the parliamentary level in such a limited period that there simply is no time to think through alternatives, formulate policies in adequate detail, or evaluate the effectiveness of anything set in motion. As one noted politician, Henry Kissinger, has admitted: 'Usually decisions are made in a very brief time with enormous pressure and uncertain knowledge'.[10] The 'quick and dirty' policy proposal, as it is known in the trade, is the result. The sheer scale of governmental activity, the rapidity of domestic and international events, the pace set by pressure groups, and the ever present awareness of the next election, contribute to the problem.

Very few people, even those in the Public Service—which is there to help prepare and administer policies—get the opportunity to see something through from start to finish. They just do not have, or are not given, the time. There is also little time available to monitor the operation of policies or to evaluate their effectiveness. While there are sometimes political reasons behind this, time pressures play a real part in it. As a result, very little is known about how satisfactory many policies are in achieving the goals which inspired them. Often it is only after a massive breakdown in the system, or a serious scandal, that their ineffectiveness comes to light. The inadequacy of much welfare administration partly stems from this lack of proper follow through.

This is particularly evident in the sphere of international relations. Over the last century and a half diplomatic procedures have shifted from gravity and ceremoniousness to haste, complexity and nervous urgency. Karl Barth claims: 'The work accomplished in this whole field has increased tenfold in the last 150 years and what have we gained? We find ourselves if not in evil at least in most incompetent hands, not because they work too little ... but because they work too much and in a way which is far too complicated and excited.'[11] If it were only a game diplomats were involved in, or matters of peripheral importance, this might not matter too much. But when the future of life on this planet is at stake the situation is alarming. Indeed, Jacques Ellul suggests that the general acceleration of life in modern societies must lead to a closing of the gap between the pent-up feelings of people and the explosive tempo of society—by means of the outbreak of war.[12]

Conclusion
It would not be difficult to cite other examples of the kinds of difficulties mentioned above. But it is clear enough already that the whole fabric of social and political life is affected by the pace of life, rate of change, and pressure of time today. Whether we are looking at encounters between small groups of people or at interactions between large national groupings, whether we are observing the behaviour of voluntary associations or industrial organisations, the result is the same. There is a decline in the quality of social relationships and in the stability of economic and political arrangements. These no longer possess the depth or strength that once they displayed.

One sign of this is the increasing turnover in personal relationships, both inside and outside marriage; the membership of voluntary organisations, religious and otherwise, also undergoes constant change, and not only by reason of mobility. The demise of small, and even large, firms takes place with increasing frequency; governments tend to come and go more often than they did in the past. But there are other signs as well, viz, the shallowness of much family life and social intercourse and the widespread poverty of political imagination and achievement. All is not well in these areas of life today.

Footnotes

1. Further interesting observations on this may be found in J. Holt, *Escape from Childhood: The Needs and Rights of Children* (Dutton: New York, 1974) pp. 32–33.

2. I have not found any recent figures on this but an American survey conducted between 1948 and 1958 showed a 30 percent decrease in these areas. See J.P. Robinson and P.E. Converse, 'Social Change as Reflected in the Use of Time', p. 41.

3. A. Toffler, *The Third Wave*, (London: Pan, 1980) p. 66.

4. See *The German Tribune* (10th February, 1980) for a report of the West German survey.

5. On the Australian statistics, according to which communication difficulties appear to be on the increase, see further J. Krupinski, 'Family Conflict and Family Disruption', *The Family in Australia: Social, Demographic and Psychological Aspects*, J. Krupinski and A. Stoller (eds.), (Sydney: Pergamon, 1974) p. 254.

6. F. Hirsch, *The Social Limits to Growth* (London: Routledge and Kegan Paul, 1976) pp. 77–78.

7. Adapted from M. Crozier, *Le Mal Americain* (Paris: Fayord, 1980) as quoted in his own translation by Jean-Francois Revel, *Encounter* (April, 1981) p. 48.

8. Professor Joseph Weizenbaum at the European Management Forum symposium in Davos, Switzerland (May, 1980).

9. Reported first in the *International Herald Tribune* (Paris) and then in *Encounter* (U.K.), the December, 1980, issue.

10. So Henry Kissinger in *The Observer* (19th June, 1977) on policy formation. On the lack of adequate policy evaluation, see, for example, the report from the Senate Standing Committee on Social Welfare, *Through a Glass Darkly: Evaluation in Australian Health and Welfare Services* (Canberra: Australian Government Publishing Service, 1979).

11. K. Barth, *Church Dogmatics Vol. III: The Doctrine of Creation, Part 4* (Edinburgh: T. & T. Clark, 1961) p. 556.

12. J. Ellul, *The Technological Society* (New York: Knopf, 1964) p. 422.

5

The Erosion of
Thought and Leisure

It may seem strange to suggest that our capacity to think is on the decrease today. Or our ability to engage in recreation. Surely we devote a greater part of our time to education than any previous society! The length of time children attend school has dramatically increased during this century. Even more marked is the proportion of students now attending tertiary institutions. Adult education courses have also proliferated in recent years. We must add to this the wide range of books and magazines produced on almost every conceivable topic, the growth in public libraries, and the availability of radio programmes, tapes (and soon videos) on educational subjects.

Whether or not we have more free time than our predecessors, surely there can be no doubt about the increased options people have as to how they will use their leisure. Technology has invented a whole new species of leisure pursuits, never more so than now through the possibilities opened up by the silicon chip. A larger selection of hobbies and clubs are now available to the ordinary person. The car, tourist boat and aeroplane have brought other places and cultures within the average person's reach. Have not all these brought about a new awareness of the riches available to us in our leisure hours and maximised the amount of satisfaction?

Unhappily it is not so simple. Quite apart from whether extra schooling, tertiary study and adult education courses have made us better educated or whether the leisure and tourist industry have heightened the quality of our leisure, the pressure of time negates many of our best intentions and desires in these two areas.

Decision-making and reflection

'The first casualty of war', the saying runs, 'is truth.' Truth or wisdom is also a casualty of lack of time. The less time we have, the less opportunity there is to think. The less opportunity there is to think, the less likelihood we will form sound judgments. The less sound judgments we make, the less adequate decisions we will make.

Lack of time affects the quality of our decision-making at even the most mundane levels. As we acquire more and more possessions and demand more and more services, for instance, extra time is needed to decide what goods and services to procure. So many decisions must be made that we reduce the time allowed per decision for acquiring information. This produces a decline in the quality of our decisions. Surveys conducted in the 'fifties showed a 13 per cent increase in impulse buying of non-expensive items compared with a decade before, and only 25 per cent of expensive goods were found to be purchased on the basis of fully deliberated decisions. I have not come across more recent figures but see no reason why this tendency should have weakened.

In this decrease in the quality of decisions about goods and services, we have a paradigm of what is taking place in many areas of life. We are spending less and less time thinking about the ultimate purpose of economic growth. We have little time to decide our attitudes to various political problems. And we fail to find time to think through, or do something specific about, many important social issues.[1] It is no different with the basic problems facing the churches today.

As a result of the pace of modern life, most people have little energy for utilizing the various sources of information which would help them form sound judgments. For all the increasing number of books published each year, and the accessibility of books through libraries, the average working person rarely reads to gather information. The worker's only opportunities for reading are in the train or bus or at home after work. Under such circumstances he or she does not look for anything demanding, merely something to distract from the daily grind. So women read love stories to make up for the emotional life they lack, men read adventure stories to satisfy their craving for a less predictable existence, and both read mystery stories to compensate for the banality of their daily routines. Only with rare exceptions will a working person look for something to 'improve his mind', demand an effort from him, or give rise to reflection, awareness or sustained thought. Jacques Ellul claims primary responsibility for this rests not with the individual himself but with the very condition of his life. The problem recurs at all economic levels and in all professions. It is childish to believe, for instance, that the lawyer or doctor can do any real reading outside of his work, for his work overwhelms him.[2]

Most clergy read less theology than their more thoughtful parishioners. Politicians, by the time they have read all the reports, papers, memos, agendas, background briefings required of them, have little time left to read any substantial analyses of society or government. And teachers rarely get to read the books set down for course preparation, let alone other material. Strange as it may seem, students who do little but read, and many mature age participants in adult education programmes, are not really any better off. They do not have time to properly digest what passes before them, or to follow up insights which might lead them into a more profound understanding of issues.

Our century has certainly produced an enormous range of aural and visual materials. Alongside the telephone, telegraph and camera, we now have radio, teletype, television, microwaves, communications satellites, visual display units, home computers, xerox machines, and others on the way. We are subjected to a huge number of messages via these various media, but there is a limit to the amount we can absorb. The resultant 'communications overload' can also create severe personal and social problems.[3]

The materials from which we draw information—newspapers, magazines, television reports etc—have taken on a propagandist character. To an extent this is an inevitable concomitant of our increasingly technological and mass society. But time pressures also play a part. In newspaper reporting, for instance, rigid daily deadlines and the sheer number of stories dictate that only the briefest amount of time be given to researching, interviewing and writing. Everything is done in haste. The shallowness of the reporting and the volume of material presented prevent readers coming to a full understanding of the issues discussed.[4]

More considered appraisals are expected to come from academics. But staff participation in departmental and campuswide administration, the increased amount of paper work involved in running courses, the continuing emphasis upon specialised research as opposed to just plain study, and the heavier workloads imposed upon lecturers by staff cuts, long working hours and exhausting demands, leave little time for thought. Time to think is the scarcest of academic resources.[5] One notable social commentator complains that, as a result of the present intensity, haste and acceleration of academic exchanges, 'symptoms of degeneration and debility ... in the general trend of intellectual production and consumption' are everywhere to be seen.[6] Another goes as far as to say that 'intellectual self-discipline is in the process of decomposition'.[7]

In the theological area few Christian thinkers have time to think or write in any sustained or creative way. Most are too overworked or overcommitted to write anything but the occasional article. Those who do deal mainly with questions of an esoteric technical kind arising out of professional theological debate, or take their agenda from the general intellectual climate with its superficial identification of basic issues. Genuinely fresh insights with wide-ranging practical implications are rare. When it occurs it is often rushed into print in a partially developed form. Matthew Arnold counselled well when he urged:

> Let us think of quietly enlarging our stock of true and fresh ideas, and not, as soon as we get an idea or half an idea, be running out with it into the street, and trying to make it rule there.[8]

Creative activity and play

It is not only things of the mind which suffer when time is short. Take appreciation of the created order. Conservationists and bush-walkers apart, little time is given over to walking and driving for pleasure. These pursuits are generally carried out with some object other than pleasure in view. Even when surfing or hiking we are in danger of merely using the natural world for our own benefit and not appreciating it for its own worth. 'Can't I just be in the woods without any special reason?' the Catholic contemplative Thomas Merton asks. For this 'is something too excellent to be justified or explained! It just is ... We are not "having" fun, we are not "having" anything' and 'there is no clock that can measure the speech of this rain that falls all night on the drowned and lonely forest'.[9]

Most people allow little time for developing their creative gifts. While something of a renaissance is taking place in the arts and crafts area, only a minority are involved; housewives make up a significant proportion of this group, along with some students, young-marrieds and retired people. Learning to play musical instruments (except the guitar) has dropped over the last two decades. Self-made entertainment within the family or among friends has suffered as a result. The standards of excellence paraded before us in the media are certainly an inhibiting factor. Since they cannot attain such high performance levels, many people will not even try. Even if they do overcome their inhibitions, most do not have the time to develop their abilities. Artistic efforts are not regarded as important enough to take priority over 'useful', socially endorsed or financially rewarding activities.

So there are a large number of people who are capable of creative achievement but never get round to doing anything. Just think of all the poems that have never been written, songs composed, yarns told, films shot, cartoons drawn, interiors designed, pots thrown, crafts enjoyed, plays staged, furniture made—all for want of a little time and perseverance. As Jon Stallworthy expresses it, in his poem 'Lament .

Because I have no time
To set my ladder up, and climb

Out of the dung and straw,
Green poems laid in a dark store
Shrivel and grow soft
Like upturned apples in a loft.[10]

Even when we do make the time, the demands, tension and haste of life today all too easily interrupt us and affect the quality of our creative efforts. Too many things that come from our hands or minds are half-finished or finished too quickly, for both we ourselves and our creations have lacked the leisure to ripen. All of us have lost out here and our world is the poorer for it—it is a culturally greyer, more conformist place as a result.

What has happened to play? Children still engage in it, but it has become a serious, realistic affair in our age of television and progressive education. Close imitation of people and situations, rather than free-flowing fantasy, predominates, along with play with a purpose, useful play, the game.[11] Competitive sport for children has taken its toll on unstructured play. At one time in our street our younger son was the only one in his age-group free to play after school and on Saturday mornings. All the other kids were involved in practice, classes and matches.

Adults do not go in for play much at all. Hobbies and sports, both products of the industrial revolution—yes. But play—no, except on rare occasions with the children. When they have leisure time, which is not very often, adults prefer the craftsmanlike world of the hobby or the structured and competitive atmosphere of sport. Here the aspirations and energies which find no outlet at work can be expressed. Here adults find the challenge, achievement and meaning denied to them in the workaday world. All that is to the good. But such activity should not be equated with genuine play. Play too can be absorbing, can draw on our resources, can have its special rules and participants. But it also contains an indispensable carefree element, and a thoroughgoing uselessness, that mark it off from the hobby or sport. We, of all the people who have ever lived, can least afford to do without this Play is healing to the work-structured, achievement-orientaced fact-obsessed soul. It restores the spirit. It sets things in perspective and puts us back in touch with basic elements in our make-up In the long run, it actually links us up with reality.[12]

Conclusion

Play has a wider significance also, as Johan Huizinga argues in his highly original book *Homo Ludens*.[13] Play, he says, is at the source of our most significant cultural contributions: law, poetry, science, philosophy, the arts, social rituals, festivals, conventions. According to Huizinga, the play-element in culture has been on the wane since the eighteenth century. Yet, he argues, 'real civilization cannot exist in the absence of a certain play-element', and 'to be a sound culture-creating force this play-element must be pure'.[14] Play must have its aim only in itself, and its spirit must arise from inspiration rather than careful calculation.

Widening the argument, Joseph Pieper identifies not just play but leisure as the basis of culture.[15] It is in leisure, he says, that our most creative moments are experienced. Innovations in science, in art, and in other spheres surface when the mind and spirit are relaxed and open to the subconscious. It was said of Einstein that much of the time he 'just used to sit and think'. Most of us are fast losing the capacity to enter into this kind of experience. Even when we have the time, we feel we should be 'doing' something and our activity should produce some tangible benefit. When we try to relax we feel guilty and tend to apologise for, or justify, our behaviour if others are around.

Yet it is only as we cease our restless 'doing' that we will discover what is to be done. Only as we stop and listen to the voice within will we have something to go around and do. The genuinely original and fruitful life has its source right here. So does the future well-being of our civilisation as a whole. 'For it is only by withdrawing from external activities for a short or long season that we can register those deeper creative rhythms which are denied or suppressed in our "normal" existence. It is in such zones of peace and quiet alone that there disclose themselves those fertilizing liberalizing ideas by which the life of society is renewed and maintained ... Unless in the days to come the same respect is paid to "idle" contemplation as is paid today to systematization and planning, culture will wither away through lack of vision and inspiration.'[16]

Footnotes

1. So S.B. Linder, *op.cit.*, p. 67. To feel the full force of Linder's argument, the whole section, pages 64–76, should be read. He also documents the surveys which the text goes on to mention.

2. J. Ellul, *A Critique of the New Commonplaces* (New York: Knopf, 1968) pp. 262–263. Cf. J. Moltmann, *Theology and Joy* (London: SCM, 1973) p. 33 and P. Valery, *op.cit.*, p. 203.

3. D. Bell, *op.cit.*, pp. 316–317.

4. How Ellul reaches the paradoxical conclusion that a person is better off not reading such materials makes fascinating and compelling reading. See J. Ellul, *Propaganda: The Formation of Men's Attitudes* (New York: Vintage, 1973).

5. Cf. M. Thornton, *The Future of Theology* (London: Hodder and Stoughton, 1969) p. 49 and S. de Grazia, *On Time, Work and Leisure* (New York: Doubleday, 1964) pp. 253–254.

6. P. Valèry, *op.cit.*, pp. 138–139.

7. Th. Adorno, *Minima Moralia* (London: Verso, 1974) p. 29.

8. Quoted in J.H. Buckley, *The Triumph of Time: A Study of the Victorian Concepts of Time, History, Progress and Decadence* (Cambridge, Mass: Belknop Press, 1967).

9. T. Merton, *Raids on the Unspeakable* (Norfolk: New Directions, 1966) pp. 13–14.

10. J. Stallworthy, 'Lament', *Voices: the Third Book* (Harmondsworth: Penguin, 1968) p. 172.

11 On the important distinction between 'play' and 'games' see further J. Passmore, *The Perfectibility of Man* (London: Duckworth, 1970) pp. 295–299.

12. See further D.M. Winnicott, *Playing and Reality* (Harmondsworth: Penguin, 1971) pp. 46–75.

13. J. Huizinga, *Homo Ludens* (London: Paladin, 1970).

14. *Ibid.*, p. 233.

15. J. Pieper, *Leisure: The Basis of Culture* (London: Faber, 1952).

16. L. Hyde, *Spirit and Society* (London: Methuen, 1949) pp. 87–88.

6

The Undermining of Religion and Spirituality

The final dimension of life affected by our modern view of time is the most fundamental of all. For whatever damage we may have done to ourselves physically and psychologically, socially and politically, intellectually and creatively, religiously and spiritually we have suffered far more. It is at this level that our over-regulated, hyper-paced way of life has most deeply affected us.

The decline in religious sensitivity

I am using the word 'religion' here in the widest sense. Our religion is whatever we allow to give basic meaning to our lives, provide us with a set of values and become a focus for our strongest feelings, however unconsciously and however superficially. No one is without religion in this sense. But the religions to which modern men and women have become addicted, and the spirituality that corresponds to them, are generally tawdry affairs. For the most part they are centred upon the acquisition of wealth and status, power and control, health and fulfilment, family and a name. All of these are very short-term goals. They provide a solution to our desire for meaning, values and commitment of only the most limited and shallow kind. They rarely sustain people in any deep personal crisis and do not carry anyone beyond the threshold of death. They have neither the personal depth nor temporal breadth to warrant our serious attention. In the last analysis they are illusory and fail to deliver what they appear to promise. They are a lie and a delusion.

That is why it is disturbing to find people congratulating themselves every time a speed record is broken, as if going faster were some end in itself; we fail to think about what use it is to gain time like this. Similar congratulations are voiced every time a new remedy is invented, as if living longer were also an end in itself; we fail to work out what it is we are actually living for. People do not know what to do with their time because the spiritual foundations of their lives have been destroyed. As Ellul says: 'No one knows where we are going, the aim of life has been forgotten, the end has been left behind. Man has set out at tremendous speed to go *nowhere*.'[1] 'Indeed', comments his compatriot Valèry, 'there is an element of suicide in the feverish and superficial life of the civilised world'.[2]

The going itself, movement for its own sake, has taken the place of more fundamental questions about who they are and where they are heading. Those who are caught up in the busy life have neither the time nor quiet to come to understand themselves and their goals.[3] Since the opportunity for inward attention hardly ever comes, many people have not heard from themselves for a long, long time. Those who are always 'on the run' never meet anyone any more, not even themselves.[4] Confronted with the harmful things they do to others, they do not have time to be troubled with remorse. Confronted with the suspicion that their lives are not heading in the right direction, they are unwilling to stop and explore alternatives. Thinking is impractical—it only wastes time and prevents them from getting on with the things that lie to hand. Yet the really practical course of action for a traveller uncertain of his way is not to continue with the utmost speed in the same direction—it is to stop and consider how to find the right path.[5] Unfortunately most never pause long enough to discover where the basic answer to life lies. 'Where shall the word be found, where will the Word resound?' asks T.S. Eliot, 'Not here, there is not enough silence'.[6]

The flight into busyness is often an attempt to escape from life's deeper questions, to avoid being disturbed by them. Rather than finding time for solitude we prefer, in the words of Judith Wright:

> ... the shouting, the running, the eating, the drinking—
> never alone and thinking,
> never remembering the Dream or finding the Thing, always
> striving with your breath hardly above the water
> ... to go away, to be quiet and go away, to be alone in a strange
> place in spring,
> shakes the heart.[7]

Most people have a deeply rooted dread of time and are afraid to look into its face. That is why they are constantly endeavouring to forget themselves, ignore the past and avoid looking too deeply into the future.[8] The busyness in which they attempt to hide from themselves and God, and the constant fatigue that accompanies their behaviour, are more than just symptoms of an inadequate sense of self and a deficient vitality.[9] They are signs of the judgment of God. As the Bible reminds us over and over again, those who turn away from God will find that their works are vain and that they exhaust themselves for nothing. This is what we see taking place before our eyes.[10]

The subversion of spiritual life

Not only non-Christians are in this position today; many Christians are victims also. They may be more in touch with certain aspects of their inner selves and the needs of others around them. But their own deepest needs and desires often remain foreign to them and they gauge the real plight and potential of others in only the most superficial way. Their relationship with God is more at the acquaintance level than that of deep familiarity, and only in the haziest way have they grasped the plans God has for them in this life. They are in too much of a hurry—'doing the Lord's work' as much as anything else—to stop and enter more deeply into their inner selves. Such a process takes time, for the real self is submerged beneath layers of family, social and denominational conditioning. Only with a more measured approach to life and regular experience of solitude can one penetrate these layers.

When busy Christians do stop for 'quiet times' in their own
homes or 'worship services' with their fellow Christians, they still
feel the pressure of all the things they have to do and fit into their
work-dominated schedules. Quality time with ourselves, with
others, with the world, and above all with God, cannot be rushed
and timetabled in this way. It is in the nature of schedules and
modern work to vitiate spiritual life. A person's life is not made up
of watertight compartments: work in the morning, a break over
lunch, more work in the afternoon, family recreation in the early
evening, spiritual refreshment from then on. So it is a mistake to
think that a typical day in our kind of world does not alter the
texture of the remainder of our time and affect our capacity for
spiritual experience. It is very difficult to leave behind the modern
world's planned, strictly utilitarian attitude to time, as well as its
hyperactive rhythms and routine character.[11]

Many Christians as well as non-Christians have a dread of
time and are afraid to stand still. This is not so much because they
are attempting to hide from themselves and from God in any
general sense. Indeed they are grateful that they have found him,
and themselves in him. But there are still aspects of themselves
and of him that they are not prepared to face.

Some lack the assurance that God, or for that matter their
fellow-Christians, accept them as they are. Despite the fact that in
hymns like 'Just as I am ...', in passages like Romans 5, in books
and sermons on the theme of 'grace', they are assured that this is
so, they still cannot quite believe it. With this lack of belief comes
a danger, as it always does. It is the same danger which Jesus and
Paul initially fought against in their own day. For if you lack
assurance of your acceptability and worth, the temptation is to try
to earn approval both from others and yourself by your own
efforts. The easiest way to go about this is by doing additional
things for them. This is one reason why people take on so many
extra tasks and responsibilities that God never required of them.
This is why some continue to do more in their churches than they
really need to. This is why many Christians find it difficult to say
'no' to demands made of them by their fellow believers.

Others have such an over-refined conscience that they have to do something themselves about every need they hear about or see. They assume that to come across a need *ipso facto* carries with it an obligation to meet it. Otherwise they live under a sense of guilt that will not leave them alone. Such people are only vaguely aware of their physical or psychological limits and of their responsibility to family and church. They also fail to reckon with God's capacity to raise up others to step into the breach or with the fact that, however much we may wish it otherwise, 'the poor are always with you'. They fail to see that, even if we had all the time in the world, no competing responsibilities towards our families, or friends to distract us, and no needs of our own to attend to, that there would still be an overwhelming number of people, organisations and situations that require our help.

Then there are those who feel themselves to be indispensable when, in fact, they have too high an estimate of their own abilities or importance. This leads them to think that no one else can do the job at hand as well as they can. Therefore they find it hard to delegate any of their responsibilities to others who could do it, or give little thought to training up others to take their place. Where they carry this attitude over into their church, or to some other organisation to which they belong, they tend to encourage an imperialistic attitude to the group's activities. That is, they desire it to not only do all that similar groups do but often wish it to enlarge its activities in a whole range of time-demanding ways. Unwilling to let others around them take over some of their responsibilities, or even God himself to take some of the weight, they increase their own burden and suffer all the time pressures that go with it.

Behind all these, of course, there often stands an unaccepting, overdemanding or arrogant parent, whose influence has deeply ingrained these attitudes in our psyches. They are not easily removed. Only the patient grace of God and loving, balanced and sensible commitment of a small group of other Christians can begin to deal with them.

Conclusion

Losing our grasp of time, we are in danger of losing ourselves as well. By seeking to exploit time for largely tangible ends, and to value speed rather than substance, we have turned life topsyturvy. We are finding it harder and harder to maintain our equilibrium, and it is little wonder that as we hurry through the brief span of time allotted to us we feel 'forever disoriented or off balance; unsure of our ideas, institutions and values; unsure of our relations to others and to society; unsure of our purpose and identity'. As the world has accelerated, 'it has become increasingly plain that, if the psychic cost of slowly changing societies was the stultification of personality, the psychic cost of rapidly changing societies is the disintegration of personality'.[12]

Michel Quoist eloquently captures the essence of our problem:

> I went out, Lord.
> Men were coming out.
> They were coming and going,
> Walking and running.
> Everything was rushing, cars, lorries, the street, the whole town.
> Men were rushing not to waste time.
> They were rushing after time,
> To catch up with time,
> To gain time.
>
> Goodbye, sir, excuse me, I haven't time.
> I'll come back, I can't wait, I haven't time.
> I must end this letter—I haven't time.
> I'd love to help you, but I haven't time.
> I can't accept, having no time.
> I can't think, I can't read, I'm swamped, I haven't time.
> I'd like to pray, but I haven't time . . .
> You understand, Lord, they simply haven't the time.
>
> The child is playing, he hasn't time right now . . . Later on . . .
> The schoolboy has his homework to do, he hasn't time . . . Later
>   on . . .
> The student has his courses, and so much work, he hasn't
>   time . . . Later on . . .
> The young man is at his sports, he hasn't time . . . Later on . . .

The young married man has his new house, he has to fix it up,
    he hasn't time . . . Later on . . .
The grandparents have their grandchildren, they haven't
    time . . . Later on . . .
They are ill, they have their treatments, they haven't time . . .
    Later on . . .
They are dying, they have no . . .
Too late! . . . They have no more time!

And so all men run after time, Lord.
They pass through life running—hurried, jostled, over-burdened,
    frantic, and they never get there. They haven't time.
In spite of all their efforts they're still short of time, of a great deal
    of time.
Lord, you must have made a mistake in your calculations.
There is a big mistake somewhere.
The hours are too short,
The days are too short,
Our lives are too short . . .[13]

That is the issue! Has God made a mistake in his calculations? A big
mistake somewhere? Or somewhere, somehow, have we? It does not
occur to most of us that the problem of time is a critical problem at all,
let alone one for which we are partly responsible. We are, of course,
aware that life is more hectic than we would prefer it to be. We pause
to regret this every so often but then rush off to attend to whatever is
next on our list of responsibilities. But we treat it as a fact of life rather
than as a condition that can be changed. And we seldom regard the
condition as one which we have had a significant part in shaping. We
forget that life has not always been so rushed and ignore or defer the
challenge of those who have committed themselves to a simpler, less
harried way of life. 'I'll do something about it when the children have
grown up', we say, or 'when I've finished my studies', 'when the house
is paid off', 'when I've realised my ambitions', 'when I've reached the
top'. Or, most unlikely of all, 'when I retire'. In the meantime we comfort
ourselves with the thought that, as working hours continue to decrease,
our free time is expanding and that one day, as a result of technological

inventions taking place in our society, we will find ourselves enjoying the promised leisure society.

But how realistic is the hope that many people place in changing patterns of work or in future technological innovations to give them the additional time they desire? Before looking more closely at the reasons for our problem with time, it would be helpful to know whether the problem is only a temporary one or more fundamental in character. If, largely without our help, it will shortly disappear, then we do not need to analyse its causes in as comprehensive a way.

Footnotes

1. J. Ellul, *The Presence of the Kingdom* (London: SCM, 1951) pp. 68-69.
2. P. Valèry, *op.cit.*, p. 201.
3. See further S. Kierkegaard, *Purity of Heart is to Will One Thing* (New York: Harper, 1956) p. 108.
4. Cf. M. Quoist, *The Christian Response* (Dublin: Gill, 1965) p. 76.
5. This is as important for societies as for individuals, as R.H. Tawney, *The Acquisitive Society* (London: Fontana, 1961) pp. 9-10 points out.
6. T.S. Eliot, 'Ash Wednesday', in *T.S. Eliot: Selected Poems* (London: Faber and Faber, 1954) p. 90. Compare also the First Chorus of 'The Rock' in the same volume.
7. J. Wright, 'The Child', *Collected Poems 1942-1970* (Sydney: Angus and Robertson, 1975) p. 36.
8. Cf. H. Thielicke, 'Our Freedom and our Free Time', *Christ and the Meaning of Life: A Book of Sermons and Meditations* (London: James Clarke, 1965) pp. 148-149; N. Berdyaev, *Solitude and Society* (London: Bles, 1938) p. 102.
9. R.L. Stevenson, 'An Apology for Idlers', in *Eight Essayists*, ed. A.S. Cairncross (London: Macmillan, 1940) p. 184.
10. P. Tournier, *Fatigue in Modern Society* (Atlanta: John Knox, 1973) p. 34.
11. J. Ellul, *op.cit.*, pp. 129-130.
12. A.M. Schlesinger Jnr., *op.cit.*, p. 280.
13. M. Quoist, *Prayers of Life* (Dublin: Gill and Macmillan, 1963) pp. 76-77. The poem is a commentary on Ephesians 5:15-17.

Part 3
Dreams of an Age of Leisure

The end of scarcity, it was believed . . . would be the freeing of time from the inexora-
ble rhythm of economic life.
In the end, all time has become an economic calculus.
As Auden put it, 'Time will
only say, I told you so'.
D. Bell, The Coming of Post-
Industrial Society

7

The Myth of
Increased Free Time

Despite the bleak situation I have described, many people insist that we have never had it so good. Look how working hours and the length of the working year have dropped, they say. And think how much further these will shrink as the technological revolution continues! Consider how labour-saving devices and service industries have given us extra leisure time. Think how the car and rapid communication systems have multiplied the number of things we can do in a short space of time. And how part-time work and early retirement are giving more free time to some members of society.

So it is said, said often, and almost uniformly believed—side by side with the complaints people make about having too little time to do the things they really want to do. Where, then, does the truth lie? Who is deceiving whom? What is the real state of affairs?

Have working hours really decreased?

During the last century, time spent in paid employment has certainly decreased in advanced industrial democracies.[1] In the United Kingdom, United States and Australia 100 years ago, a 60-hour week was the norm. The working week had dropped to around 50 hours a week by World War I. In the 1920s the 44-hour week was uniformly introduced despite employers' opposition and legislative delay. In Australia at the beginning of 1948 the 40-hour week was uniformly introduced. Many people have since gained a shorter working week—eg, around 37½ hours per week in the Public Service and 35 hours per week in some blue-collar unions. But the 40-hour week has remained the legal standard and movement towards a general 35-hour week is clearly going to be a protracted affair. Overall then, there was a dramatic decline in legal working hours during the half-century before the Depression but there has been only a minor fall in the half-century since. A levelling out in the hours laid down for work has occurred.[2] Although we are in a considerably better position than our forbears last century, we are only marginally better off than our grandparents.

However, such figures do not tell the whole story. They show only how long a person can be legally required to work, not how long he or she actually spends on the job. In the late '60s, for example, the average working week in the USA was about 48 hours: considerably more than the legal requirement, only a little less than the pre-Depression level, and more than in the immediate post-war period. Furthermore, the number of people working 48 hours or more per week had risen over the preceding 20 years, with self-employed workers averaging about 10 hours more per week than other employed people.

In Australia during the '60s, average working hours were only a little lower, and in 1981 the average number of hours worked per week by adult males was around 41.0; this figure included 1.5 hours overtime. The 1981 figure represented a rise of almost half-an-hour per week on 1979 figures, perhaps because reduced staff ceilings were forcing people to work longer. When female members of the labour force are included the figure needs to be adjusted downwards, for they work approximately two hours per week less. The 1981 figure did not cover professional people or those in managerial positions—both groups tend to work long hours. Also, it should be noted that the 23 per cent of the workforce who worked overtime did on average 7 hours per week overtime.[3] This indicates that probably a third of our male workforce spends well over 40 hours a week on the job—as did their predecessors 50 years ago. The remainder of workers are spending fewer hours at work (and Australian workers almost 3 hours per week less than their American counterparts), but even so they have gained only an hour or so a day of free time over the past two generations.

We also need to remember that, with the spectacular increase of women in the workforce, we now have over a third more of the population working than in the early part of the century. This means that, despite the modest decrease in the number of hours worked by many people, there has been a big increase in the number of hours supplied to the labour market by the average couple of working age.

What about early retirement schemes, the late ages at which many begin work, holiday breaks and long service leave? Haven't there been substantial leisure time gains here? Some, yes, but not nearly as large as you might think.

Certainly more young people enter the workforce later than did their counterparts at the beginning of the century.[4] And with high unemployment many young people are prolonging their educational years. In doing so, however, they have merely put off one kind of work to continue another. The length of schooling and amount of homework has increased, as have the number of training and school-to-work transition programmes. The average student at high school, college or university works about the same number of hours as his peers who are employed. Many, of course, work far harder.

At the other end of the work cycle, can we expect to live longer after retirement? A century ago in Australia, life expectancy was 52 years for men and 55 for women. Now it is approximately 68 and 75 years respectively. But this statistical increase is mainly due to the century-long decline in infant mortality rates, a trend that now appears to be coming to a close; it is primarily because more people are living that life expectancy figures have risen so dramatically, not because people are living longer.[5] Actual life expectancy for the bulk of Australians has scarcely increased at all during this period. In America it has actually been decreasing since the 1950s.[6] Although the average

Australian may live a little longer than his turn-of-the-century counterpart, he tends also to stay longer in the workforce; so the one virtually balances out the other and little free time is gained. While early retirement schemes have the potential to alter this situation, as yet they are too few to make any significant difference. Where they are available, the people who avail themselves of them, or are forced to take them up, often look for re-employment.

It is undoubtedly in the areas of longer vacations, time-off arrangements and long service leave that the most noticeable advances have been made. A generation ago most workers had only two weeks' annual vacation; now the majority have four weeks. (Many people in the United States are less well off than those in the United Kingdom and Australia in this respect.) Paid sick leave—generally used up whether there are grounds for it or not—now commonly amounts in this country to ten days a year on full pay and ten days a year on half pay; in some areas the allowance is increased after three years' service to twenty days on full pay and twenty days on half pay. Maternity leave is available in many places, providing three months' leave on full pay with the option of remaining on unpaid leave for a further nine months. Provision of three months' long service leave after ten or fifteen years' service—a benefit in which Australia leads the world—is becoming more widespread.[7] Australia also has more public holidays during the year than any comparable Western country, and the combining of a statutory holiday with a Saturday or Sunday has established the convention of the Long Weekend.

Once again the additional time acquired by these means is not all gain. Due to the increasing pressure of work, people generally find they take longer to unwind on holidays than before: 'a week to ten days' is the period many people specify. And at least part of the reason for the notorious 'sickie' syndrome in our society is the nervous frustration and boredom engendered by the work situation.

Shiftwork has been increasing in most industrialised countries, and surveys conducted suggest that this trend is likely to continue. Between a quarter and a third of all workers are now

employed on shift or at night. The social and psychological disadvantages of shiftwork are serious and people who work the same
number of hours doing it as those working regular hours are much
worse off. This is another case where the figures denoting hours
worked do not tell the whole story. There are hidden costs involved.

Given our greater mobility nowadays, much more time is
spent than previously in moving from one house and job to
another. Moving generally requires a lot of work, most of it
outside the hours of employment, and a large amount of time.
Re-settling demands still more time and effort.

All in all, we do not seem to have much more free time —
before, during or after our paid working life—than our forbears.
To a large extent, then, the radical decline in working hours that
we hear so much about is a myth of our own making.[8]

Has free time really increased?

Every now and again you come across euphoric statements about
technology's contribution to the creation of a 'leisured society'.
So, for example, the claim that 'for the first time in the history of
mankind there is well on the way a civilisation not topped by a
leisure class, but a civilisation characterised by universal leisure'.[9]
All is not as it seems in this respect, any more than with the decline
in working hours.

Political theorist Sebastian de Grazia tells us that in the
Middle Ages, indeed from Classical Antiquity, the number of
holidays or 'holy days' was around 115 a year. Although some
people in those times worked long hours, this was true only
during certain periods in the year. Winter months were less hectic
and, as in certain trades today, inclement weather often provided a
welcome respite from labour. Most urban citizens worked a short
day. For instance, in ancient Rome afternoons were generally
reserved for social and recreational purposes and scarcely anyone
laboured at night. De Grazia concludes that, alongside mediaeval
Europe and ancient Rome, 'free time today suffers by comparison,
and leisure even more'.[10]

It is the effect of the industrial revolution upon working
hours that has distorted our understanding of how much more

free time we have in comparison with earlier societies. As we shall see in more detail later, the widespread introduction of machines increased the length of the working day for many people. Without doubt our free time is greater than of those who worked in the factories in Manchester or the sweatshops of New York in the middle of the nineteenth century. But, taking the longer view, much of our gains in the last hundred years have only rectified the abnormal situation created by the industrial revolution.[11]

De Grazia conducts a comparison between the free time possessed by a male American worker in the '60s and a typical, not severely exploited, worker 100 years ago. Despite the advantage of an additional 31 hours per week off legal working hours, the modern American is found to be not much better off. More people in the '60s were working overtime than 100 years earlier (many worked about six hours per week overtime). More people in the '60s were taking on second jobs to augment their wages (this occupied a further two or three hours per week). People were taking longer to get to and from work (an extra hour a day or five a week for the average commuter). Almost another six hours per week were taken up with maintenance jobs in and around the home. Working men helped more with household chores than did their forbears (generally spending 2.5 hours per week on this).

All this added up to a net gain of about 8.5 to 9.5 hours per week, or 1.25 to 1.5 hours per day, additional free time—a small yield over such a long period of time. But today's heightened work tempo, increased noise levels and crowded urban conditions have an impact on these few extra hours of free time. For instance, we take longer to unwind at the end of the day and at the weekend. How much time shall we deduct for this? De Grazia's suggestion of 1.25 to 1.5 hours per day seems reasonable.

The upshot of all this is that there does not appear to have been any gain in genuinely free time for most Americans in the post-Depression to pre-Vietnam period. Indeed, comparison between a restricted 1931–33 survey and a 1965–66 national one actually showed up a two-hour decrease in 'leisure'.[12]

What is the position in Australia? Somewhat brighter. If we average out the number of hours worked per day over 365 days a

year—an artificial but statistically helpful way of making comparisons—we find that in the mid-'70s the typical male Australian
worked 3.3 hours per day as opposed to the 3.8 hours per day
worked by his American counterpart; the free-time figures were
5.8 and 5.0 hours per day respectively. In other words, men here
worked quarter of an hour less a day and had three-quarters of an
hour a day more free time. Unless de Grazia's calculations for
factors eroding free time are less applicable here, this still does not
put us at any great advantage over people living at the turn of the
century. As yet we do not have the statistics to make full
comparisons, but it would be surprising if our free time is not
affected by similar considerations to the ones he mentions.[13]

A survey taken in 1975 indicates how working women and
housewives compare with men in number of hours worked. On a
typical weekday the amount of free time enjoyed by working men
in Australia was 3.9 hours, for working women 3.7 hours, and for
housewives 5.0. On weekends these figures rose to 6.7, 7.4 and
7.8 respectively.[14] The figures for housewives may seem too low,
but the amount of housework created by people who are at home
all day needs to be borne in mind.

But surely labour-saving devices have improved the free time
situation, especially for women? Surprisingly, it doesn't quite
work out that way. Some household chores do consume less time
than before. For example, food preparation and ironing take less
time owing to the introduction of pre-prepared foods and non-
iron fabrics rather than because of labour-saving devices. But such
gains are offset by the fact that, among the middle-class particularly, homes and gardens are larger, material possessions requiring
maintenance and servicing are more numerous, and standards of
personal and household presentability are higher:

> All told, the conventional assumption that the advent of home
> appliances and other conveniences would divert large amounts
> of time from home management chores to leisure and recrea-
> tion seems purely wrong. Naturally labour-saving devices *do*
> save both time and drudgery. In fact, they probably make a
> major contribution in permitting women the 'luxury' of out-
> side employment while maintaining a household at a tolerable
> level. Nevertheless, for the woman who stays at home, it seems

that expectations concerning the level of household care have risen significantly in the past 30 years and that, in an affluent society, there is a good deal more at home to take care of.[15]

There have been marked increases in time turned over to shopping, household errands and the chauffeuring of children. Many spend more time than previously shopping. Working women give only about half as much time to household chores as full-time housewives—in both Australia and America about 28 hours compared to 52 or 53 hours per week; adjustment of figures to allow for this suggests that women at home now devote more rather than less time to such things.

Access to a car certainly cuts down the time it takes to *do* certain things, but it also increases people's expectations concerning what they can and should do. The greater availability of the car has resulted in a decline in its use for recreation. It is mostly used for tasks: shopping, running errands, chauffeuring. Families with more than one car devote less time to personal interaction than others.[16] Then there is the time that has to be spent in looking after one's vehicle. In the last two or three decades, the car has probably created more rather than less work.

Much the same could be said about the telephone. While it has decreased the time it takes to fulfil a wide range of obligations and carry out a large variety of tasks, it has also multiplied the number of obligations and tasks that we attempt to perform. While it enables us to keep in touch more easily with people, it has increased the amount of time given to incidental contacts and passing acquaintances.

Our accelerated rate of change and rapid pace of life do not necessarily improve the speed and efficiency with which many things are done. In isolated cases they can even be counter-productive.

Commuting time provides a good example. Although people can now travel to and from work at speeds which were inconceivable a century ago, this has not resulted in shortened travelling times. For, as public transport systems gave more rapid access to city centres, people simply moved further out of town, creating our suburban sprawl. City traffic is still so congested that the average speed at which cars travel through a typical modern city is around 15 kph, the speed at which a bicycle moves![17]

Our time gains overall must be offset against time wasted in strikes and unemployment, queues and traffic-jams ... all of which are products of our large scale technology and highly integrated society. So while technological improvements and increased inter-dependence do speed up some processes, the centralisation involved often works against, rather than for, greater efficiency. Little wonder that for all our increased speed many of us find that, like Lewis Carroll's Alice, 'It takes all the running you can do to keep in the same place'.

Conclusion

What has improved over the last few decades is the quality rather than quantity of household work, travelling and consumption time. Home maintenance is considerably less onerous than it used to be, travel is more comfortable and people now have a greater range of ways in which they can use their free time. It is this that people have preferred to seek rather than any substantial realloca-tion of time by reducing the number of hours spent at work and so increasing the amount of time available for recreation and other 'leisure' activities.[18]

Footnotes

1. For detailed information on the decline of the British working week see M.A. Bienfeld, *Working Hours in British Industry: An Economic History* (London: Weidenfeld and Nicholson, 1972). J.D. Owen, *Working Hours: An Economic Analysis* (Toronto: Lexington, 1979) discusses the American situation. Also see A.A. Evans, *Hours of Work in Industrialised Countries* (Geneva: International Labor Organisation, 1975).

2. For more on this see J.P. Robinson and P.E. Converse, 'Social Change as Reflected in the Use of Time', *The Human Meaning of Social Change*, A. Campbell and P.E. Converse (eds.) (New York: Russell Sage Foundation, 1972) p. 45 ff and, more fully, J.P. Robinson, *op.cit.*, pp. 46–61.

3. Based on figures for October, 1982 issued by the Commonwealth Trading Bank in its leaflet *The Australian Economy* (released in January, 1983). More detailed breakdowns may be found in the *Official Year Book of Australia* (Canberra: Australian Bureau of

Statistics, Vols. 1–65, 1901–1981). See also the report in *The Canberra Times* (23rd December, 1980).

4. Figures on the length of schooling, and the numbers involved, covering various European countries and the United States up to the early 1970s, are cited in M.J. de Chalendar, *Lifelong Allocation of Time* (Paris: Organisation for Economic Co-operation and Development, 1976) pp. 17–22. For comparative Australian figures see the Report of the Interim Committee for the Australian Schools Commission, *Schools in Australia* (Canberra: AGPS, 1973) pp. 26–29.

5. Y.R. Mendelsohn, *The Condition of the People: Social Welfare in Australia 1900–1975* (Sydney: Angus and Robertson, 1979) p. 232. This was also the conclusion of a report presented to the 17th National Conference of Physiotherapists in Melbourne during May, 1980. See also J. Norelle Luckiss, 'On Liberty and the Health of the Community', *Community Health in Australia* (ed.) R. Walpole (Harmondsworth: Penguin, 1979) pp. 1–3.

6. See further N. Elliot, *The Gods of Life* (New York: Macmillan, 1974).

7. So the report *Long Service Leave in Australia* (MIT Association of Australia, 1977).

8. Cf. Staffan B. Linder, *op.cit.*, p. 137.

9. G. Soule, *Time for Living* (New York: Viking, 1955) p. 122. Soule comments further on gains in time introduced by technology, pp. 59–61.

10. S. de Grazia, *op.cit.*, p. 83.

11. On changes introduced by the industrial revolution, see G. Langenfelt, *The Historic Origin of the Eight-Hour Day* (Stockholm: Almquist and Wiksell, 1954) pp. 46–53 and 98–107.

12. J.P. Robinson and P.E. Converse, *op.cit.*, p. 79. Their contribution contains a valuable summary of all the data up to the beginning of the 'seventies.

13. See again the report on *Australians' Use of Time*, p. 17, together with the figures in I. Manning, *The Journey to Work* (Sydney: Allen and Unwin, 1978) remembering that these do not include time spent walking to and from public transport.

14. These were obtained by averaging out the data supplied for the years 1973–5. See the updated estimates from J.P. Robinson and P.E. Converse, *op.cit.*, Table 1 in R. Conway, *Land of the Long Weekend* (Melbourne: Sun, 1978) p. 187.

15. The figures discussed here come from the Cities Commission report cited above. Their suggested adjustment is based on surveys discussed in the article by J.P. Robinson and P.E. Converse, *op.cit.*, pp. 48–50, from which the quotation also comes (p. 50). Further support for the view expressed here comes from an American survey, ranging over the period 1926–1968, summarised in K.E. Walker, 'Homemaking Still Takes Time', *Journal of Home Economics* (61, 1969) pp. 621–624 and from a similar independent survey, ranging over the years 1920–1970, by J. Vanek, 'Time Spent in Housework', *Scientific American* (N.S. 231, 1974) pp. 116–120. The same holds true for improvements in the technology of personal cleanliness, as J.D. Owen, *op.cit.*, p. 37 points out.

16. See again J.P. Robinson and P.E. Converse, *op.cit.*, pp. 51–54 and J.P. Robinson *op.cit.*, p. 71.

17. J.M. Thomson, *Great Cities and Their Traffic* (London: Gollancz, 1977) p. 22. More generally on this see I. Illich, *Energy and Equity* (London: Marion Boyars, 1974).

18. This is the conclusion of J. Owen, *op.cit.*, pp. 31–43.

8

The Illusion of a Timeful Society

Our present situation with respect to time is different from the way we like to picture it. We tell ourselves, and are told by others, that we have more free time than earlier generations, yet the facts and figures do not bear out our claim. Our style of life also bears witness against us. And we contradict ourselves by complaining so often about our lack of time. We are guilty of 'double think' and refuse to face up to the reality of our predicament.

There are two other ways in which we try to avoid the plight we are in. When reality bears in too hard upon us in any area of life, our temptation is to search for a solution in our fantasy world. We begin to dream and in our dream find the answer to our problem. But it is an answer which does not translate back into the here-and-now of everyday life. There is a half-truth here which we should not ignore. The answer to many of our problems does have its origins in the dreams, imaginings and fantasies which break out of the closed system that our reason and our machines erect. But it does not lie in them alone. Such hints of a solution as they provide must be brought into creative interaction with the real problems themselves, so that out of the fusion of the two a new way forward starts to emerge.

Where dreams remain dreams, it is a different story. The trouble is that such dreams are generally triggered by some aspect or other of the everyday world and therefore look, or at least feel, as if they have something to offer it. Yet they never really return to it. They do not lead to any fundamental change. In relation to time, there are two main dreams that people entertain.

Turning back the clock

'Nostalgia', someone has said, 'isn't what it used to be.' He was wrong. Nostalgia has never had it so good. Almost everyone is into it. Everywhere you look you come across evidence of it. It is big business, in fact, all over the Western world. The nostalgia industry is well and truly up, off and away.

Some examples. These days you'll find many younger middle-class people, particularly couples, searching high and low for antique or mock-antique furniture, often paying quite exorbitant prices for it. Items which their parents discarded as old-fashioned, inefficient or even junk now grace the homes of the up and coming, we're-getting-there generation.

There's a new interest among such people in tracing their ancestry as well. Public libraries and the archives of genealogical societies swell with the growing number of requests for information about family antecedents. Overseas, places like Somerset House have become a place of pilgrimage for many tourists. Out of all this activity comes not just a plethora of genealogical charts but increasing interest in the compilation of family histories so as to preserve as much of the past as possible.

We have also seen a preference for period themes in numerous films and television productions.[1] This has been equally true in England, North America and Australia, but especially in our own country. Over the last decade we have seen, again particularly in Australia, mounting interest in the republication or reproduction of works by important early authors, dramatists, poets and painters. On a broader front, we have the revival of interest in the—largely imported—dress styles and musical fashions of the 'fifties and 'sixties. In giving names to their children, parents are going further back still, to the 'twenties or earlier, the period of their grandparents. Around the craft scene, or counter-culture, interest in hand-made or small-scale domestic manufacture has taken people even further back, into some of the methods employed in late pioneering days.

There is also a burgeoning interest in retaining relics and monuments of the past. This has long been a part of the English national consciousness, and for some time part of the North American as well. But it is a relatively recent phenomenon on the Australian scene. Through the work of the National Trust, local councils and local entrepreneurs, we now have well preserved houses and estates, restored townships and diggings, replicas of earlier times and places or colonial design entertainment centres. All are popular and well patronised. Even in older societies like North America however, interest in preserving or reproducing the more recent past has escalated in the last decade or two. The provision of holiday farms for the urban resident is just one example of this at work.

One of the sources of this all-pervading nostalgia is our longing for a simpler way of life, for a time when things changed less quickly, relationships were closer, life was more manageable, and there was less hurry and regulation of our lives. At the heart of this longing lies the wish 'If only we could turn back the clock ...!' The first difficulty to this is that we cannot turn back the clock and reintroduce a more agrarian, country-town or close-knit neighbourhood existence. The second is that our portrait of such an existence is sentimentalised and romanticised anyway. In the third place, most of the people who hark back to such a society never lived in it: the families have been urban dwellers for generations. In Australia, for example, it is now clear that the influential 'bush' legend was largely the creation of a group of alienated city artists.[2]

Another source of the current wave of nostalgia is the vacuum that exists between the present and the recent past for most people in our society and for our society as a whole. Ronald Conway has some perceptive remarks about this in the Australian context. 'The progressive collapse of supportive, articulate kinship continuities since World War I ... has led so many Australians either to repress or tritely conventionalise their family history ... Much of the ephemeral, shallow futurism of Australia in the fifties and sixties—half imported, half the product of ocker chauvin ism—can be explained by a refusal ... to explore the cellars of lost communal or personal hopes. For until we learn how to weep and mourn for yesterday's broken hope and denied traumas, we may never attain that maturity of heart which is equal to future crises.'[3] The situation is probably not so acute in North America where the degree of urban concentration is not quite so high and there has been a greater influence of ethnic family patterns. In England, it is the gap between Britain's pre-World War I Empire and present small power status that produces the problem, a gap that is both movingly and pathetically displayed in the youthful idealism of the last night of the Proms each year.

In both these respects, nostalgia acts as an anaesthetic to dull the sense of personal and social life. In so doing it displays all the marks of the dream, the dream that once upon a time things were different and that in our imagination we can enjoy them as different now. At one time, social rituals and traditions not only preserved this link between past and present but stimulated fresh ways of carrying what was valid in the past into changed circumstances. But both have suffered in recent years. As Robert Nisbet comments:

> The great effect of ritual is its capacity to bind past and present in a single act, with an emphasis, of course, on the present ... But when ritual declines and disappears, the sterile spirit of archaism or nostalgia takes command.[4]

Nostalgia is a signal that all is not as it should be. Where it is indulged in for its own sake, it becomes purely a way of escaping from the present situation into an imagined alternative. Only where it becomes a stimulus to wrestling with the problem it betrays can it replace the dream of a solution with its reality.

Placing hope in the future

The reverse reaction to nostalgia is an unduly optimistic fixation on what lies ahead. Whereas nostalgia sidesteps the difficulties of the present by living in a dreamworld created out of the past, this approach is confident that the answer to those difficulties will come as a byproduct of progress itself. For all its realistically sounding political or technological trappings, however, this alternative constructs a dreamworld of the future in which it places all or most of its hopes.

One version of this hope comes from Sebastian de Grazia, whose demolition of the myth of increased free time we have already examined. He argues that genuine leisure—which he differentiates from mere free time by defining it as a 'state of being', not 'a way of calculating a special kind of time'—is not fully realizable in a democracy. It is an ideal, not an idea, one which 'few desire and fewer achieve'.[5] Democracy and leisure are, he concludes, incompatible. Egalitarianism, which gives everyone a say and places everyone on the same level, is the enemy of leisure, aided and abetted by the philistine approach to life encouraged by industrial production and universal education. Only if work were separated from machinery, the doctrine of progress abandoned, and people's craving for fun replaced by something more creative, would leisure become a real possibility. In a democracy each of these hopes is vain. Since the population at large would resist any appeals to change their society's present goals, priorities and structures, only an authoritarian government could bring about the changes that are necessary. But that would bring other difficulties in its wake, increased bureaucratisation of life for one, and is unlikely to happen anyway.

What, then, does de Grazia advise? He suggests that, since the sophisticated, aristocratic leisure he has in mind is beyond the capacity of most people, the few who really want it should be politically encouraged and assisted in various ways to enter into it, leaving the masses to enjoy their ephemeral fun. We should seriously promote the emergence of a leisured minority such as existed in ancient Greek and Roman times. If this entails the taking away of prestige from the machine, the reduction of egalitarian ideas in education and a less democratic approach to politics, so be it!

De Grazia's solution is that of the radical conservative. The aristocratic temper of his ideas, while rightly recognising the presence of inequalities among people, reduces the possibility of all but an educated few gaining the benefits of a new understanding of time. What is more, he sees the solution only in terms of leisure enjoyed, not in any serious reappraisal of the nature of work and therefore of time more broadly considered. But the essential weakness of his suggestion is its faith in the ability and will of the political process to steer society away from its present technological, egalitarian and democratic concerns. Nothing in the political behaviour of the advanced industrial nations presently provides encouragement for his hopes.

Alvin Toffler proposes a different solution. He is a technological rather than political prophet. While he does not suggest that we blindly accept the current changes, he does not ask for radical new bearings on the future. To a large extent his answer is to 'get with it', throw away more, become more mobile, turn over more relationships, improvise more ad hoc organisations, process information more quickly. In order to cope, our bodies must become more bionic, our experience more simulated, our relationships more kaleidoscopic. Education, industry and politics must all be realigned to project us into the future more effectively. We must learn to run faster and embrace our future more eagerly:

> The only way to maintain any semblance of equilibrium during the super-industrial revolution will be to meet invention with invention—to design new personal and social change-regulators. Thus we need ... an array of creative strategies for shaping, deflecting, accelerating or decelerating change selectively. The individual needs new principles for pacing and planning his life, along with a dramatically new kind of education. He may also need specific new technological aids to increase his adaptivity. The society, meanwhile, needs new institutions and organizational forms, new buffers and balance wheels. All this implies still further change, to be sure—but of a type designed from the beginning to harness the accelerative thrust, to steer it and pace it ... helping people not merely to survive, but to crest the waves of change, and to gain a new sense of mastery over their own destinies.[6]

The rhetoric is magnificent, the promise seductive. But Toffler grossly overestimates the degree to which our bodies, nerves and minds can adjust to the kind of treadmill society he envisages. One would have thought that the limits of our adaptability were already transparently obvious.

There are others besides Toffler who claim that the problem of time will more or less solve itself as a byproduct of the social changes that are already beginning to take place. Futurologist Herbert Kahn has forecast that in the United States by the year 2000 people will have a 7.5 hour working day, four days a week, for 39 weeks a year, with 10 legal holidays and 13 weeks' vacation.[7] But, as more realistic commentators like Daniel Bell have pointed out, the cybernetic revolution of the '60s has not produced the expected jumps in productivity and leisure, and the micro-chip revolution of the '70s seems to have increased the number of unemployed rather than distributed a lessened workload amongst all workers.[8] It is true that some consumer-directed inventions like the home computer and video recorder bring certain advantages in relation to time, eg, reducing the amount of time of certain tasks and freeing people from the schedules of television stations. But there are grounds for thinking that such machines also increase the number of calculations attempted and programmes watched. This means that the time gained or freed is only put under new pressure.

Other technological prophets point to the potential contained in recent innovations: job-sharing, part-time work, flexi-time, the nine-day fortnight. It is true that many more people are now taking up part-time rather than full-time employment, and in the majority of cases—85% to 90%—it is by choice.[9] Job-sharing looks less hopeful. Although an increasing number of workers would welcome it, overt union pressure and alleged administrative difficulties are rendering its prospects doubtful. Similar difficulties confront moves for a nine-day fortnight or four-day week. Initial enthusiasm over this solution to employment problems in older depressed industries or highly automated ones has given way to a more guarded attitude. Most workers found themselves too much at a loss on the additional days off, especially if their wives were out at work.[10] Flexi-time arrangements have certainly loosened up work schedules and led to a civilizing of the workplace. Flexi-time's popularity is evident. Where it is available, most people take advantage of it—but often not to the extent they could. For, so ritualized do our behaviour patterns become in our attempts to cope with the complexity of modern life, that 'even a substantial change in one of the important time constraints on the individual (like flexi-time) may produce relatively little effect'.[11] The complex timings that are made available under a well-designed flexi-time scheme to maximize benefit to the firm and worker demand that more attention be given to time measurement and correlations; so flexi-time actually reinforces clock time.[12]

Some rather cynical and short-sighted observers have been heard to suggest that rising unemployment is providing a solution to the time problem. But there is all the difference in the world between enforced and freely chosen non-work time. As more than one study has shown, the physical and psychological cost to the unemployed renders the majority impotent to enjoy the additional time they have at their disposal. For instance, a survey conducted in Australia in 1981 found that 49% of the unemployed contacted 'had disorders of a severity comparable to that found in psychiatric and outpatient clinics'.[13] Too much free time of the wrong kind can be just as harmful at all levels of the personality as too little.

Another false hope stems from the proponents of a 'steady-state' economy. Quite rightly these point to the finite, limited character of many natural resources. They argue that, as these raw materials come to an end, the creation of a growth-controlled economy will result. This economy will keep pace with available resources not outstrip them. As a consequence of this, people would spend less time at work than they presently do and have more time available for leisure. But the hope overlooks the increasing shift from the production of goods to the production of services, and now from the production of services to the production of information. Services and information form the base of the new type of economy that is developing and at present these show no signs of providing a 'steady-state' situation. Their growth and corresponding demands upon people's time both at work and at leisure have virtually wiped out any gains made by the cybernetic revolution over the last two decades.

Conclusion

Both the desire to turn back the clock and to place hope in the future are doomed to fail. We cannot simply look over our shoulder at what we have left behind or cross our fingers about what lies around the corner. These are the solutions of dreamers, not realists. In our individual lives, as much as in society at large, we cannot settle for one or other of these alternatives or, as often, a contradictory amalgam of the two either. Some people do lose themselves in the past or try to recreate it. Others do pin all their hopes on the future. Neither face up to the fact that our problem with time is in fact a legacy of the past and one that, all things being equal, is only going to get worse in the future. This we shall now go on to see.

Footnotes

1. Eg, films: Picnic at Hanging Rock, The Getting of Wisdom, My Brilliant Career, Eliza Fraser, The Irishman, Breaker Morant, The Picture Show Man, Newsfront, The Man from Snowy River; T.V.: Against the Wind, The Timeless Land, Ride on Stranger, Water Under the Bridge, The Power and the Glory, Jonah, 1915, Sara Dane.

2. G. Davison, 'Sydney and the Bush: An Urban Context for the Australian Legend', Intruders in the Dust: The Australian Quest for Identity (ed.) John Carroll (Melbourne: OUP, 1982) pp. 109–130.

3. R. Conway, op.cit., p. 4.

4. R. Nisbet, The Twilight of Authority (New York: Oxford, 1975) pp. 89–90.

5. S. de Grazia, op.cit., p. 5. Also see pp. 328–389.

6. A. Toffler, op.cit., pp. 337–338. His general view of change is set out in his more recent book The Third Wave, esp. pp. 23–32.

7. H. Kahn and J.A. Wiener, The Year 2000 (New York: Macmillan, 1967) pp. 123–127. See also pp. 57–61, 86–98 and 213–217 on leisure, work and time respectively. For Australia there are the more general predictions in H. Kahn and T. Pepper, Will She Be Right? The Future of Australia (Brisbane: University of Queensland Press, 1980) pp. 116–130.

8. D. Bell, op.cit., pp. 456–466.

9. So Mary Beasley in a paper read to the Australian Institute of Political Science Summer School on 'The Future of Work'. Reported in The Canberra Times (26th January, 1981).

10. See further D. Maric, Adapting Hours to Modern Needs (Geneva: International Labor Organisation, 1977).

11. M. Shapcott, P. Steedman, 'Rhythms of Urban Activity', *Timing Space and Spacing Time*, Vol. III: *Human Activity and Time Geography*, eds. T. Carlstein, D. Parkes and N. Thrift (London: Arnold, 1978) p. 67.

12. D. Parkes and N. Thrift, 'Putting Time in Its Place', *op.cit.*, Vol. 1: *Making Sense of Time*, p. 126.

13. Jobless Action survey reported in the Canberra-based newspaper *Hard Times* (16th July, 1981).

Part 4
The Emergence of Clockwork Man

The clock, not the steam engine, is the key machine of the industrial age.
L. Mumford, Technics and Civilization

9

Advances in the Measurement of Time

It seems as if our problem with time will not simply resolve itself. This leaves us with no option but to confront it and try to understand how it arose. Where should we begin to look for an explanation of our predicament?

The answer must lie among the forces that have shaped the modern world and its attitudes.[1] For, as the theologian Emil Brunner says, 'the haste and rush which characterise our life are something typically modern'.[2] Other social commentators agree. According to one: 'The most fundamental dividing line between modern, industrial societies and traditional, non-industrialised ones, appears to lie in the value accorded to time ...'[3] Another agrees that 'In no characteristic is existing society in the West so sharply distinguished from earlier societies, whether of Europe or the East, than in its conception of time'.[4] A third comments: 'Speed ... tempo, precision, duration and other concepts (are) of little concern to pre-industrial people ... In these temporal phenomena of modern society we have a situation which is unique to our time'.[5]

Somewhere along the line of modern development, unprecedented tendencies have been set in motion. We need to determine whether external factors bear the major responsibility here, or internal drives for which we are accountable—or some combination of the two. Given the complexity of contemporary life, it is no easy task to disentangle such elements or to weigh their relative significance.[6]

In this section we will look first at the development of time-measurement devices and the change these made in ways of perceiving time. Then we will examine some crucial changes that took place in our Western understanding of reality, and the internal adjustments that accompanied them. Next the impact of industrialisation in every sphere of life comes in for attention. Finally, we will look at the impact these have had upon our attitude towards time, and use of it.

It is difficult to avoid over-simplification in describing in a few pages a set of changes that took place over many centuries, and some may wonder at the value of the exercise anyway. Is it really necessary? Does not our problem lie in the present, not in the past? Yet there is no alternative if we want to understand why we think and act as we do. Omitting to evaluate the past short-circuits even the best current attempts to overcome our difficulties with time and, indeed, is symptomatic of our time problem. Reaching back over the centuries is no mere antiquarian exercise but an essential pre-requisite to getting ourselves out of our present bind.

So while some may be tempted to overlook what follows in favour of the more practical sections that follow, I would encourage you to persevere with it. If here and there you find the material more demanding than to this point, do not let this deter you. The roots of some of our personal problems have a long history and are often complex in character. The situation with our time problem is no different.

The earliest clocks
Early cultures had various methods for measuring periods of time.[7] One way was to observe the heavenly bodies: sun, planets, moon and stars. By this means a professional navigator today can estimate the time correctly to within about a quarter of an hour, though such precision would not have been present or necessary in pre-modern civilisations. Another way was to indicate the length of a particular period in terms of the time it took to complete some

familiar task. This method survives today in such expressions as 'You could do that in the time it takes to skin a rabbit'. An alternative way was to place different-sized sticks in the ground to mark the passage of the sun. When the sticks were coupled with a calibrated plaque, the sundial made its appearance. This method was in use in Hellenistic times, and by the Middle Ages it had become very dependable. A fourth technique involved reference to natural processes which take place at a steady rate, eg, the burning of wood, the flow of water—just as in some societies today events are indicated by how many cigarettes they are away. The water clock and hour glass are only more sophisticated versions of this time-measurement method. They were refined into fairly accurate measuring devices, though the first-century stoic philosopher Seneca remarked that 'it is easier to find agreement between two philosophers than between two water clocks'![8] The hours in a Roman or Greek 'day' were variable, and this remained the norm well into the early modern period. All days had the same number of hours but, taking sunrise as their starting-point and sunset as their terminus, they lasted longer in summer and contracted in winter.

When did the clock as we know it arrive? Most researchers place its invention in the latter half of the thirteenth century. Clocks were first installed in public buildings. Before their appearance bells had announced the time of day to each city's inhabitants, alerting them to the danger of fire or an approaching enemy, calling them to arms or to peaceful assemblies, telling them when to go to bed and when to get out of it, when to go to work, when to pray and when to fight, marking the opening and closing of fairs, and celebrating the elections of popes, the coronations of kings, and victories and wars.[9] For residents of monasteries and convents, bells rang out the times for worship, work, meals, prayers, waking, resting and special occasions.

At first, clocks did not alter the rhythms of secular and religious life significantly. After all, they had only hour hands to mark the time and were not particularly accurate. They perpetuated the pattern of seasonal variations in the length of hours and were only gradually equipped with mechanisms for striking the hours and quarters. Lacking sophistication, the early clocks did not so much strictly regulate, as more generally shape, people's lives. They helped establish general co-ordination and daily routine, but not in a precise or harried way.[10] (Astronomical information was also provided by some public clocks, and clocks possessed astrological and symbolic value for many people.) Throughout mediaeval times the day remained by far the most important unit of time.[11]

During the Renaissance and Reformation, use of clocks spread, fostered not only by clocks' usefulness but also by civic pride and mechanical interest. During this time the first domestic clocks made their appearance. Admired by their upper class owners as much for their ornamental as their practical value, they also gradually attracted the attention of scholarly and better educated people. Interestingly, many clockmakers were attracted to the Reformation. A good proportion of them found their way to Switzerland when they began to suffer persecution for their new-found religious beliefs.

By the early seventeenth century the champions of the scientific revolution had become engrossed with the clock:

> Clockmaking was the first industry to put into practice the theoretical findings of physics and mechanics. At the same time, it set the pace for the general development of applied mathematics and played a role of prime importance in the evolution of scientific instruments.[12]

The scientifically minded of the period saw the clock as the machine *par excellence*. But until the introduction of the pendulum in 1658 and the balance-spring in 1674, clocks and pocket-watches were unreliable timekeepers. Much more attention was devoted to embellishing them than to making them work precisely.[13] Craftsmen devoted their energies mainly to elaborating their mechanisms and embroidering their appearance rather than developing their accuracy. For their owners, clocks were as much status symbols and playthings, decorations and elaborate toys, fashionable ornaments and sophisticated gadgets, as useful instruments. Like a child's first wristwatch today, they elicited admiration rather than conformity in behaviour.

Mass-produced timepieces

Public attitudes to time-keeping began to change as growing numbers of business people purchased and used clocks. Even so, not until the late eighteenth and early nineteeth centuries did clocks start to function widely in the way we know them. Only then did they become the main agents for co-ordinating large groups in society and for regulating the lives of individuals. Pocket-watches were common by 1800 among artisans and the burgeoning middle-classes. Use of wristwatches was not widespread until the last quarter of the century, and only in our own century have they achieved the status of necessity. The first wristwatch was made in Switzerland in 1865, and by the 1880s American factories were turning out thousands.

Speaking of the nineteenth century, time historian Cipolla remarks:

> People became very conscious of time, and, in the long run, punctuality became at the very same time a need, a virtue, and an obsession. Thus a vicious circle was set in motion. As more and more people obtained clocks and watches, it became necessary for other people to possess similar contrivances, and the machine created the condition for its own proliferation.[14]

In this way the wristwatch and clock became the most widespread mechanical aids in our society.

During this century, and especially in the last few years, we have seen the increasing sophistication in time-keeping devices. Stopwatches enabled even smaller units of time to be measured. Computerised clocks introduced more precision. Quartz and atomic clocks developed this to an even greater accuracy. Now that the latest watches include stopwatch facilities, and the means of clocking time in other time zones, the ordinary person can avail himself of some of these refinements.

Watches and clocks have also been linked with other mechanical and electrical inventions. This has widened the scope of their usefulness. Already in the last century a machine enabled employees to 'clock on' and 'clock off' at work. More recently the radio clock or oven clock provides two services at once for the worker and housewife.

With the advent of the digital watch in the last decade, people's passion for accuracy in timekeeping appears to have increased. The use of recorded time services has increased rapidly in the last few years. As a telephone company spokesman explained, 'Once a person gets hold of a digital watch with seconds as well as minutes and hours, they like to think they are precise'.[15] While this concern for precision may not necessarily carry over into behaviour—to some extent people are simply fascinated with the novelty of the digital watch—it reflects an attitude which is deeply embedded in the modern mind.

The digital watch signals another change in our thinking about time. Instead of the circular hand movements of the more traditional timepiece, we now have a succession of numbers, together with the preset or hourly 'bleeper'. This has tended to reduce our awareness of the 'flow' of time, and increased our sense of its atomistic, mechanical nature. The practical effects of this change on our general outlook and behaviour remain to be seen.

Protests against the clock

Protests against the clock have consistently arisen, particularly among more artistic observers. Already at the beginning of the modern epoch, through Shakespeare and other dramatists of the period, the clock steps on to the Elizabethan stage. With its appearance mortality and love are both felt to be more poignant and there is a new immediacy and insistence.[16] The new approach to time more and more intruded itself into literature. By the eighteenth century, in Sterne's *Tristam Shandy*, we have the hero's father described as one of the most regular men who ever lived. *Moll Flanders* is also one of fiction's great timekeepers.

Before long, however, the Romantics on both sides of the Channel were vehemently rejecting the clock-bound nature of life. So strongly did some feel this that they altogether excluded clock-time from representation on stage or mention in verse. Indeed Baudelaire went so far as to regard the clock as a symbol of evil and man as its defenceless victim. To him

> Its metallic, impersonal quality was more horrifying than any power thought of as personal; the rapid motion and insect-like

chatter of the second hand was more awesome to the ears than the resonance of bells ... The rhythm of the clock and of other objects and phenomena had a threatening aspect; their monotonous sound resembled the footsteps of the spectre of death ... [17]

Nineteenth century literature also shows an awareness of the ever-intrusive character of timepieces. George Eliot records Adam Bede's listening to the clock's 'hard indifferent tick'. The emblem of Dickens' Gradgrind was the 'deadly statistical clock ... which measured every second with a beat like a rap on a coffin-lid'. Lewis Carroll's White Rabbit forever consulted his pocket-watch in order to avoid being late. So 'the Victorians, at least as their verse and prose reveal them, were preoccupied almost obsessively with time and all the devices that measure time's flight'.[18] The consequences of this come to vivid expression in poems like Matthew Arnold's 'The Scholar Gypsy', which deplores 'the strange disease of modern life with its sick hurry', and 'The Future' which laments that '... repose has fled forever the course of the river to time'.[19]

As for the literature of our own century, 'In virtually every case ... the clock is summoned forth as a negative symbol of the subjective consciousness of an individual who wishes to assert his own private time against the chains of public life. Clocks in modern literature seem to exist only to be ignored, dropped, shattered, deformed or imposed upon.'[20] Typical here is the view expressed in Faulkner's *The Sound and the Fury* that 'time is dead as long as it is being clicked off by little wheels; only when the clock stops does time come to life'. Or Gudrun in Lawrence's *Women in Love* fearing 'the terrible bondage of this tick-tock of time, this twitching of the hands of the clock, this eternal repetition of hours and days ... there was no escape from it, no escape'. Other writers like Proust, Joyce and Woolf, to name only a few, along with philosophers like Bergson and Heidegger and scientists like Einstein searched for a new sense of time far removed from the rhythms of the clock.

Conclusion

Despite these protests, there is no denying the value of the clock. It is an invention which has had the most far-reaching application.

Without it life in large cities, at least as we know it, would not be possible. The clock is the heartbeat of the city, enabling it to function as an efficient organism. If clocks did not exist, there would be relative chaos at all levels of urban organisation. Large-scale co-ordination of people and activities could not take place. Even small-scale arrangements would labour under certain difficulties. Whether the clock should be allowed to possess so dominant a place in modern life, however, and so pervasive an influence on our most ordinary actions, is another matter.

But a prior question so far remains unanswered. Why did the clock not remain an ornament? Why did it not suffer the fate of other ingenious toys that craftsmen produced? Why did it not only become widespread but have a significant influence upon the way people lived? Advances in time-measurement do not in themselves provide an explanation for this. We cannot put it down simply to greater technical expertise or to mass methods of production. These certainly created the conditions for the watch and clock assuming such a central place in modern societies but they in no way made that inevitable. We have to look elsewhere to understand why it became so.

Footnotes

1. For the general remarks on this see M. Douglas, *Cultural Bias* (London: Royal Anthropological Institute, 1958) pp. 28–30.
2. E. Brunner, *Christianity and Civilization: Foundations* (London: Nisbet, 1948) p. 45.
3. H. Nowotny, 'Time Structuring and Time Measurement: On the Interrelation Between Timekeepers and Social Time', *The Study of Time II*, J.T. Fraser and N. Lawrence (eds.) (Berlin: Springer, 1975) p. 329.
4. G. Woodcock, 'The Tyranny of the Clock' in A. Naftalin (ed.) *An Introduction to Social Science* (Chicago: Lippincott, 1953) p. 209.
5. N. Anderson, *Work and Leisure* (London: Routledge and Kegan Paul, 1961) p. 14.
6. Cf. C.M. Cipolla, *Clocks and Culture 1300–1700* (London: Collins, 1967) p. 22.
7. In more detail see, inter alia, M.P. Nilsson, *Primitive Time Reckoning: A Study in the Origins and First Development of the Art of Counting Time Among the Primitive and Early Culture People* (Lund: Gleerup, 1920); H.J. Cowan, *Time and Its Measurement from Stone Age to Nuclear Age* (Cleveland: World Publishing, 1958); K. Welch, *Time Measurement:*

an *Introductory History* (Newton Abbot: David and Charles, 1972); and J.T. Fraser, *Of Time, Passion and Knowledge: Reflections on the Strategy of Existence* (New York: Braziller, 1975) pp. 1–62.

8. Seneca, *Apocolocyntosis*, p. 2. On Roman time, see further the good popular account in J. Carcopino, *Daily Life in Ancient Rome* (Harmondsworth: Penguin, 1956) pp. 160–168.

9. C.M. Cipolla, *op.cit.*, p. 38.

10. On monastic life see Dom. David Knowles, *The Monastic Order in England* (Cambridge: Cambridge University, 1940) and D. Parry, *Households of God: The Rule of St. Benedict* (London: Darton, Longman and Todd, 1980).

11. See further R. Glasser, *Time in French Life and Thought* (Manchester: Manchester University Press, 1972) pp. 55–62.

12. C. Cipolla, *op.cit.*, pp. 58–59.

13. See generally in this connection the often reported statement of Charles V of France (*c.* 1550) quoted by J.T. Fraser, *op.cit.* (1975) p. 62. Even beyond the seventeenth century sundials continued in use, partly to set clocks.

14. C. Cipolla, *op.cit.*, p. 103.

15. See the report on Telecom Australia's 1980–81 financial operations in *The Canberra Times* (12th December, 1981).

16. See most fully F. Turner, *Shakespeare on the Nature of Time* (Oxford: Clarendon, 1971).

17. R. Glasser, *op.cit.*, p. 283. For other examples see the poems of Edward Herbert of Cherbury, John Milton and John Hall—with an eye to the watch, clock and hour-glass respectively—in *The Metaphysical Poets*, ed. H. Gardner (Harmondsworth: Penguin, 1972) pp. 94–95, 176–177, 288–289.

18. J.H. Buckley, *op.cit.*, pp. 1–2.

19. See 'The Scholar Gypsy' lines 144–145 and 'The Future' lines 58–68, *Matthew Arnold: A Selection of His Poems* (Harmondsworth: Penguin, 1954) pp. 212, 187 respectively.

20. Th. Ziolkowski, 'The Discordant Clocks', *Dimensions of the Modern Novel* (Princeton: Princeton University Press, 1969) p. 188, the caveat about public time and structure being entered by D.H. Higdon, *Time and English Fiction* (London: Macmillan, 1977). For an examination of the role of time in many key modern writers see (ed.) A. Patrides, *op.cit.*, pp. 114–249.

10

Changing Attitudes to Time and Reality

Alongside technical developments in time-measurement, a transformation took place in the way people viewed time and reality. What we see happening between the fifteenth and nineteenth centuries is the gradual demise of the traditional worldview, with its partially Christian contours, in favour of the modern secular outlook. Life in general began to take on a different character.

The early modern outlook

According to the Mediaeval worldview, each person's life was a small drama played out against the temporal backdrop of a cosmic drama involving God and mankind, heaven and hell, the Creation and Last Judgment. Like the air one breathed, time was simply a natural accompaniment of all human activities; it was not viewed as resource to be self-consciously utilised and arranged. Certainly some people in earlier times had been encouraged to use 'every hour' and 'each day' wisely. We also occasionally come across extremely industrious and time-conscious men.[1] But these do not appear to reflect general tendencies in their own or later times.

During the Renaissance time was still seen primarily as the atmosphere or environment which enabled one to experience others and nature more intimately and to develop oneself more fully. Instead, people became more inclined to celebrate time and to resent the possibility of being regulated by the clock.[2]

Exponents of the new Humanism that followed developed a more serious attitude towards time. The mood was sombre and, for the first time in any widespread way, there developed a bad conscience concerning misuse and wasting of time. Careful watch began to be kept over the use of small divisions of time as well as over the total life span.[3] The human rather than the human–divine drama, and the span of one's lifetime rather than of God's eternity, now occupied the stage.

The Puritan Revolution restored a strong sense of the divine and emphasised the celebrating of life. The campaign to turn Sunday into a Sabbath gradually won favour with bourgeois Englishmen and the pioneering Americans and was in its time a significant cultural contribution. While strict Sabbath-keeping suppressed certain sporting and aesthetic elements, it emphasised enjoying God, helping others, relaxing mentally and bodily, and sanctifying the natural world.[4] The Puritans prohibited holidays which did not coincide with Sunday, thereby inadvertently preparing the way for the more routinised way of life required in industrialisation. They also encouraged awareness and use of small units of time. The idea of 'redeeming the time' played a prominent part in Puritan rhetoric. Likening time to money, Richard Baxter urged his readers:

> Use every minute of it as a most precious thing, and spend it wholly in the way of duty ... Remember how gainful the Redeeming of Time is ... in Merchandise or in trading, in husbandry or any gaining course ...[5]

We should beware of reading our modern notion of busyness into statements such as this. The diary of another Puritan, Richard Rodgers, shows that this was far from his mind. In it he allots as much time for 'eating, recreating, idle talk and journeys' as for direct engagement in the Lord's work.[6] It remains true, however, that Puritans like Baxter were attuned to the mores of the rising commercial and trading groups in society.

The modern viewpoint emerges

All these developments bring us to the threshold of our modern view of time. The first decisive step took place in the late seventeenth century during the Scientific Revolution. The person responsible was Isaac Newton, who formulated the notion of mathematical time: time made up of a sequence of equally divisible units. 'Absolute true and mathematical time', he wrote, 'of itself and from its own nature flows equably without relation to anything eternal.'[7] This understanding of time is artificial, having little to do with the way we actually experience events. It sees time as not only completely external to us, but fractionatal as well. In short, Newton put into conceptual form the understanding of time that the now-perfected clocks and watches of his day implied.

Newton maintained strong personal religious beliefs, but his approach to time smoothed the way for a deistic outlook. God could be seen to have simply set time and the world going, much as a craftsman makes and winds up a clock and then leaves it while he gets on with other things. The corollary of such a view is that man, too, can get on with other things and not worry much about God. Although Newton never drew this conclusion from his theory, at a practical level some men of his era did. Turning their backs on the Puritan conviction that it was essentially God's achievement through Christ which justified a person's life and gave him or her a sense of worth, they set out to justify themselves to themselves and others, no longer through religious good works (since the Reformation had closed off that route to them) but through their secular jobs. It is precisely here that we have the source of the 'Protestant work ethic'. This ethic arose, not through a Calvinist insistence on the importance of good works for gaining assurance of one's divine election, but in a secularised distortion of it among the upwardly mobile but formally religious middle-classes.[8]

In the eighteenth century the Enlightenment brought a more resolute secularising of life. Belief in a supra-natural universe existing alongside this one, and in life after death, decreased. People began to see their brief span of years in a finite context rather than in an eternal one. The more people confined their sights to the material and temporal horizons of this world, the stronger the temptation to realise all their goals, and find all their values, within this world. Their desire for immediate gains placed a growing pressure upon the time at their disposal. A more intensive use of everyday time and a stronger belief in human progress eventuated.[9]

With the appearance of Methodism, time became a matter of concern in religious circles. The very name 'Methodist' implies a regulated sense of time, and Wesley had the distinction of being described as the first busy man. 'John Wesley's conversation is good,' said Dr Johnson, 'but he is never at leisure. He is always obliged to go at a certain hour. This is very disagreeable to a man who loves to fold his legs and have out his talk, as I do.'[10] Wesley made much of people's mortality, of the fact that they had so little time in life. He also employed images of time as a medium of exchange, though with little emphasis on commerce. For the Christian life was a matter of 'saving all the time you can for the best purposes' and 'buying up every fleeting moment out of the hands of sin'.[11] It is important to remember here Wesley's influence upon British evangelicalism, as well as his successful ministry in America.

These emerging attitudes found their embodiment in Benjamin Franklin, who favoured and perhaps even coined the expression 'time is money'. Franklin, who maintained a life-long interest in clocks, crystallised the new attitude to time:

> Since our Time is reduced to a Standard, and the Bullion of the Day minted out into Hours, the Industrious know how to employ every Piece of Time to a real Advantage in their different Professions: and he that is prodigal of his Hours is, in effect, a Squanderer of Money.[12]

According to Franklin time was a medium of exchange for the pursuit of primarily secular ends. His fully commercialised view of time helped mould the ideology of the New World, with its faith in human progress. Franklin and his compatriots were fashioning a new social order. For them time was a kind of human resource on the one hand and almost a divine force on the other.

Later modern developments

The Romantic Movement in Europe in the late eighteenth and early nineteenth centuries was in part a reaction against these trends. It emphasised an inner sense of time which had nothing to do with technical inventions like the clock or scientific notions of a mathematical kind; it espoused a less optimistic view of the course of history; and it stressed the unity between people, the world and the divine order (the last two sometimes merged more than in traditional religious thinking), rather than the individual's isolation from his natural and spiritual environment. Rousseau, who formed a bridge between the Enlightenment and Romanticism, was probably the first commentator to sound a note of alarm about the increasing regulation and haste of modern life.

Later in the nineteenth century, a new philosophy emerged. Among some social thinkers, 'utility' became the chief value in personal and social life. A key figure here was Jeremy Bentham, who became the father of the 'science' of administration and bureaucracy. With the earthly 'happiness of the greatest possible number' as the goal, Bentham and his fellow utilitarian thinkers developed a passion for 'order' and 'efficiency' in the management of society. Their schemes depended upon the measurement of processes and inducements in as exact a manner as possible. Consequently

> ... man himself could now be regulated. When the rule was applied by the engineer—the utilitarian *par excellence*—not only was work broken down in detail, but it was measured by detail, and paid for in time units defined in metric qualities. With this new rationality came a unique and abrupt break from the rhythm of work in the past. With it came a new role of time.[13]

Utilitarian attitudes began to affect people's attitude to their free time. The view gradually prevailed that only useful activity was valuable, moral and meaningful. Unless their rest and recreation achieved something 'worthwhile', people felt guilty. Relaxation as an end in itself, pure play and idleness all came under censure or suspicion. The hobby, competitive games and leisure activities started to supplant them.

The evolutionary theory propounded by Charles Darwin at once modified and reinforced attitudes towards time.[14] It not only reinforced a view of life bounded by birth and the grave but made the length of the time seem even shorter. Compared with the

aeons of time involved in evolution itself, man's lot seemed very
insignificant indeed. Partially affected by this point of view, for
many historians a purposeful view of the passage of events gave
way to a straightforward linear view of time—a record of simply
'one damn thing after another'. As for the mass of people:

> Some time during the nineteenth century, in the industrialised
> nations of the West, the use of the worker's time on the one
> hand and, on the other hand, his individual destiny in time
> came to be seen as two separate issues ... this amounted to a
> cleavage between what people do and what they are.[15]

More than anyone else in the nineteenth century, Karl Marx saw
this cleavage most clearly. As Sidney Hook notes: 'Marx was
particularly sensitive to the place and importance of time'.[16] In the
first place, Marx embraced the scientific, technological view with
its emphasis upon 'this worldly' time. As well, he claimed that the
entrepreneur's exploitation of workers' time lay at the root of
capitalist development. He also discerned the centrality of the
clock in the industrial process. 'The clock', he commented, 'is the
first automatic machine applied to practical purposes; the whole
production of regular motion was developed through it'.[17] Marx
foresaw the alienating and socially destructive effects of the
mechanisation of work, but he failed to speak out against the
excessive regulation of time. As J.T. Fraser sums up: 'From the
sixteenth century on, clockwork became the bourgeois—later the
communist—ideal, a quasi-religious object for both, and the
paradigm of praiseworthy conduct'.[18]

Among Christians, individuals like Shaftesbury worked tire-
lessly to improve working conditions and alleviate social hard-
ships. But the churches did not challenge the sense of time
associated with the new economic era. On the contrary, middle-
class nineteenth-century Christians advocated tighter and tighter
control of time. They became excessively concerned with punctuality. In the family home of that extraordinary missionary in
China, Hudson Taylor, there was a typically strict policy about
turning up to meals on time. As Taylor's father used to explain:

> 'If there are five people and they are kept waiting one minute,
> do you not see that five minutes are lost that can never be found
> again?'[19]

E.P. Thompson sums up the dominant Christian attitude to time during this period. A scrutiny of sermons, homilies and tracts reveals that throughout the nineteenth century the propaganda of time-thrift continued to be directed to the working people, the rhetoric becoming more debased, the apostrophes to eternity becoming more shop-soiled, the homilies more mean and banal. In early Victorian tracts and reading matter aimed at the masses, one is choked by the quantity of the stuff ...[20] In other words, nineteenth-century churchmen compounded the time problem. They did not assist in its solution.

Conclusion

During the last five centuries, we have seen a gradual foreshortening of the time boundaries within which people see their lives taking place. The erosion of the Christian world-view by a humanist one narrowed people's gaze to the brief span of life allotted them. The influence of evolutionary ideas made that span seem even less significant. In addition, scientific thought reduced time to a mechanical affair. With utilitarian notions carrying the day in both capitalist and communist countries, work and leisure came under great regulation and stricter account of their profitability. As a result the importance of small, artificially reckoned units of time rapidly increased. Meanwhile both businessmen and churchmen extolled the virtues of discipline in the use of time and attacked idleness.

But all of this still does not add up to our present view of time or explain the shortage of time so many experience. No more than advances in time-measurement does it account for our predicament. There is still a missing factor.

Footnotes

1. On the first, see Seneca, 'On Saving Time', *Epistulae Morales*, (ed.) R.M. Grummare (London: Heinemann, 1953) I pp. 3–5. On the second, Pliny the Elder, *Natural History* (intro.), H. Rackham (London: Heinemann, 1958) I pp. x–xii.

2. For a thorough discussion see R.J. Quinones, *The Renaissance Discovery of Time* (Cambridge, Mass: Harvard University Press, 1972). There is also his briefer treatment, 'Time and Historical Values in the Literature of the Renaissance', *Aspects of Time*, (ed.) C.A. Patrides (Manchester: Manchester University, 1976) pp. 39–56.

3. See W. Sombart, *The Quintessence of Capitalism* (London: Unwin, 1915) pp. 104–108, quoting the fifteenth century L.B. Alberti's work, 'On the Family'.

4. This aspect of Puritanism, frequently neglected, is rightly stressed by R. Lee, *op.cit.*, p. 171 and W.U. Solberg, *Redeem the Time: The Puritan Sabbath in Early America* (Cambridge, Mass: Harvard, 1977).

5. R. Baxter, *A Christian Directory* (London: 1673) pp. 274–277. See also *The Poor Man's Family Book* (London, 1697), (6th edition) pp. 290–291.

6. R. Rodgers, 'A Garden of Spirituall Flowers', in *Two Elizabethan Diaries*, (ed.) M.N. Knappen (Gloucester, Mass: Peter Smith, 1966) p. 88. On Puritan attitudes generally, see E.P. Thompson, 'Time, Work-Discipline and Industrial Capitalism' in M.W. Flinn and T.C. Smout (eds.), *Essays in Social History* (Oxford: Clarendon, 1974) p. 61. Thompson overestimates the extent to which concern with time was central or unique to Puritan teaching.

7. I. Newton, *Principia Mathematica*, Definitions: Scholium I (Berkeley: University of California, 1962) I p. 6.

8. For a more balanced assessment of the evidence see the comments of, and works cited by, M.J. Kitch, *Capitalism and the Reformation* (London: Longman, 1967) pp. 164–180 (especially the treatment of time on pp. 164–170). Unfortunately even modern evaluations of the Puritan attitude to time follow Weber uncritically here. See, for example, J.T. Fraser, *The Voices of Time: A Co-operative Survey of Man's View of Time as Expressed by the Sciences and the Humanities* (London: Penguin/Allen Lane, 1968) quoting R.H. Knapp, 'Time Imagery and the Achievement Motive', *Journal of Personality* (26, 1958) p. 426 and 'Attitudes Towards Time and Aesthetic Choice', *Journal of Social Psychology* (56, 1962) p. 79.

9. See A.H. Mendilow, 'The Time Obsession of the Twentieth Century', *Aspects of Time*, (ed.) C.A. Patrides (Manchester: Manchester University, 1976) pp. 69–74. On the connection between the idea of progress and the economic motif there is the discussion by B. Goudzwaard, *Capitalism and Progress: A Diagnosis of Western Society* (Grand Rapids: Eerdmans, 1979). On the change in metaphysical thinking about the universe, see A.O. Lovejoy, *The Great Chain of Being: The History of an Idea* (New York: Harper, 1960) esp. pp. 242–287.

10. See J. Boswell, *The Life of Samuel Johnson* (London: Dent, 1949) II pp. 167–168.

11. J. Wesley, 'On Redeeming the Time', *The Works of John Wesley* (London: Cordeaux, 1811) p. 181.

12. From 'Poor Richard's Almanac' (1751) in *The Papers of Benjamin Franklin*, (eds.) L.W. Larrabee and W.J. Bell (New Haven, Connecticut, 1961) cv. 86–87. For a series of more recent, similarly inspired statements see G.M. Lebhar, *The Use of Time* (New York: Chain Store, 1958) pp. 83–146.

13. D. Bell, *op.cit.*, p. 224. This was a far cry from the sort of efficiency talked about by Adam Smith, *An Inquiry into the Nature and Causes of the Wealth of Nations*, ed. R.H. Campbell and A.S. Skinner (Oxford: Clarendon, 1976) pp. 19–20, for he sought to preserve a place for natural rhythms of work (pp. 99–100).

14. Cf. F.C. Haber, 'The Darwinian Revolution in the Concept of Time' in J.T. Fraser, F.C. Haber and G. Mueller (eds.), *The Study of Time* (New York: Springer, 1972) p. 385.

15. J.T. Fraser, *op.cit.*, (1975) p. 378.

16. S. Hook, *From Hegel to Marx: Studies in the Intellectual Development of Karl Marx* (Ann Arbor: University of Michigan Press, 1971) p. 32.

17. Marx in a letter to Engels on 28th January, 1863, in *Karl Marx and Friedrich Engels: Selected Correspondence 1846–1895* (New York: International Publishers, 1942) p. 142. For Marx's doctrine of surplus value consult K. Marx, *Capital* (Harmondsworth: Penguin, 1976).

18. J.T. Fraser, *op.cit.*, (1975) p. 377.

19. Dr and Mrs Howard Taylor, *Hudson Taylor in Early Years: The Growth of a Soul* (London: China Inland Mission, 1911) p. 47.

20. See again E.P. Thompson, *op.cit.*, p. 64.

11

The Industrialisation of Work and Leisure

We have seen how developments in time-measurement provided the technical means for approaching time differently, and how changes in worldview led to a growing desire to make the most of it. However, these changes alone do not fully explain the drastic shortage of time and frantic pace of life we experience today. Industrialisation provides the missing link.

The impact upon work

Before the industrial revolution, small-scale domestic and workshop production was based on a flexible approach to time. Tasks themselves were regarded as that which should define time, not vice versa, and a variety of jobs were undertaken by all workers in a team. Mondays as well as Sundays were usually taken off or worked more lightly.

The formation of the large factory required greater co-ordination of the workforce, so that machines could be operated properly; also more intensive use of time, so that machines could be used to their maximum capacity. In the beginning, while towns and factories remained small, the bell-tower and whistle seemed sufficient for the task. Then came the clock, first placed in a tower and later hung up wherever work was to be done. It provided the means whereby industrialists could co-ordinate the movements of large numbers of men to the regularity of machines. Through timekeeping, as well as through division of labour, fines, incentives, and closer supervision of workers, a new conception of time developed.[1] Though it was one which possessed many advantages in terms of efficiency, and facilitated the affluent way of life which many enjoy today, its disadvantages have not received as much attention.

With the industrial revolution came a rise in the number of hours ordinarily worked. In England the general pattern of working hours, established in 1495 during the reign of Henry VII, was superseded. As well, there were now fewer holy days which people could take off, and there was a vast difference between working in a tightly regulated factory and working out in the fields. Some factories established a 12-hour to 14-hour day for their workers. Previously a 10-hour day had been the norm.

Gradually the mechanisation of work time spread throughout the community. Not only blue-collar but white-collar workers, not only wage-earners but those on salaries and stipends, not only people in business but those in professions, gradually absorbed the new ethos. All work came to be visualised in terms of the time dimension.[2] As de Grazia notes, 'the modern factory is fundamentally a place of order in which stimulus and response, the rhythm of work, derive from a mechanically imposed sense of time and place'.[3] The typical office is also highly regulated: as Aldous Huxley remarked: 'Today every efficient office [is a] prison in which the workers suffer ... from the consciousness of being inside a machine'.[4]

In time the newer salaried professionals became as much a part of the system as anyone, and self-employed professionals found it hard to resist the constraints which society's timetables imposed upon them. Witness the daily schedules of doctors and lawyers, for instance, with their division of the day into small fractions. In this way the tentacles of time spread out and encircled the whole working process. 'Time rules the work economy, its various rhythms and motions.'[5]

The 'industrialised' approach to time has affected many activities related to employment. So that numbers of people can get to and from work on time, for example, social organisation of a highly sophisticated kind has become necessary. Our transport systems operate on complicated timetables, with exact timekeeping and the highest possible speeds their goals. The farther workers' homes are distanced from their places of employment, the more complex these systems must become. So 'in his travel to and from work the worker is chained by time'. Even those driving private cars to work must follow regular timetables prescribed by the pattern of working hours and traffic flow. Patterns of sleeping and waking are also drawn into the orbit of work-controlled time. The alarm clock or pre-set clock-radio beside the bed has become a necessity. This regulation was by no means all damaging. In some measure it was both needful and helpful. Public transport systems, for example, could not function without it. But its penetration of so many aspects of the individual's life should have been a cause for concern.

Returning to the service area of the economy, Theodor Veblen points out that 'schedules of time, place and circumstance rule throughout'.[6] The more people wish to avail themselves of such services, and the farther they are geographically separated from those who supply them, the more necessary it becomes for consumers and producers of services to make mutual arrangements, co-ordinate and plan ahead. This also affects services of a cultural kind. In the area of education, for instance, the school system has become as tightly organised as the modern factory. Bells, clocks, timetables and schedules are just as intrusive.

The effects upon free time
Even free time feels the pressure of the clock. The attitude to time in the factory or office accompanies people to work, follows them home, and—increasingly—stays with them during their evenings, weekends, public holidays and vacations. The phrase 'free time' indicates that we measure leisure's value in relation to work. It is not so much what leisure time offers in itself that is prized, but the release it provides from work. Similarly the expression 'spare time' suggests something unexpectedly given and highlights the difference between work-occupied and unoccupied time. The ancient Greeks defined leisure differently. For them it was the

dominant reality and work was regarded as secondary. One worked to have leisure rather than had leisure in order to work. The word they used for work meant 'non-leisure'. The ancient Hebrews used a special term, 'sabbath', to describe a non-work time; for them non-work time possessed independent significance. These ancient cultures fixed their attention on the state or quality of leisure rather than the type or amount of time available. But today 'leisure' is something which flows from, and prepares for, work. We relax, take a break, go away on vacation, in order to recover from work and regain strength for more work. Use of the military term for a holiday—'leave'—makes this connection clear.[7] In West Germany recently a man was prosecuted by his employer for returning from holidays too tired to recommence work efficiently. As the holiday was paid for by the employer, the court ruled that its purpose was to refresh the employee for further work.[8]

With industrialisation comes the fixing of times for celebrations and holidays. In his epic account of life in northern Queensland, *Poor Fellow My Country*, Xavier Herbert gives an example. As foreign-based industrialists moved in to take over locally owned cattle stations, the date of the annual race carnival—the high point of the station-hands' and town-dwellers' year—became more firmly fixed:

> Originally the date had depended on when the season ended. That was before the Vaiseys took over. Since then it had rather been that the end of the season was fixed by that date; as if Lord Alfred Vaisey, in his financial wisdom, had seen it as a means to more efficient work of his properties and further profit in reduced wages bills, since the common workers were employed only during those six weeks ...[9]

Before industrialisation the timing of holidays and leave-of-absence was determined to a large extent by seasons, the weather and personal requirements. Remember the brother in George Eliot's *Adam Bede* who, with scarcely any forethought, took time off to go on a week's walk to visit relatives in another village? With the coming of the factory, however, certain weeks in the year were earmarked for workers' holidays and all machinery was shut down during these weeks; leave-of-absence during other periods was refused except under extreme circumstances, eg, 'compassionate leave'.

Industrialisation at first affected only work time; social life preserved its traditional patterns. But gradually leisure time came under pressure from the clock. This arose partly from the need to co-ordinate with others at a distance, partly from the invasion of free time by the productive process. According to Jacques Ellul:

> Leisure time is mechanised time and is exploited by techniques which, although different from those of man's ordinary work, are as invasive, exacting, and leave men no more free than labour itself.[10]

During their free time people tended to reproduce behaviour patterns developed in the work situation and shaped by the kind of time inherent in it. Working class culture appears to be a combination of release from, and reproduction of, the rhythms of work,[11] with the first often understandably dominating. In middle-class circles there is a greater tendency to reproduce the workplace's intensive use of time, an intensity to which we become addicted. For example, psychologically many of us find it difficult to operate at a slower pace on weekends and holidays. We find it hard to switch into second, let alone first, gear at such times, while to stop altogether—except in front of a TV set—is virtually impossible. Business and professional people frequently find that the managerial, achieving performance required of them at work is just as much expected of them in their free time activities, eg, running voluntary organisations, always winning at sport.[12]

The preference for mass-produced rather than self-made free time activities also affected the use of time. The large-scale commercialisation of leisure activities in our society has led to a more standardised, co-ordinated approach to free time, though this is now under a certain amount of challenge through the introduction of innovations like video machines and cable television. Packaged holidays scrupulously allot so much time to this and that as they whisk their patrons at a whirlwind 'if-it's-Tuesday-this-must-be-Belgium' speed through their chocolate-box assortment of sights. Sports have become tied, sometimes inappropriately, to the clock or stopwatch. Precise measurement of time that elapses from the beginning to the end of an event does not speak directly of the event, but instead measures it by units appropriate to a quite different type of occurrence, remote from human involvement. Watches and clocks are not constructed to accord with a sequence of vital acts. They are only mechanical, repetitive agents, external and indifferent to the existence of human activities and their time.[13]

The intensification of time-use

Reforms in the calendar and improvements in time-measurement spelt the end of irregular work patterns shaped by fluctuations in workers' physical energy, variable seasonal conditions and occasional religious celebrations. These reforms also made possible the arbitrary re-arrangement of activities on a vast scale. This process was furthered by the creation of a national Standard Time or, in large countries like the United States and Australia, of several fixed time-zones, so ending the fluctuations in local times that lasted until almost the end of the last century, and in a few places even longer. Around-the-clock shift work and 'hourly' or 'piece' rates of pay emerged. Echoes of the old way of thinking survived only in the terms 'overtime', 'time and a half', and 'double time'.

The mechanical view of time as a series of interchangeable units broke through the rhythms and limits of natural, personal, social and religious time, imposing itself upon virtually any time during the day, week or year. Change was furthered by such inventions as the gas light and electric light, which for the first time in human history made it feasible to use night-time hours for the purposes of work on a mass scale. (The emergency situation in wartime pushes this tendency to extremes.) Intensified use—or, as one writer has called it, 'colonisation'—of time has become part and parcel of daily life in all societies like our own. The last great frontier of human migration is occurring in time—a spreading of wakeful activity throughout the 24 hours of the day.[14]

Utilitarian philosophy advocated efficiency as the administrative ideal, and throughout the nineteenth century mechanisms

devised to increase efficiency grew more complex. The Bundy
clock (invented in 1885 and named after its creator) was a
refinement of a technique introduced by Wedgwood a century
earlier for determining the exact amount of time an employee
spent on the job. The early twentieth century saw the development of time-and-motion study techniques applicable to management and production by Frederick Taylor and Frank Gilbreth.[15]

The management sciences have been intimately involved in
the application of clocktime to work and discipline.[16] The
slow-motion camera and transistorised computer increased the
sophistication with which time-and-motion studies could be
conducted. Sometimes such studies went past the elimination of
unnecessarily time-consuming or disorganised work, beyond the
mere breakdown of work into its simplest details. Industrial
engineers began to reach out for a simple, comprehensive system
to encompass all time and motion. The devisers of the
Methods-Time-Measurement system, for instance, sought a cata-
logue of defined work motions (reach, move, turn, grasp, position, disengage, etc) with a scale of predetermined time values for
each motion, all pinpointed neatly on one handy card. The goal
was to establish a standard performance time for every job in
industry. Such a system overlooks the fact that a worker's
'natural' rhythms in the use of his hands may in the end be far
more efficient than one 'best' way.[17]

The totalitarian threat implicit in the modern view of time
comes to its clearest, and most frightening, expression in techniques such as Methods-Time-Measurement. The human being is
disregarded; everything is rigidly controlled under an abstract
notion of time and movement.

The application of time-and-motion measurement makes
itself felt in all areas of life. It is particularly noticeable in sport. An
obsession with records marks sporting endeavours in both
amateur and professional circles. 'Scientific' training is based on
the slow-motion camera, computerised clock, precision
measuring instruments and biofeedback devices. The stopwatch is
no longer adequate. Differences between competitors are no
longer reckoned in tenths but in hundredths of a second. Things

have reached the stage where a gold medallist in the Winter Olympics in 1980 won a 15-kilometre cross-country skiing event by a mere 0.001 of a second, a difference so infinitesimal given the distance involved that the entire business took on a ridiculous air. Preoccupation with the fractional clicking of the clock dominates the sportsman's whole existence. Sport has become, as the title of a recent book puts it, 'a prison of measured time'.[18]

The intensification of time use in sport is indicative of the increasing regulation of modern life. It is significant that the last Olympic Games were watched by more people than any other event in our times. For, beyond the interest in sport itself, and the patriotic fervour the occasion elicited, this unique international event symbolised the clock-ruled, pace-dominated, achievement-obsessed character of the world in which we live.

Economic considerations continue to force an intensified use of free time upon us. The Swedish economist Staffran B. Linder has described how this happens. Our desire for material advancement, he says, results not only in greater production during work time but in increased pressure on consumption time as well. While we take pleasure in the wider range of goods we can have, we need more time to enjoy them all. Since the marginal increases in free time that have come our way are nowhere near large enough to cope with the range of goods we have acquired, our free time becomes more pressured. In order to enjoy all our possessions we have to maximise use of our leisure time. One way we do this is by consuming several things at once! It is not uncommon to find someone attempting to listen to the stereo, read the newspaper and eat a meal all at the one time. Leisure time is scheduled like a working day so that as many hard-earned consumer goods as possible can be sampled.

We face a parallel pressure upon our time in relation to the services we rush to utilise. In the consumption-oriented economy it becomes increasingly expensive to direct labour to activities which fail to yield observable gains in productivity. Also, rising standards of living enable the suppliers of services to be more selective about the sorts of services they offer, pushing up the rewards sought for unpleasant jobs. Anyone who has watched the steep rise in the cost of hiring a plumber will recognise this trend. The result is that more time has to be devoted by the consumer to making enough money to buy services. The problem is compounded by the need to spend money on 'instrumental or intermediate activities',[19] eg, the cost of a taxi, so that more can be done in a limited period of time, or the cost of a child-minder, so that more money can be earned. As people look for more and more services to cater to their physical, psychological, educational and cultural desires, increasing pressure will fall upon their free time as well. They will schedule their leisure in order to fit in as many of these as possible.

Conclusion
To summarise:

> The tyranny of the clock ... has developed, step by step, with our successful revolution against the dictatorship of material poverty ... Economic growth entails a general increase in the scarcity of time ... Consumption gobbles up time alive.[20]

So, then, the more we go on seeking additional material goods and personal services, the less time we actually have. The more possessions a person has or services he or she requires, the busier he or she will be.[21] There has been an increasing preference for income over leisure during the last century and there is little sign of this slackening. This suggests that many people are in for an increasingly busy time in the future.[22]

Footnotes
1. Cf. S. de Grazia, op.cit., p. 452.
2. N. Anderson, op.cit., p. 54.
3. S. de Grazia, op.cit., p. 224.
4. Quoted ibid.
5. S. de Grazia, op.cit., p. 226. See further R.L. Rotenberg, The Social Organisation of Time in Complex Societies: A Case Study from Vienna, Austria (Ph.D. University of Massachusetts, 1978) p. 329 ff. Rotenberg distinguishes between a variety of temporal constraints which affect people: institutional ones (eg, times decreed for starting and

stopping work), social ones (eg, use of the car), bureaucratic ones (eg, governmental regulations about opening and closing hours) and environmental ones (eg, location of facilities).

6. Theodor Veblen, *The Theory of Business Enterprise* (New York: Kelley, 1960) pp. 13–14.

7. Cf. J. Moltmann, *Theology and Joy* (London: SCM, 1973) p. 32.

8. Recounted in L.R.B. Elton and H. Messel, *Time and Man* (Oxford: Pergamon, 1978) p. 104.

9. X. Herbert, *Poor Fellow My Country* (Sydney: Collins, 1975) p. 66.

10. J. Ellul, *The Technological Society*, p. 401. See also S. de Grazia, *op.cit.*, p. 452

11. J. Clarke, 'Style', *Resistance Through Rituals: Youth Subcultures in Post-War Britain*, S. Hall and T. Jefferson (eds.) (London: Hutchinson, 1975) p. 76.

12. See further H. Wilensky, 'Work, Careers and Social Integration', *International Social Science Journal* (12, 1960) *passim*, and F. Emery and C. Phillips, *Living at Work* (Canberra: AGPS, 1976). For a brief summary of some of the literature on the 'Compensation' and 'Generalisation' ('Spillover') hypotheses, see further G. Smith, 'Leisure: A Study of Its Relation to Work and Society', *Zadok Papers*, Series 1 (S14, 1979) pp. 10–11.

13. Cf. P. Weiss, *Sport: A Philosophic Inquiry* (Edwardsville: Southern Illinois University Press, 1969) p. 118.

14. M. Melbin, 'The Colonisation of Time', *Human Spacing and Human Time II: Human Activity and Time Geography*, T. Carlstein, D. Parkes and N. Thrift (eds.) (London: Edward Arnold, 1978) p. 100.

15. See F.W. Taylor, *The Principles of Scientific Management* (New York: Harper and Row, 1929) and F.B. Gilbreth, *Motion Study* (Princeton: Von Nostrand, 1911). Excerpts and summaries of their views may be read in (eds.) A. Tillett, T. Kempner and G. Wills, *Management Thinkers* (Harmondsworth: Penguin, 1970) pp. 75–107.

16. J.P. Clark, 'Temporal Inventories and Time Structuring in Large Organisations', *The Study of Time III*, J.T. Fraser, N. Lawrence, D. Park (eds.) (New York: Springer, 1978) pp. 391–418.

17. S. de Grazia, *op.cit.*, pp. 231, 232, 236.

18. J. Marie Brohm, *Sport—A Prison of Measured Time* (London: Ink Links, 1978).

19. F. Hirsch, *Social Limits to Growth* (London: Routledge and Kegan Paul, 1976) p. 74 and I. Illich, *The Right to Useful Unemployment and Its Professional Enemies* (London: Marion Boyars, 1978) pp. 63–64.

20. S.B. Linder, *op.cit.*, p. 4 and S. de Grazia, *op.cit.*, p. 211, respectively. Cf. also G. Becker, 'A Theory of the Allocation of Time', *Economic Journal* (75, 1965) pp. 493–517. On acquisitive tendencies in modern life generally see, inter alia, R.H. Tawney, *The Acquisitive Society* (London: Collins, 1961) and F. Zweig, *The New Acquisitive Society* (Chichester: Rose, 1976).

21. I am taking account here of the reservations expressed about Linder's one-dimensional treatment of time as a resource which is traded off simply with money by F. Stuart Chapin Jnr, *Human Activity Patterns in the City: Things People Do in Time and Space* (New York: Wiley, 1974).

22. Cf. E.H. Phelps-Brown, *A Century of Pay* (Macmillan: London, 1968). I am aware that his conclusions are based on figures relating to the period between 1840 and 1950 only and that Australians have always shown a greater preference for leisure than people from many other countries. But the statistics outlined in chapter 1 show that little change has taken place in the U.S. since and that Australians are only marginally better off.

12

The Deifying and Impoverishing of Time

If the analysis of the last three chapters is correct, the pressure of time in everyday life is not primarily the result of the development or distribution of clocks and watches. More significant were changes in worldview leading to a less God-centred and grace-based approach to life in favour of a more man-centred and work-justifying attitude. Also crucial was the impact of mechanical inventions and administrative techniques that went hand-in-hand with this alteration in viewpoint in the wake of the industrial revolution. These new personal attitudes and industrial forces fuelled each other and generated their own momentum. They led in turn to a more intensive accumulation of goods and services, and to a greater sophistication and penetration of time-measurement devices.

This means that the situation in which we have landed ourselves with respect to time arises partly from our own false set of priorities and partly from forces outside us which possess their own momentum. Our difficulties with time are a symptom of certain deeper problems, ie, the quest for self-worth and the approval of others by means of performance at work or by the amassing of material goods, and the runaway development of the machines and techniques we have developed to gain these ends. Having consciously shaped our desires in certain new directions, we become further shaped by the very mechanisms created to achieve those desires, and the mechanisms in turn create still further desires that we seek to satisfy.

Time as an idol

This has had a significant effect upon the way we view time itself. For one thing we have made too much of it. We have elevated 'clock-time' into a more important place in our lives than it warrants. Even before the Industrial Revolution, Jonathan Swift discerned that a new idol had arisen. In his fable *Gulliver's Travels* he records his hero's capture by the Lilliputians. Fascinated by various aspects of Gulliver's clothing, the Lilliputians note:

> Out of his pocket hung a great silver chain, with a wonderful kind of engine at the bottom. We directed him to draw out whatever was at the end of that chain; which appeared to be a globe, half silver, and half of some transparent metal: for on the transparent side we saw certain strange figures circularly drawn, and thought we could touch them, until we found our fingers stopped with that lucid substance. He put this engine to our ears, which made an incessant noise like that of a water-mill: and we conjecture it is either some unknown animal, or the god that he worships: but we are more inclined to the latter opinion, because he assured us (if we understood him right, for he expressed himself very imperfectly), that he seldom did anything without consulting it. He called it his oracle, and said it pointed the time for every action of his life.[1]

Anyone who has worn a watch will recognise the force of these observations. Clock-time has become tyrannical and all-pervasive. Our pattern of life is largely controlled by the clock and calendar.[2] Mechanical, manageable time has a tight grip on us and our society. It is sobering to consider, for instance, how much prior programming has shaped even our careers. 'Who tells us how to spend our time, when to do what, how long a working life is to last, when to live and when to die?'[3] How much are our actions and choices really under our own control?

Given this, it is not surprising some writers have no hesitation in declaring that we have turned time into a quasi-religious affair. 'The time-cult is the master-concept of our day', claims Wyndham Lewis.[4] 'Time is the idol that rules our life', says Erich

Fromm.[5] Or as another vividly puts it: time is a 'one-faced monster-God'.[6]

The anthropologist E.T. Hall perceptively notes that for us the contents and limits of a period of time are generally 'sacrosanct'. In a non-Western culture a person simply starts at some point and goes on until he has completed his task or until something else intervenes. But if we allocate a certain amount of time to an activity, we are unwilling to rearrange our programme; we are not able to continually alter the way we divide up our time, even though an activity may call for such flexibility. 'Once set, the schedule is almost sacred, so that not only is it wrong, according to the formal dictates of our culture, to be late, but it is a violation of the informal patterns to keep changing schedules or appointments or to deviate from the agenda.'[7] Anyone who has attended classes in a school or university, worked in an office or factory, or participated in conferences or conventions, knows how true this is. No matter how important may be the person or event which turns up unexpectedly and needs attention, almost always the programme will be adhered to; 'the show must go on ...'.

For many people a diary has become their most important book and its loss causes the owner himself to feel lost.[8] As for the watch, we become oddly wedded to it in a quite physical as well as psychological sense. How else do we explain the fact that it stays part of us in a way that no other piece of clothing or machinery does, surviving changes of clothes and even undressing? In the strictest sense it has become an extension of ourselves. We all have 'pacers' these days, whether we have a heart condition or not. We would also just as surely 'die' without them. Idols not only enslave their admirers, however, they also transform people into replicas of themselves. So people 'actually became like clocks, acting with a repetitive regularity which had no resemblance to the rhythmic life of a natural being. They became, as the Victorian phrase put it, "as regular as clockwork".'[9] It is not surprising that wind-up clockwork toys have become so popular in our century, nor that as grownups we should surround ourselves with 'big toys', for when we look at these inventions we gaze at an image of ourselves.

Time as a commodity

On another level we have made too little of time. Rejecting its real significance, we have transformed it into a commodity like all the other resources—material, technical and human—available to us. We regard it as an exploitable tool for serving our compulsively work-oriented and possessively materialistic ends. We can earn it, spend it, save it, waste it.[10] It can be added, subtracted, divided, saved, lost, filled, killed or stolen.[11] It is measured and bought and sold.[12] No longer does time possess value because of the opportunity it offers to discover, appreciate and share the essential human experiences which make up the kind of life God has given us. Instead it becomes dominated by, and traded off against, a different set of things or values which are first produced and then consumed in time. A day becomes prized not because it opens up the possibility of working and relating, giving and receiving, thinking and imagining, resting and praying, but for how much can be crammed into it so that goals of less intrinsic worth can be achieved.

This attitude leads to as severely diminished a view of the past as of the present. The past, whether humanity's or our own, is seen to deserve attention only in so far as it is practically 'useful'. It has no value in its own right and is not worth talking about simply because it is there. It is not even significant as part of the continuing story of which we ourselves are the present characters. Since it is difficult to draw lessons from it, to turn it to present profit, history is neglected, and study of it becomes a luxury. Those who have the inclination to do so can indulge in historical reading and research if they wish, but for most people it is simply irrelevant. According to J.T. Fraser we have turned the oppressive modern emphasis on tradition into an equally oppressive modern emphasis on no tradition.[13] As for one's personal history, it too is thought to have no value in itself. Aside from providing the occasional anecdote, related to entertain others or merely pass the time, one's past is important only for what it can contribute to the present. Only past experience which yields knowledge that is immediately and practically relevant—'know how'—is worthwhile. Since the greater part of our personal history fails to pass that test, looking backwards on it is thought to be a waste of time.[14]

Inability to understand our shared history as a coherent process leaves individuals feeling alienated and purposeless. According to Patrick White, Australians in particular have failed to link up their individual present with their cultural past.[15] Many people find it difficult to identify the changes which have taken place in their own personal histories. 'It now requires a special effort, special skill and training, or a particular frame of mind to ... reconstruct one's own personal biography according to a unified and significant pattern.'[16] If we neglect to do this we are in danger of becoming, in T.S. Eliot's words, 'people to whom nothing has happened, at most a continual impact of external events'.[17] Failure to appreciate the past ultimately issues in a significant loss in personal identity. A disconnected past leads to a confused present. Only by finding out where we have come from can we discover who we are. Without an appreciation of the past we are aimless, shortsighted and uncertain.[18]

To treat time as a commodity leads to a circumscribed view of the future as well. For just as the past becomes reduced to what is presently useful, so the future becomes narrowed to what seems presently practicable. If the past is regarded as a stockpile to be raided when expedient, the future is viewed as a blueprint to be effected as soon as time permits. The only future most societies and most people look forward to is what we may term the 'manageable future'. The future under their consideration is not very far ahead, and the results looked for are in the short, not long, term. Only those things which are a projection from known, present circumstances are taken seriously. All else must be set to one side, including the radically new and especially the purely imaginary. Such thinking is said to be idealistic—it does not face the facts. Clearly this outlook leaves little room for the one who wishes 'to dream the impossible dream'. Except here and there, chiefly in the scientific/technological area, society quite literally has no time for such a person. In so doing it cuts itself off from most of the really creative possibilities that the future contains and which the present so desperately needs. The future becomes 'an already overloaded present, multiplied as it were by some growth factor. The more the future is planned, the more it is filled up with activities, wishes, plans and desires, the more it comes to resemble the overloaded present which it was intended to expand ... As with a busy man's schedule that has already been filled up for months in advance, a society preoccupied with its future is likely to find itself "booked up in advance"'.[19]

Like society at large, individuals are often booked up days, weeks, even months in advance. Annual planners, once seen only in the offices of businessmen or professional people, are now entering lounge rooms and students' quarters. Just as some people go into financial debt in order to get all they want to own, so many go heavily into time debt to achieve all they want to do. As a result they shut out any chance of spontaneity and adventure. Philip Slater comments: 'The desire to borrow more time is the sign of an unlived life'.[20] Thus a lack of proper personal identity can arise as much from a circumscribed view of the future as from a diminished view of the past. Our dreams, visions and imaginings—not arbitrarily severed from present realities but not determined by them either—are as crucial as our memories.

In such a situation, present realities such as job[21] and possessions[22] become the things which tell myself and others who I am, what my place is in the world, where I have come from and where I am going.[23] And it is not only material things which can be the object of this attitude but also services of various kinds, even causes and people as well.[24] The same thing happens with respect to time, in large measure because of its manipulation by the work-economy and because of our own acquisitive attitudes. For if the value of time is measured by how much is produced and consumed, and if the individual's life is perceived as merely an accumulation of such things as consumer goods, useful relationships, and powerful positions, 'the status of the self is of purely instrumental, technological value, just like any other commodity. Caught within the formidable pressure of time, and the social world, the self is reduced to the status of what it can provide, accomplish and achieve'.[25] So time, when regarded as a commodity like the goods produced in time, ultimately converts people into commodities themselves.

Conclusion

Where do we turn from here?

We have traced the root causes of our time problem and seen something of its repercussions in our understanding of time itself. The picture that emerges is not a happy one and the causes of our present predicament are exceedingly complex. For our problem with time is a direct consequence of our whole Western way of life. That way of life has brought us a number of very real benefits. But it has also created for us some very severe difficulties. It is only lately that we have begun to recognise certain of these, eg, what two hundred years of industrial and urban development has done to our material environment. The burden of my argument is that our temporal environment has been just as catastrophically affected and that it is also starting to take its revenge. We have upset the delicate balance of the temporal rhythms and framework within which we live and are now beginning to pay the price for so doing.

Is that state of affairs inevitable or can something be done about it? What steps do individuals or groups take to break out of this circle? How well or how poorly do they succeed? These and related concerns will occupy us in the following chapters.

Footnotes

1. J. Swift, *Gulliver's Travels* (London: Dent, 1940) pp. 31–32.
2. Cf. S.G.F. Brandon, 'The Deification of Time', *The Study of Time*, J.T. Fraser, F.C. Haber and G.K. Mueller (eds.) (New York: Springer, 1972) p. 375.
3. H. Nowotny, *op.cit.*, p. 418. Cf. the remarks of S.D. Nollen, 'The Changing Workplace', *Across the Board* (April, 1980) pp. 6–21.
4. Wyndham Lewis, *Time and Western Man* (London: Chatto and Windus, 1972) p. 17.
5. E. Fromm, *To Have or To Be?* (New York: Harper and Row, 1976) p. 129.
6. T. Ungari, in J.T. Fraser, F.C. Haber and G. Mueller (eds.), *op.cit.*, (1972) p. 475.

7. E.T. Hall, *The Hidden Dimension* (New York: Doubleday, 1966) pp. 182,183.

8. Cf. S.B. Linder, *op.cit.*, p. 22.

9. G. Woodcock, *op.cit.*, p. 211.

10. E.T. Hall, *The Silent Language* (New York: Doubleday, 1959) p. 29.

11. K. Lynch, *op.cit.*, p. 128.

12. G. Woodcock, *op.cit.*, p. 210.

13. J.T. Fraser, *Of Time, Passion and Knowledge*, p. 380.

14. Cf. H. Meyerhoff, *Time in Literature* (Berkeley: University of California, 1960) p. 108.

15. Cf. V. Brady, 'Patrick White's Australia', *Intruders in the Dust*, ed. J. Carroll (Melbourne: OUP, 1982) pp. 198–201.

16. H. Meyerhoff, *op.cit.*, p. 109. He adds 'The experiential links between one's past and present have often been disrupted as much as the theoretical connection in history'.

17. T.S. Eliot, 'The Family Reunion', *Complete Plays and Poems* (New York: Harçourt, World and Brace, 1952) p. 234.

18. This may be explored further in C. Lasch, *The Culture of Narcissism: American Life in an Age of Diminishing Expectations* (London: Sphere, 1980) pp. 3–8. Lasch gives a fully drawn, if one-sided, portrait of the kind of personality this produces. In the Australian scene, it is interesting to note how static, episodic and purposeless many Australian films have been. See J. Clancy, 'Australian Film: Renaissance in the Seventies', *Intruders in the Dust*, ed. J. Carroll (Melbourne: OUP, 1982) p. 170.

19. H. Nowotny, *op.cit.*, p. 337.

20. P. Slater, *Earthwalk* (New York: Doubleday, 1974) p. 47.

21. See further S. Weiss and D. Riesman, 'Work and Automation', *Contemporary Social Problems*, R.K. Merton and R.A. Nisbet (eds.) (New York: Harcourt, World and Brace,1966) pp. 579–580.

22. E. Fromm, *op.cit.*, passim.

23. Studs Terkel, *op.cit.*, p. 393.

24. Cf. also S.B. Linder, *op.cit.*, p. 40.

25. H. Meyerhoff, *op.cit.*, pp. 114–115. On time as a commodity, see further G. Lakoff and M. Johnson, *Metaphors We Live By* (Chicago: University of Chicago, 1980) pp. 6–8.

The Solution:
Time Regained

Part 5
Breaking Out of the Time Prison

Whereas man can evade phi-
losophising on the subject of
time, he is compelled by life
to come to terms with it and
to decide what he is to make
of it.
R. Glasser, Time in French
Life and Thought

13

The Legacy of
Pre-industrial Attitudes

It may seem strange to begin the quest for a solution to our problems with time through an enquiry into selected pre-industrial ways of life. Few people in the fully developed societies consider that they have anything to teach us. This only shows how much we are historically sealed off from earlier societies and how culturally shortsighted we have become.

There are two main reasons for approaching the issue this way. Firstly, it reminds us how historically unusual and culturally bound is our modern view of time. Technically simpler cultures, especially those unaffected by the Judaeo-Christian understanding of time, have a very different approach to it. Indeed it is hard for us to understand how unimportant time can become in a non-industrialised, non-Western setting.[1] Secondly, in certain circles in the West today there is a nostalgic longing for pre-industrial modes of living. While this rarely leads to any decisive break with our Western way of life, there is a vague feeling abroad that we have something to learn from earlier cultures, about time as well as about their attitude to the environment.

We begin therefore by looking at two cultures, one nomadic and one agrarian, both of which manage to survive into the twentieth century. Although these have particular relevance to people living in Australia, they may properly stand for those indigenous and immigrant peoples with whom the populations of other Western societies are in closer contact. In any case, Australian Aboriginal and rural Greek attitudes towards time both possess an intrinsic interest.

Australian Aboriginal attitudes

For the Aboriginals the cycle of seasons is paramount. Time is not seen as a linear affair progressing from some point in the past to another point in the future. Rather it follows the annual rhythms of nature. Apart from concern with the coming seasons, there is little interest in the future. The past is, like the not-so-far-away 'olden times' of children, a repository of wisdom and skill. As for the 'Dreaming', that mythical dimension of life which dominates and permeates all traditional Aboriginal thinking, it is 'independent of the directorial flow which characterises every life' and to that extent seems 'independent of the importance placed on past and future'.[2] Most attention is given to the present, with its practical daily concerns. Ceremonial rites are oriented to the present, sanctifying and empowering it rather than fixing attention on the past or propelling the participant into the future. Within this present, activity and non-activity alternate in a regular way, governed by the rhythms of the natural world. No value distinction is drawn between activity and non-activity.

Differences in approach to time are fundamental to many problems and misunderstandings in Aboriginal/white Australian interrelationships. Aboriginals are frequently labelled as lazy and unreliable because they lack the conditioned response to the demands of lineal time upon which the Westerner has patterned his or her life.[3]

In the main, Aboriginal people (living traditionally/tribally) have no need to measure time accurately or to carefully programme its use. For them everything has its own natural time and pace. Time periods can be marked quite satisfactorily in less specific ways than we employ.[4] Aboriginal people are not 'goal-setters' in the way we are; goals pertain to the future and time-measurement. Aboriginal tribes never plant and harvest, preferring to commit themselves to nature and take what they can when it becomes available. An Aboriginal group spends its time in one social 'space', whereas we pass through a number of different environments every day, eg, home, shops, work, club, church, and strict time co-ordination is needed for us to negotiate our way through these. In an Aboriginal tribe regular contacts need not be governed by time limitations because members see one another daily. Few plans need to be made, since the external rhythms of nature cannot be altered and the tradition-kinship system determines what one does in time.

The important thing is for the individual and group to fit in with natural and social necessities. Time takes its quality from the activity or inactivity currently prevailing. The monthly cycle of the moon is the chief rhythm followed. Not only timings, but possessions, relationships and business are all geared around this regular cycle. Aboriginal groups have adapted weapons, chattels and the institution of property to these conditions. They have also shaped ordinary activities like socialising, trading and celebrating so as to accommodate to their itinerant and rhythmical way of life.[5] Since the timing of natural events such as the coming of spring could vary, fixed time references are not employed.

Aboriginal languages reflect this approach to time. In their modern forms they display some evidence of European modes of thinking (eg, counting numbers higher than two, reckoning days beyond tomorrow and yesterday, occasional mention of clock time). But Aboriginal languages traditionally have a different temporal atmosphere. Speaking of the Adnyamathanha tribe, a linguist reports:

> There is no word for 'time' in the sense of time in 'time passes', only a word which is translated 'time', meaning 'occasion', 'event'. Likewise the language permits of no numbering of days. Indeed, it appears that there is no concept of linear measurement of any kind. Time can nevertheless be pinpointed to some extent by reference to 'morning', 'afternoon', 'night', 'sun', the form of the verb making it clear whether or not the afternoon is completed (ie, the afternoon past), or not (the afternoon to come).
>
> My informants can give me a word for 'how many', but they say it is not often used and, indeed, some I have questioned do not know it. It is also suggested it comes from English. The word

'when' also appears to have restricted use, though it has now become more necessary through the introduction of counted time. 'When' an event happened is pinpointed by reference to another event which happened at that time. Sentences beginning 'When I was a child' or 'When the whites came' require no translation for 'when': the event or state is mentioned and related events follow in the discourse.

It is arguable as to whether there are tenses, as we generally understand them, in this language and in some others. What seems to be much more important is whether an event being talked about is a real, identifiable event or not, and if it is, whether or not it is completed. The future is talked about in the same form as generalisations about the past (which, of course, do not refer to a specific event). 'We used to gather wild pear root' and 'we will gather wild pear root' both appear in the same form. There are both verb morphemes and adverbs which express that an event was of some duration, or that it often occurred, but these do not point to any absolute time concept.[6]

Certain aspects of the Aboriginal way of life are attractive to the world-weary Western soul—the greater accord with natural rhythms, the regular alternation of work and rest, the less harried pace at which things are done. In these respects the Aboriginal exhibits a more civilized approach to life than his 'more advanced' fellowmen. But we would be seeing Aboriginal culture through a romantic haze if we did not recognise its real disadvantages. Though free from mechanical bondage, it is subject to natural determinism. For all the balance it has forged between human beings and their environment, it leaves little room for choice or variation. Long periods of enforced idleness, a semi-nomadic existence, and a limited sense of past and future restrict the development of a full personal, social and cultural life. We need to discover how those qualities we admire in Aboriginal society can be incorporated in our own technological civilization. There is no way we can simply return to the Aboriginal approach to time.

Rural Greek attitudes

We now turn to modern-day rural Greece. Given their shared Western culture, it would be true to say that the rural Greek and other Europeans have more in common than the rural Aboriginal

and other Australians. The Greeks also share a common religion
—Christianity—with their neighbours, whereas tribal Aboriginal'
religion differs greatly from that of white Australians. Migration
from Greece to countries like the United States and Australia have
also brought old and new world cultures closer together.
However, Greece's rural areas have not yet felt the impact of the
industrial and technological revolutions, and it comes as no
surprise that the attitude to time in these areas differs noticeably
from that in more 'advanced' societies. In Greek towns and cities
the old attitude to time survives to an extent. Anthropologist
Margaret Mead describes the Greek attitude to time thus:

> Greeks 'pass' the time; they do not save or accumulate or use it.
> And they are intent on passing the time, not on budgeting it.
> Although city people say that this picture is changing, that they
> are now made aware of the need to use time, the attitude is still
> widely prevalent, even in the area of private life among the
> urban groups.
> The clock is not master of the Greek: it does not tell him to get
> up, to go to the field. In most villages, in spite of recent
> changes, the peasants still get up at sunrise or dawn to go to the
> fields, and return at sundown. The day is made for work. At
> night women visit and gossip; men join them or go to the
> coffee house; there is story-telling, and ardent political discus-
> sion; and as for any work done after dark, 'the day takes a look
> at it and laughs'. Wherever there is no law to the contrary, a
> man opens his store in due course, not by the clock; however,
> in the cities he now functions under clocked time because he
> comes under government and union regulations. Even in the
> United States, though conservative Greek businessmen have
> adapted their business life to the time of the clock, in their
> private life and at social gatherings they function irrespective of
> the clock ...
> Greek men and women work expeditiously, as a rule, but do
> this best at their own rhythm; any need to hurry is external and
> interfering; it introduces fuss and disturbance. Efficiency can
> usually be found when it is not a conscious end ...
> For the Greek traditionally, to work against time, to hurry, is
> to forfeit freedom. His term for hurry means, originally, to
> coerce oneself; and a visitor arriving out of breath may say: 'I
> have hurried', but the form in which the word is more often
> used is 'Don't hurry'. One does not admonish another to coerce

himself, and a mother does not constantly ask her child to hurry
up, unless perhaps she is following the new books on child
training which say that a baby must not be allowed to set his
own pace ...
There are many clocks and watches in Greece now, both in the
city and the village. Watches are an important part of a man's
trappings, and of a girl's adornment. Clocks are necessary to
complete the furnishing of a house. It is not essential as a rule
that they keep good time, or that they run at all. If they are in
good running order, and are in use, their function is one of
reference; they do not shape the household life. They give
information and satisfy curiosity; they do not tell the wife that
it is now time to start cooking or serve the meal ...
Villagers speak of hours and minutes, but these are merely
references to the passing of time, rather than its measure.
Visitors, asking how far it is to the next village, find that 'five
minutes' may mean half an hour or two hours, but they find the
answer 'A cigarette away' does provide an accurate measure.
In spite of the prevalence of timepieces, the church bell and the
school bell, and even a cannon blast, continue to have active
functions in calling adults or children to pre-arranged gatherings or communal village work. Even in the cities, people are
called 'Englishmen' when they turn up on the dot at meetings
or appointments.[7]

Most Australians and North Americans are unaware how alien
their attitude to time seems to people who have migrated from
Greek villages and towns. For Greek-born newcomers the culture
shock is considerable. If only we had eyes to see it, we could learn
much from rural Greeks' casual, less clockbound approach to life.
Didn't Zorba become the envy of us all? Among rural people there
is greater resonance with the natural rhythms of day, season and
year. More allowance is made in work situations for personal
preferences and temperament. Social occasions are allowed to
follow their own inherent courses. Value is placed on personal
freedom, and on celebrating what the moment brings, at the
expense of strict regulation by the clock.

But these values are in jeopardy today in Greece. They are
constantly yielding ground, retreating in the face of technical and
bureaucratic intrusion.[8] There is no possibility of our perpetuating
the Greeks' simpler approach to life. Our society is structured in a

way that prevents us from doing so. But we can attempt to find new patterns which preserve valuable pre-industrial attitudes.

Conclusion

If we were to pursue this investigation of pre-industrial attitudes to time further, eg, by exploring Spanish or West Indian attitudes, or those from the Arabian countries or Indian sub-Continent, related differences would appear. To give just one example: ie, anthropologists have also noted the contrast between Spanish and Anglo-Saxon attitudes to time. Whereas an English clock 'runs', a Spanish clock 'walks':

> Such a simple difference as this has enormous implications for approaching differences in the behaviour of English-speaking and Spanish-speaking persons. If time is moving rapidly, as Anglo-Saxon usage declares, we must hurry and make use of it before it has gone. If time walks, as the Spanish-speaking say, one can take a more leisurely attitude to it.[9]

One has only to remember the central place of manana in Spanish life, the deferring of things till a later time which do not have to be done now or do not bring immediate benefits, to begin to appreciate further differences between it and Anglo-Saxon ways.[10]

In all these instances, we have things to learn from lifestyles which are quietly disappearing before our eyes. These ways of life conserve attitudes towards time which we do well to learn from before they vanish altogether. Here and there we can imitate them directly, eg, allowing meals and social gatherings to develop their own rhythms. In other cases we can translate these into terms more suited to our technological society, eg, encouraging work patterns which possess more flexibility, socialising and opportunity for leisure. At the most basic level we can preserve the spirit which animates them and refuse to allow our freedom to die the death of a thousand qualifications at the hands of the clock, diary, timetable and schedule.

Footnotes

1. The general thesis of E.T. Hall, *The Silent Language* (1959) mentioned earlier, is again relevant here.
2. So I. Holm and R.R. McConnochie, 'Time Perspective in Aboriginal Children', *Aboriginal Cognition—Retrospect and Prospect*, eds. G.E. Kearney and D.W. McElwain (Canberra: Australian Institute for Aboriginal Studies, 1976) p. 282.
3. M. Boyes-King, *Patterns of Aboriginal Culture—Then and Now* (Sydney: McGraw Hill, 1977) p. 51 n. 15.
4. For a fictional representation of this, see the comments about reckoning time in X. Herbert, *Poor Fellow My Country* (Sydney: Collins, 1975) p. 431.
5. Cf. W.E.H. Stanner, *After the Dreaming: The 1969 Boyer Lectures* (Sydney: Australian Broadcasting Commission, 1969).
6. I am indebted to Dorothy Tunbridge, a doctoral student at the Australian National University, for this information.
7. (Ed.) M. Mead, *Cultural Patterns and Technical Change* (Deventer, Holland: UNESCO, 1953) pp. 90–91.
8. See further (ed.) M. Mead, *op.cit.*, pp. 108–114.
9. L. Saunders, *Cultural Differences and Medical Care* (1954) p. 116.
10. For more detail see M. Mead, *op.cit.*, pp. 179–180, 190–191. Although written a quarter of a century ago, Mead's portrait of life in rural Greek and Spanish-American settings still possesses value. Although some changes have taken place in the cities or among more upwardly mobile groups, elsewhere older attitudes continue to linger on.

14

The Protest of the Counter Culture

In considering the legacy of pre-industrial societies, we have made a start towards refurbishing our approach to time. This can be carried further by turning to pockets of anti-industrial critique in the most fully developed countries. They have something to teach us as well.

In the 'sixties and 'seventies a strong protest movement opposed to many aspects of Western life emerged in advanced industrial societies. One target of criticism was the all-consuming materialism and affluence of people in highly developed countries. Another was our industrially based work environment and leisure activities. Concern was also expressed about bureaucratic encroachment upon private and social life. Implied in such protests was rejection of the existing Western attitude to time.

We will look now at two of the protesting groups: the Hippie sub-culture which flourished in the 'sixties, and the broader alternative lifestyle movement which emerged in the 'seventies and continues in the 'eighties. We will also look at the latter's influence on the middle-classes, and at some similarities between the Hippie movement and traditional working-class responses to industrialisation. Throughout, we will attempt to identify those elements which can help us develop a more satisfactory view of time and more liberated use of it.

'Dropping out'—the Hippies' reaction

According to one observer, the Hippies wanted to subvert modern industrial time.[1] Their determination to experience the 'existential now' led them to reject both past and future. They rejected modern society's utilitarian, goal-driven and emotionally controlled way of managing self and social relations, preferring to celebrate open expressiveness and immediate gratification of wishes and desires.

The Hippies refused to value the past, even for its 'know-how'. They refused to plan ahead, even for the 'manageable future'. Their focus was the present alone.[2] The Hippies refused to adopt a measured, planned approach to the present. They sought the spontaneous in place of the routine, the anarchic in place of the punctual, the random in place of the appointment, the 'happening' in place of the organised event.

Yet alongside their preoccupation with the present, the Hippies wanted to experience a different dimension of time. The key used to open the door to this other dimension was the hallucinogenic drug. Drugs offered a way of discovering the real self below the layers of civilised controls, of revealing new vistas of perception and feeling beneath the rational consciousness. They lifted the user outside the traditional time scale, into a free-floating, almost timeless, world where relationships between things were by association rather than in sequence. Here all three modes of experiencing time—past, present and future—coalesced into a prolonged 'now'. Marijuana users found their time awareness was either minimal or completely absent. LSD users reported that their awareness of time was 'absent', that time seemed to stop; they seemed to experience past, present and future all at once.[3]

All this looks like an attempt to escape from time altogether, and in that bible of the hipsters—Henry Miller's *Tropic of Capricorn*—that is the way it is often talked about. But it was really an endeavour to make the present moment eternal. The Hippies aimed to hold on to the present, to expand it and magnify its value. 'The hipster', said Norman Mailer '[lived] in that enormous present which is without past or future, memory or planned intention'.[4] Or as the philosopher John Passmore put it, what the adherents of this new mysticism wanted was 'Paradise Now'.[5]

It would appear that consistent drug use permanently alters the user's attitude to the ordinary world. Managing time arrangements becomes more difficult, and efficiency in doing things suffers. Heavy marijuana users tend to adopt a very inactive, slowed-down style of existence. Simon and Garfunkel caught this Hippie mood perfectly in their song *Feelin' Groovy*:

> Slow down, you move too fast.
> You gotta make the moment last ...

For the Hippies music provided another way of enlarging the present. The music they listened to and promoted cut across the structured characteristics of classical European and popular American composition. The stream 'pulse' sound of rock 'n' roll lent itself to being stopped, faded or easily changed and carried the listener out of his everyday world into a semi-mystical or ecstatic one.[6] The motor-bike represented another sort of ecstasy. It catapulted the rider into a kind of never-ending, experience-packed present. There was no sense that the bike and its rider were coming from anything in particular or heading anywhere in particular. What was important was the going itself. The mechanical 'trip' complemented the chemical or musical 'trip'. Both got you to the same destination. The way in which the mechanical can be combined with a mystical extension of the present is nowhere more powerfully delineated than in Robert M. Pirsig's high ideas road novel *Zen and the Art of Motorcycle Maintenance*.[7]

The Hippies were reacting against a number of disturbing trends in Western society. They did so instinctively rather than rationally, expressing their feelings through living an alternative lifestyle rather than by formulating an alternative philosophy. Their cult of spontaneity and the mystically expanded moment was a significant contribution and its value should not be underestimated. By stressing the importance of spontaneity at all levels of human interaction and in all areas of human activity, they were bringing to the fore a seriously neglected aspect of personal and social life. Their quest for a fuller experience of time other than the one-thing-after-another attitude that guides most people was also fully justified; there are other dimensions of time than the mere succession of moments that we experience throughout each day. In both these ways the Hippies entered an important corrective to the dominant attitude.

But how successfully did the Hippies break away from the general tyranny of time? One difficulty they encountered was the temporary nature of their release. For drugs offer no permanent solution: they have to be resorted to again and again. And you cannot 'freak out' on a motorcycle or succumb to the spell of music all the time. Another difficulty was that the new world entered into was not so much a totally different universe as a pleasurable intensification of everyday experience.[8] Indeed, the Hippies' preoccupation with the present resembled the narrow focus which is characteristic of most people's outlook today. They experienced no recovery of the past, no creative entry into the future, only an expanded present. It is interesting to note that the Hippies bypassed ascetic meditation techniques in favour of hallucenogens. They were in too much of a hurry to take the longer Eastern route. Showing how typically Western they still were, they preferred the shorter, faster 'trip'. Their quest for mystical experiences merely rendered them less able to deal with the ordinary concerns of life.

If the Hippie lifestyle produced simply a less regulated life and a slower pace, this would be all to the good. But, as Aldous Huxley wrote of his experiences under mescalin, drug experience is 'incompatible with action and even with the will to action, the very thought of action'.[9] There is certainly room in a fully rounded life for appreciation of the present moment and for intensification of it through mystical awareness. But there is also a need for alertness, resolve and perseverance. The basic problems of life, including the time problem, have to be steadily confronted, not just sidestepped or temporarily evaded.

The Hippies did not last. The more political mood of the Vietnam generation overtook them. After that had spent its force, a broader-based minority movement arose, characterised by the search for a more integrated alternative lifestyle.

'Living it up'—a working-class counterpart

The Hippie movement was largely a middle-class phenomenon. But some of its features were already present in working-class culture, which preserves a number of pre-industrial attitudes as part of an instinctive reaction against the work patterns imposed by the industrial revolution. Middle-class Hippies, coming from backgrounds already firmly indoctrinated with industrialised attitudes to work and leisure, had to 'drop out' of society to look for the alternative they desired. Working-class people, on the other hand, did not have to do this—for they had never fully 'joined up'. Long before Hippies discovered the value of 'doing nothing' and participating in unplanned 'happenings', long before they discovered the thrill of motorcycle speed and pulsating musical rhythm, working-class young people were enjoying these as part of their non-work relaxation.

Drinking also has been a noticeable feature of working-class life since the beginning of the industrial revolution. Alongside its factories, every nineteenth-century city had its gin houses. Alcohol provided a sure and speedy escape from the pressures that filled most people's daylight hours. Long before the Hippies realized drugs could open up a new world of experience, many working-class people were intermittently drinking themselves into a pleasant state of oblivion. (Today, for middle-class people as well, alcohol is the chief way of breaking free from the time and other constraints of the workaday scene.) Studies indicate that many alcoholics are reacting to their regulation and speed at work. Drink speeds up their leisure time so that it moves at the same pace. In other words, alcohol helps them overcome their withdrawal symptoms. While they are at work, their time rate is faster than that of the majority of people: they tend to work faster than others, they are more irritated by slowness in others, more bored when time is moving slowly; they are interested in the control and ordering of time, and in planning, scheduling and arriving early for appointments. Alcoholics are also seeking release from the uncertainties of the present. The past is often seen as the most pleasant, influential, exciting, receptive period of their lives, and it seems closer to them than it does to other people. Given a choice, they would like to live in the past.[10] The present produces anxiety which the alcoholic seeks to escape. As for the future, the alcoholic tends not to think about it much. Indeed, some alcoholics say they never think of it at all. Alcohol promises an escape from the chains of everyday time, but it only helps people to evade their problems and gain a temporary respite. It does nothing to change the pressures, and in the long run it weakens the drinker's power to do anything about these pressures.

'Scaling down'—the alternative lifestyle proposal

The alternative lifestyle movement, which continues in the 'eighties, has a less individualistic, more social orientation than did the Hippies. The random, casual togetherness of the Hippies, and their occasional 'happenings', have been replaced by the intentional household and commune. There is a strong preference among counter culture people for a rural or semi-rural rather than an urban setting. Instead of the quest for an enlarged consciousness and sensual gratification, there is a desire to live in harmony with the natural rhythms of the environment and the body. There is also a great deal less hurry. The 'trip'—whether cross-country or into the soul, whether fuelled by petrol or acid, whether the result of mechanical acceleration or chemical 'speed'—has been replaced by a desire to stay in one place and settle into a long-term commitment to others and to the neighbourhood or soil. Meditation along Eastern lines—the longer, slower route to self-awareness—has become popular. This movement seems to be attracting older, more markedly middle-class recruits than the Hippie movement did.

Among those searching for an alternative lifestyle, there is disquiet about generally accepted attitudes towards time. Much of their rejection of the 'rat race' seems to be a rebellion against time constraints and pressures.[11] The flight from the city and from a regular job involves rejection of a clock-dominated, haste-ridden way of life in favour of more natural patterns. Personal relationships—which are governed by rhythms arising out of the quality of interchange between people, not by the hands or digits on a watch—are highly valued. Punctuality is scorned and social arrangements are fluid. Meditation provides a shift into a different kind of time; its intrinsic rhythms are unrelated to the passing of seconds, minutes and hours.

However, with their concern for conservation, their interest in politics and their long-term devotion to communal life, representatives of this movement often display a deeper commitment to past, present and future than the average member of the establishment culture. Indeed, the counter culture response to the general view of time in Western society is far more substantial than that generated by the Hippie movement. It attempts to provide a permanent alternative. It does not rely on intermittent experiences and on an *ad hoc* way of life, but places emphasis on enduring concern for others and serious respect for natural and biological rhythms. Unlike the Hippie movement, it concerns itself in some measure with politics, at the level of ideas and also of practice, demonstrating concern with society at large.[12] Past and future are granted significance, without loss to the importance of the present. The counter culture's recognition that the world of everyday time is not the only one, that there is a mystical realm also able to be experienced now, is something it shares with the Hippies. But it approaches this mystical realm from a more religious, less purely chemical, point of view and tries to relate it to the world of ordinary experience.

These features of the alternative lifestyle approach to time are commendable and appealing. They are vital elements in any attempt to restore a proper understanding and use of time. The counter culture has pointed the way here in several significant respects.

But the movement fails to provide a general solution to the problem of time. Certainly in such a highly urbanised country as Australia it is plausible to argue that more people should live in rural or semi-rural areas and rediscover the values and difficulties inherent in such a way of life. For all the myths with which they have invested the 'bush', few Australians have ever come to terms with their land. It is also important that more people in advanced Western societies should be able to fashion a different kind of livelihood and working environment for themselves than our prevailing structures allow. The difficulty is that we cannot simply transfer the counter culture attitude toward time into our industrial-bureaucratic urban context. Yet that is where most of us will continue to live, surrounded by highly developed machines and their products, large-scale organisations and their schedules. We cannot all return to a simpler agrarian way of life nor to a small-scale craft approach to work and employment.

In the long run the tyranny of time has to be tackled and broken in the cities, in the midst of technological and bureaucratic conditions. We certainly need to develop a greater respect for biological rhythms and a deeper sense of community. But we should treasure the human as well as natural past and seek to recover and conserve worthwhile urban cultural values (values that the development of surburbia has considerably eroded) as well as those more characteristic of a rural environment. As well we need an openness to the future that does not altogether exclude technological advance and large-scale social co-ordination. Although there is another time dimension which exists beyond the everyday one we experience, this is not the timeless world of mystical awareness but the timeful world of God's growing kingdom and his Spirit's everyday operations.

'Tuning in'—a middle-class response

Certain aspects of the alternative lifestyle movement have penetrated middle-class circles and influenced a minority within them. Concern for the environment is now widespread, for example. It is unfortunate, though, that many middle-class people involved in the ecology movement should engage more in hectic political agitation than in relaxed appreciation of the natural world. There is also an interest in biological rhythms. It is a pity, however, that many preoccupy themselves with their biological rhythms in such a pseudo-scientific way.[13] But not all people who become concerned about these things fall into the trap of carrying over the tempo of modern life into their search for a lifestyle more in harmony with natural and bodily cycles.

Other signs of counter culture influence on middle-class life are the widespread practice of meditation, use of drugs such as cannabis and cocaine, and interest in mystical Eastern religions and philosophies.[14] Meditation techniques such as TM and Raj Yoga are now well known. Public lectures on these practices are well attended and private firms, community organisations and government departments are all promoting meditation for dealing with stress induced by work and home pressures.

It is hard to quarrel with any attempt in our superficial and materialistic society to withdraw in solitude to explore one's real nature and spiritual reality. But the emphasis in the '80s on meditation *techniques* is troubling. It continues that fascination with artificial means, methods and programmes that has bedevilled our society over the last two hundred years.[15] In doing so, it imports part of the problem into the very 'solution' being proposed. Also, placing the emphasis upon meditation as the method for dealing with work-engendered stress conveniently locates the problem in the *individual*, not in the system of which he is a part. The message is clear: 'You are the one who has to adapt to the system; the system doesn't need to be changed in order that you can enjoy a more natural, humane and sociable life'. No wonder business, bureaucratic and government organisations are prepared to mount expensive conferences on meditation techniques and to encourage, even pay for, people to attend them.

As for the attraction of mystical religions and the use of cannabis to enter the mystical realm, it needs to be repeated that entering into an experience of timelessness, whatever peace of mind and stability it may give, cannot yield a lasting solution to the tyranny of time. At best it can provide only an intermittent withdrawal from, and socially inadequate response to, the problem. Only entry into a new dimension of time which interprets the past, gives direction in the present, and contains possibilities for the future would overcome this. Among the various options that are available, the Judaeo-Christian approach to time offers the greatest promise of doing this.

Conclusion

The protest of the counter culture is a reminder that all is far from well in our industrial society. This is as true of what it has to say about time as it is of any other aspect of its critique. Certain facets of working-class life—which have been too quickly blamed and too little understood—should have persuaded us of this much earlier. The Hippie's attempt to escape from the problem through drugs, and the worker's attempt to blot it out through alcohol offer no solution. But their refusal to allow the clock to regulate the whole of their lives, especially their free time, is a healthy one. Leaving room for the spontaneous, the unplanned and the openended is part of the answer. So is the quest, whether through drugs, drink or any other means, to experience a different kind of time. While the occasional drink does help us to unwind from the unnatural regulation and pace of modern life, drugs of any kind do not give us entrance to the new dimension of time we both seek and need.

The alternative lifestyle movement is a better guide here. Meditation is a crucial part of the answer to our problem with time. But the content of that meditation needs more careful attention. The timeless world of Eastern religions is eventually a cul-de-sac, for it does not lead back into the world of everyday life with any realism or vitality. It simply helps people to cope better with the world as it is or offers them an illusory or one-sided alternative to it. Still the contemporary counter culture's quest for a less affluent, more communal and less bureaucratic, more natural way of life should catalyse us all to develop a more modest, sociable, participatory and environmentally conscious lifestyle. If we attempt to do this in the cities as well as in the country, and with the help of technology rather than without it, that is because we do not regard the city or the machine, for all their dangers, as inherently suspect.

Footnotes

1. Paul E. Willis, *Profane Culture* (London: Routledge and Kegan Paul, 1978) p. 168.

2. Stuart Hall, *The Hippies: An American 'Moment'*, Occasional Paper (University of Birmingham, October, 1968) p. 12.

3. Stephens Newells, 'Chemical Modifiers of Time'. *The Future of Time*, eds. H. Yaker, H. Osmond and F. Cheek (London: Hogarth, 1972), pp. 380–381.

4. N. Mailer, *Advertisements for Myself* (New York: Putnam, 1968) p. 271. The language of timelessness, or of interest in time, occurs in H. Miller, *Tropic of Capricorn* (London: Panther, 1964) p. 117.

5. J. Passmore, *The Perfectibility of Man* (London: Duckworth, 1970) pp. 304–327.

6. Paul E. Willis, *op.cit.*, pp. 78, 169.

7. Robert M. Pirsig, *Zen and the Art of Motorcycle Maintenance: An Inquiry Into Values* (London: Bodley Head, 1974).

8. Cf. S. Hall, *op.cit.*, p. 16.

9. Aldous Huxley, *The Doors of Perception* and *Heaven and Hell* (Harmondsworth: Penguin, 1959) p. 35. See further the quotation from Baudelaire, cited in O. Guinness, *The Dust of Death: A Critique of the Counter Culture* (London: IVP, 1973) p. 242.

10. F.E. Cheek and J. Laucius, 'Time Worlds of Three Drug-Using Groups—Alcoholics, Heroin Addicts and Psychedelics', *The Future of Time, op.cit.*, pp. 338, 340. See also S. Newells, *op.cit.*, pp. 378–379. On the attitudes to time characteristic of the working-class subculture, see two articles: P. Corrigan, 'Doing Nothing', and G. Murdock and R.M. McCron, 'Consciousness of Class and Consciousness of Generation', in *Resistance Through Rituals: Youth Subcultures in Post-War Britain*, S. Hall and T. Jefferson (eds.) (London: Hutchinson, 1975).

11. So B.S. Gorman and A.E. Wessmann, *The Personal Experience of Time* (New York: Plenum, 1977) pp. 47–48.

12. On the link between mysticism and politics, see especially T. Roszak, *Where The Wasteland Ends: Politics and Transcendence in a Post-Industrial Society* (New York: Doubleday, 1972) pp. 99–107.

13. For a pseudo-scientific approach see B. Gittelson, *Biorhythms: A Personal Science* (New York: Arco, 1976).

14. Influential here have been the writings of much-read academic popularisers like Erich Fromm and Alan Watts. See, for example, E. Fromm, D.T. Suzuki and R. de Martino, *Zen Buddhism and Psychoanalysis* (New York: Harper, 1960) and A. Watts, *Hidden Cloud, Unknown Whereabouts: A Mountain Journal* (London: Cape, 1974).

15. The most powerful exposé of this comes from J. Ellul, *The Technological Society*.

15

The Limits of Time
Management Principles

Neither pre- nor anti-industrial approaches to time are able to solve our difficulties with time. Has any attempt been made within advanced industrial societies to find a satisfactory answer? Within the dominant culture of Western countries, only one systematic attempt to deal with the time problem has emerged. This is 'time management'. Unlike its counter culture alternative, this feels at home in the city. Indeed it promises to make life tolerable there, even in the workplace. Time management, therefore, faces the problem at its point of greatest tension and claims to relieve that tension without requiring any radical break with one's general style of life.

Time management has its roots in the time-and-motion studies first conducted in the business sector in the early 1900s. The current approach goes beyond those early studies by taking into account people's personalities as well as their jobs. At first time management was applied only to people employed in middle and upper management positions in private enterprise. Now it is seen as applicable to all levels of employment—to people in government organisations, professional groups and religious and charitable work, and to leisure time as well as working hours. At its most expansive, the time management approach offers itself as a complete solution to the time difficulties we have already identified.

Practical ways of saving time

Early advocates of time management made a number of dubious recommendations. One gave the following advice: reduce sleep by two hours a day, spend up to an hour a day less over meals, in small talk and at leisure, and gain an additional hour a day by moving closer to your work place.[1] He estimated that 'thrift' along these lines would add five and a half years of usable time to the average 40-year-old's life! However, unless people are over-sleeping, the first piece of advice contains real health dangers. The second idea puts at risk relaxation, friendship and family together-ness. The third suggestion is quite sensible, provided the quality of life does not suffer. Later time management advocates varied as to where they put the emphasis: on accumulating extra time for use, or on maximising efficient usage of all time.[2]

Over the last two decades the time management approach has gained sophistication. There are numerous books by leading people in industry, business and administration who wish to make public their personal time-saving discoveries, and conferences and seminars on time management have become compulsory for many people in employment.

Two key points are made by time management advocates: 1. To become an effective worker (or to engage in effective leisure) you have to start with your use of time, not with planning your job (or your relaxation).[3] 2. To handle time successfully involves not so much learning how to manage it as how to manage yourself.[4] These twin pillars of time management rightly stress the importance of time and the way it affects our most fun-damental choices.

It is important for us to understand how we are actually spending our time. Most of us have little idea of where our time goes. Only by 'logging' it in some way, over a representative period, will we find out what happens to it. That done, we need to define our short-term, intermediate and long-term goals. These goals should be based on a realistic assessment of our skills and weaknesses, along with a clear understanding of the objectives of the organisations or professions to which we belong. Having determined our goals we need to list required tasks in order of priority and eliminate those which can be handled by others or do not really need to be done at all. Where we have little choice in the matter of our responsibilities at least we may be able to question our superiors about why they ask us to undertake time-consuming tasks which have only doubtful value. When formulating priorities we must distinguish between genuinely important tasks and merely urgent ones. We must become opportunity oriented rather than problem oriented. We should set aside time for exploring new possibilities as well as fulfilling responsibilities.

Time management experts tell us we ought to identify time-wasting activities and find more efficient ways of carrying them out. It would be hard to find an aspect of the work situation which has not been scrutinised from this angle.[5] Attempts have also been made to grade time-wasting activities according to their importance.[6] Having pruned time-wasting activities and discovered more efficient ways of doing tasks, we need to make wise use of the 'discretionary' time gained. First we need to consolidate this time into sizable blocks. This prevents it from being frittered away on insignificant tasks and enables it to be put to concentrated use on important projects. Some sort of schedule then has to be drawn up to cover daily, weekly, monthly and annual use of time. Blocks of time need to be reserved for important thinking, writing and forecasting. We should arrange meetings so that they do not distract us from important tasks, and we should build flexibility into our programmes so that we will be able to deal with contingencies without time-consuming reorganisation.

If these guidelines are properly applied to the work situation, there should be ample time to do other things: spend time with the family, enjoy leisure and educational activities, take regular holidays, become involved in civic affairs or voluntary work ... Well-managed on-the-job time leaves evenings, weekends and holidays free for other interests and responsibilities. Staying back at the office at night, taking work home on the weekend, or cancelling a holiday to remain on the job is a sure sign that a person is not handling his or her time well. 'Workaholism' is based on several fallacies: that the best achievers spend longer on the job than others, that the harder we work the more we get done, that the most active employees produce the best results, and that doing many jobs right is more important than doing the right job.

Time management experts tell us that if we put their principles into operation there will be no need for us to work longer, harder, more intensely or more busily. And if we apply these same principles to other activities we will perform them more efficiently and so have extra time for anything else we might care to do. Suitably modified, the time management approach can be implemented productively in running a home, studying for a degree, organising one's leisure or planning for retirement.[7] It is even applicable to the way in which individuals order their devotional lives or churches organise their activities.[8] In principle, every area of life can benefit from responsible time management.

The time management approach endeavours to be both comprehensive in scope and practical in character. It promises a way through the problems posed by our increased pace of life and regular work environments. Its advocates have relied less on theoretical reflections about the nature of work and leisure than on the actual experiences of people who have learned to cope with life the hard way. A good deal of what is advocated in time management manuals is simply codified common-sense. It is a mark of how far we have strayed from the obvious truths that such a wholesale rediscovery or systematisation of common-sense has become necessary.

Deeper issues that are overlooked

But time management has its troubling aspects. Two in particular stand out, and they are fundamental to the approach. They concern: (1) its advocates' attitude to time generally and to free time especially, and (2) their understanding of the personal framework within which people operate and of our present social and cultural conditions.

Time management fails to challenge the view of time prevailing in advanced industrial societies. Indeed, it wholeheartedly endorses it. The language it uses and the concepts with which it is associated come from the world of commerce and industry. Some examples:

> [The individual] cannot delay the clock or hasten it. He cannot buy time or give it away. He has exactly as much as everyone else ... No respecter of persons or position, the minute hand moves relentlessly on ... Can we settle for anything less than the best in the matter of how we utilize those precious resources, including time ... entrusted to our care?[9]
>
> For the amount of time which any single individual can employ profitably is obviously limited no matter how industrious he may be, but ... by [rightly] using some of my time I can induce others to use their time more productively ... Time-thrift pays as it goes. You get your dividends daily. You don't have to await the journey's end to collect ... Yesterday is a cancelled check, tomorrow is a promissory note. Today is ready cash. Use it![10]
>
> So for purposes of time management, consider that you are paid by the hour, whether you actually are or not. To find your rate, take your annual salary, in thousands of dollars, divide by two, and that is roughly your hourly pay ... if you have in the back of your mind a specific measure of their dollar cost, you'll find it much easier to prevent their [the hours] getting out of hand ... Lay claim to the time you save. Plan it.[11]
>
> [Time is] a unique resource ... one cannot rent, hire, buy or otherwise obtain more time. The supply of time is totally inelastic. No matter how high the demand, the supply will not go up ... time is totally perishable and cannot be stored ... time is, therefore, always in exceedingly short supply.[12]

Works by Christian authors do not differ in this respect from works by those with different philosophies.[13]

Allowances certainly have to be made here. To some extent words are chosen merely to drive the point home in a vivid and forceful way. To some extent they reflect the thinking of the work-oriented audience for which they are intended. And to some extent the commercial terms used have lost their original associations and become part of everyday discourse. But such terms occur too frequently, and too much is built upon them for these factors to explain away their presence. No, the time management approach itself reinforces the centrality of the watch and clock in modern life.

Note the movement's predilection for schedules, planners, time-charts and such pretentiously titled inventions as the Personal Time Investment Analysis Worksheet.[14] One recent series of seminars on the subject was titled 'How to get 26 hours out of every day'! Throughout the time management literature, time is treated as a scarce resource, one that must be exploited for all its productive worth and consumed as intensively as any other commodity. This 'managing' is premised on a clock-based way of life; it is really 'scheduling' into which flexibility needs to be built. Free time becomes permeated by planning and the ever-ticking watch. As one time management expert says: 'How do you find time for [tranquillity] in today's busy world? The same way you find time for anything else in life that's worthwhile: you plan for it, you set a time for it, and then you do it.'[15]

In Christian time management literature leisure is regarded as having its justification in its relationship to work. According to one writer: 'We do not work in order to have leisure. We have leisure in order that we might get on with our work ... The industrial planners tell us that a time away from work allows us to return to our job with a greater level of efficiency'.[16] Here we have striking testimony to the way in which the secular viewpoint is simply identified with, or assimilated into, the Christian one.

The second defect in the time management solution is that it operates within strict limits. While it points out to people that their difficulties with time often have a source outside themselves (eg, interruptions or demands by other people, poor lines of communication, uncertain exercise of authority, malfunctioning or overly intensive technological inventions, inefficient institutional arrangements and structures), it is the individual who becomes the focus of most of the advice and who is seen as the fulcrum of change. Yet in most situations some sort of structural solution is also required. A few time-and-motion personnel in private industry and government administration will approach a particular section or department in a holistic way and look for a comprehensive answer to its problems; even then changes are not always arrived at in a genuinely communal fashion. In most time management practice a strong individualistic strain remains.

This individualism is even more pronounced in Christian writings. Church leaders, clergy and their spouses are rarely encouraged to sort out their time use in consultation with others (members of the family, Christian organisations, the congregation). Searching discussion with the people directly affected by their decisions is not encouraged. There is no mention of their wrestling through time issues in the company of any small group of fellow-believers who are committed to and responsible for each other's daily welfare. Generally speaking, time problem solving is left to the individual, with only an occasional reference to other people or the Christian community.

Where time management experts look beyond the individual, they look at institutional structures and not at the broader social and cultural dimensions. There is little awareness that time pressure is an all-pervading problem. While individuals and sometimes organisations are recognised as having problems, time pressure is not seen as endemic to our whole Western way of life. Our use of time is never regarded as something in need of radical questioning rather than just more careful 'managing'. The time issue is examined only in discrete contexts, not in a comprehensive way. People are not encouraged to get to the root of the problem and cannot see that other options are open to them.

So, for example, while the time management approach urges people to define their goals, it does not encourage them to think whether these goals ultimately lie outside the purely secular understanding of life. It rarely even encourages people to consider whether their penultimate purpose or goal lies outside the domain of company/bureaucracy/profession in some other field of work or some counter culture alternative. It could be argued that the new stress upon the value of meditation in some of these work environments has begun to change this state of affairs. This does open up experience of a different quality of time. But, as we have seen, it is one which generally encourages people to adapt more to their present situation rather than to challenge or transform it. Besides, interest in meditation has largely sprung up alongside rather than from within time management circles. Christianity's more dynamic view of supernatural time has much to offer here, but it is rarely expressed in the Christian time management literature.[17]

Conclusion

The overriding difficulty with the time management approach turns out to be the opposite of that of the counter culture. Whereas the counter culture fails to help people deal with the world in which most of them live, time management injects too much of the spirit of the world into the solution it offers. One leaves the realm of business out of account; the other turns too much of life, even one's spiritual life, into a kind of business. So while both have helpful insights into ways in which we can struggle against the tyranny of time, in the end both fail to dislodge the tyrant from his throne.

Some other framework is needed from which to approach the problem. This needs to be broad enough to encompass the best insights of both the counter culture and time management solutions. It also needs to be large enough to include a dimension of time beyond our everyday experience which does not take us away from our day-to-day activities so much as lead us more vitally and creatively into them. It should also be able to deal with aspects of the time problem which neither the counter culture nor time management confront. Only one framework is capable of doing this. We must now give it sustained attention.

Footnotes

1. G.M. Lebhar, *The Use of Time* (New York: Chain Store, 1958 edn.) p. 9 ff.
2. So, respectively, R. Josephs, *How to Gain an Extra Hour a Day* (New York: Dalton, 1955) which contains 243 specific suggestions for saving time, and J.A. Schindler, *How to Live 365 Days a Year* (New York: Prentice-Hall, 1954) which argues the necessity of always taking advantage of the present.
3. Cf., with respect to the work situation, the influential book of Peter F. Drucker, *The Effective Executive* (London: Pan 1970) p. 26. Drucker begins with a chapter entitled 'Know Thy Time'.

4. See the opening sentences of the preface of the book (more than 215,000 copies in print!) by Ted W. Engstrom and R. Alec Mackenzie, *Managing Your Time: Practical Guidelines on the Effective Use of Time* (Grand Rapids: Zondervan, 1967).

5. E.C. Bliss, *Getting Things Done: The ABC's of Time Management* (New York: Scribner, 1976). Bliss goes further and looks at businessmen's non-work as well as work situation.

6. So A. Mackenzie, *The Time Trap: How to Get More Done in Less Time* (New York: McGraw Hill, 1972) esp. pp. 173–178, gives a list of the top twenty time-wasters among businessmen worldwide. Time management courses frequently provide these for secretaries and other employees as well.

7. On this, see further A. Lakein, *How to Get Control of Your Time and Your Life* (New York: Peter H. Wyden, 1973) and also D. Silcox, *Women Time: Personal Time Management for Women Only* (Ridgefield, Conn: Wyden, 1980).

8. Cf. S.B. Leas, *Time Management: A Working Guide for Church Leaders* (Nashville: Abingdon, 1978); S.B. Douglass, *Practical Help for Christians in Personal Planning, Time Scheduling and Self-Control* (San Bernardino: C.C. International, 1978).

9. From the preface of Ted W. Engstrom and R. Alec Mackenzie, *op.cit.*

10. See G.M. Lebhar, *op.cit.* The quotations are from pp. vi, 14, 124.

11. E.C. Bliss, *op.cit.*, p. 104.

12. P.F. Drucker, *op.cit.*, pp. 26–27.

13. E.R. Drayton, *Tools for Time Management: Christian Perspectives on Managing Priorities* (Grand Rapids: Zondervan, 1974).

14. The 'Personal Time Investment Analysis Worksheet' occurs in the *Marc Management Series* produced by World Vision Missions Advanced Research and Communication Center, Monrovia, California. For another example, less pretentious in its description but visually demonstrating the centrality of the clock, see the page-time inventory prepared by Lee Chapman, of Executive Time Studies Inc., in 'Surveying and Controlling Executive Time', *The Small Business Administration*, No. 76.

15. *Op.cit.*, p. 112.

16. P. King, *How Do You Find the Time?* (Edmonds, W.A.: Women's Aglow Fellowship) pp. 110–111. Similarly T.W. Engstrom and R.A. Mackenzie, *op.cit.*, pp. 28–29.

17. Even when the nature of time is specifically considered, as in T.W. Engstrom and R.A. Mackenzie, *op.cit.*, pp. 21–31.

Part 6
Toward an Ecology of Time

We can redeem the time only
if we conduct ourselves in
these times . . . with a wisdom
rooted in that hope which
comes from . . . revelation.
Then, and only then, is time
set on its true course.
J. Ellul, Hope in Time of
Abandonment

16

Time in Judaeo-
Christian Perspective

If neither the time management solution nor the counter culture
solution can fully solve our problems, and we cannot return to
some pre-industrial pattern of life, where can we turn? To suggest
that there might be something in the Judaeo-Christian outlook
would not surprise those who are aware of its capacity to throw
new light on even the most complex contemporary questions.
That it has much to say about time only encourages the hope that
it has something distinctive to offer.

The Judaeo-Christian understanding of time had its origin in
the East, among the people of Israel, and it took many centuries
before it came to have a permanent home in the West. Once it had
done this, it tended both to shape the Western tradition and
become shaped by it in return. Despite the passing of its domi-
nance in the West, it still has a residual impact upon modern life
and, through some of the movements antagonistic towards it but
still affected by it, eg, Humanism and Marxism, continues to
exercise a partial and indirect influence upon it.

What we need to do is go back to the origins of the Judaeo-
Christian view and see whether these contain clues to our present
problems with time that have been overlaid or ignored in the
intervening centuries. For clues there are and it is from these that
the framework of what we might call an 'ecology' of time begins to
appear. By this I mean a view of time which integrates our

understanding and use of it with all other aspects of our existence rather than working against them.

Inadequate views of the biblical understanding

For many Christians biblical injunctions about use of time seem to underline the importance of each moment that passes. Consider the following, for example:

> Conduct yourselves wisely toward outsiders, *making the most of* (or redeeming) the time. (Col. 4:5)
> Look carefully then how you walk, not as unwise men but as wise, *making the most of the time*, because the days are evil. (Eph. 5:15)
> But exhort one another *every day*, as long as it is called 'today', that none of you may be hardened by the deceitfulness of sin. (Heb. 3:13)

Other verses stress how quickly the end times are approaching:

> The Lord is *at hand*. (Phil. 4:5)
> Besides this you know *what hour it is*, how *it is full time now* for you to wake from sleep. For salvation is nearer to us now than when we first believed; *the night is far gone*, the day is at hand ... (Rom. 13:11–12)
> He who testifies to these things says, 'Surely *I am coming soon*' Amen. Come, Lord Jesus! (Rev. 22:20)

Do not these words stress the significance of each moment and underline the importance of carrying out our obligations while there is still time to fulfil them? Many have concluded from these and other passages that God demands 'busyness' in his service and therefore find no fault with the pace of life today in itself. Lack of 'busyness' is taken as a sign of half-hearted commitment.

But the first set of passages does not encourage a busy use of time at all. What they ask for is a discerning approach to it. We are to conduct ourselves 'wisely' not hectically toward outsiders (Col. 4:5). We are to be careful that we do not use time 'unwisely', not casually (Eph. 5:15). We are to exhort one another 'constantly' not at every opportunity (Heb. 3:13). And, despite the translation, we are not called upon to 'make the most of the time'. This choice of words underlines how affected even translators are by our modern obsession with maximising time use. What we are required to do is to free ('redeem') it from unprofitable activities. Today this injunction could be directed as much against the round of superficial pursuits that so many Christians are engaged in as against wasting time in all sorts of idle or superficial ways.

The second set of passages emphasises the need for alertness not busyness. The implication drawn from this is not that we should speed up our activities but that we should refuse to allow ourselves to become 'anxious' about anything (Phil. 4:6). This is the very opposite to the state of mind of the busy person. We are also enjoined to conduct ourselves 'becomingly' in the light of our knowledge of Christ's coming, not to rush around trying to do everything before it is too late (Rom. 13:13). Busyness actually reduces the quality of our life in Christ and encourages shallowness of both understanding and character. In Revelation we are simply encouraged to live on in the 'grace' of Christ which will sustain us through to the end (Rev. 22:21).

Nevertheless until recently young children had the credo of 'busyness' drummed into them through Sunday School classes. Many middle-aged Christians still know by heart the following poem:

> You have only just a minute,
> Only sixty seconds in it.
> Didn't choose it, can't refuse it,
> But it's up to you to use it.
> You will suffer if you lose it,
> Give account if you abuse it.
> Only just one tiny minute
> But eternity is in it.[1]

This attitude was reinforced by appeals to adolescents and adults to 'use every opportunity' to spread the Christian message. Appeals were sometimes combined with warnings of a missionary nature that 'every minute thousands are going to hell because they are dying without Christ'. Great urgency was attached to each passing moment. Such warnings and appeals are rare today, but they have left their mark in the way in which many middle-aged and older Christians think about time, order their lives, and function at work. A strong sense of accountability for all time at their disposal—sometimes down to its smallest fraction—pervades their outlook. While they talk much about the importance of 'redeeming' the time, the fact is that they have very little unaccounted-for time at all. Unlike first-century Christians, who lived in a less pressured world and had to be exhorted to use their spare time responsibly, many Christians today need first to create free time so that they can actually have something to put to good use or 'redeem'.

Those lacking sympathy towards the Christian point of view do not argue that it supports our modern conception of busyness. They assert that it has no relevance to modern problems at all. After all, the biblical materials were composed two to three thousand years ago in a quite different social, economic and cultural setting. Some of them have their basis in a nomadic way of life, while others arose out of a more settled, but still predominantly rural, background.[2] Where an urban audience is addressed, it is pre-feudal in character. All this makes it improbable that the Bible could contain anything very helpful for people living in today's cities. If present-day rural Greek attitudes cannot help us much in dealing with our problems, what likelihood is there of even older Mediterranean attitudes doing so?

Yet there is something special about the biblical approach to time. The ancient Hebrews had a distinctive awareness of their presence in time and history, and this was a direct consequence of their experience of God. The early Christians took over and intensified this approach to time and, through Christianity, it came to have an important place in Western thought.[3] This view of time gave the West its peculiarly forward-looking, dynamic character. By contrast, Greek and Roman thought lacked a strong sense of progress. Only in very limited respects could historians discern development taking place.[4] Every few thousand years the cosmos decayed and a new start had to be made all over again. But in the biblical writings there was movement from a definite beginning (the Creation) to a definite end (the Last Days), with certain novel and decisive events along the way (eg, the Exodus, the Covenant, and for Christians the Incarnation and Resurrection). This conception of a forward movement in time gave impetus to social change in succeeding centuries and ultimately produced a new type of individual[5]—it fashioned what we call 'modern man'. Our emphasis on will rather than contemplation, our belief that change, development and reform are possible in personal and social life, our drive towards what lies ahead rather than preoccupation with what lies behind, our confidence in our ability to shape and plan the future: all have their origins in the biblical attitude towards time and history.

The trouble is that the Judaeo-Christian approach to time has become identified with all the problematic aspects of advanced industrial 'progress'. This is one of the reasons why many people have become attracted to more mystical Eastern attitudes to time. The question at issue is really this: does the Judaeo-Christian approach inevitably lead to the impoverishment and deification of time that we discussed earlier, or do these problems result from distortion of the approach? Could it be that, alongside the secularisation of the Reformation understanding of work into the 'Protestant work ethic', there has occurred a secularisation of the Christian understanding of time into our present endorsement of 'busyness'? Whether or not there are tendencies in the biblical writings that necessarily lead in this direction is a question we must seek to answer.

The general approach of the biblical writings
We must bear four things in mind as we approach these writings.

It is important to recognise the culturally conditioned character of all the statements in the biblical records. Some references to time are simply a reflection of the pre-feudal way of life, nothing more. We are not bound, for instance, to estimate time from sunset to sunset as the Gospel writers do. Nor are we required to use the language of 'redemption' or 'stewardship' in talking about our responsibilities vis-a-vis time simply because the Epistles employ this metaphor.

We must not presume there is a unique biblical view of time. Too many writers on the subject state dogmatically that biblical and Greek views on the one hand and biblical and modern ones on the other stand in complete opposition to one another. Closer inspection reveals an overlap between the two at some points. For example, Jewish and Christian thought also possessed recurrent elements, eg, annual cultic rites, the rise and fall of kingdoms, typological connections between events.[6] The purposeful forward movement of time contained detours, sudden jumps and retreats; it was not a purely linear conception.[7]

We must consider the possibility that the Bible contains a plurality of views on time. Some books, like Chronicles or Daniel, certainly do stress the calculation of times more than others, like Exodus or Proverbs, which stress their special quality. If this is true, partially different emphases and practical attitudes to time may be drawn from the Bible. What follows is my own view of the way in which our current dilemma can be illumined by leading biblical strands of thought.[8]

We need to take the Bible record as a whole and look for ways in which biblical perspectives, in spite of their culturally conditioned character, transcend the centuries and supply guidelines for us. By discovering various intermediate principles, attitudes, models and images of behaviour—stimulated by the Bible but modified in the light of our changed social and cultural circumstances—we can try to bridge the gap between the Bible world and our own. Other sources of knowledge of God ('natural theology' or 'general revelation') have a contribution to make, and it is not improper to corroborate or supplement the biblical material by data from the physical, biological and social sciences.

There were two ways of looking at a particular unit of time in biblical days. Time was often measured in a straightforward, chronological way.[9] For both Hebrews and early Christians, the 'day' rather than the 'hour' was the most common expression for a unit of time.[10] The Hebrews had names for different parts of the day—'dawn', 'morning', 'midday', 'dark', 'evening'—and night was divided into three watches. But no word for 'hour' occurs in the Old Testament. In the New Testament there are Greek words for the parts of the day, and a term for 'hour' is used both in a specific and general sense. By then the Roman practice of four watches during the night had taken root. In both Hebrew and Greek, particular characteristics of the day and night could be designated, eg, the hottest part of the day, the time of the evening breeze. References to the days before or after a certain day occur, and there were terms for long periods of time: the week, month and year. Less specific periods of time—'a few days', 'a short time', 'many days'—are mentioned, and there are loose phrases typical of an unregulated society, eg, 'about this time [tomorrow]'. Also there were words for non-specific units of time; these are usually translated as 'situation' or 'time'. Length of time (eg, brief or long) could be indicated. There were ways of referring to the past, eg, 'the former days', and to the future, eg, 'the coming days'. These allusions could be made more specific by the use of numbers or by references to well-known figures, eg, a past monarch. Despite what some writers have claimed, 'there is no good ground for considering chronological reckoning to be an unessential or secondary element in the biblical understanding of time'.[11]

A qualitative approach to time is also present in the Bible. Writers often place the emphasis on 'what' is happening, not on 'when' something happens. A particular time period is defined according to its content, not its position or duration on a chronological line. Just as it is not always the length of a piece of cloth that is most important, but rather its texture, so it is with time.[12] For the biblical writers, each event was charged with personal significance. Sometimes specific occasions were regarded as unique and singularly decisive; sometimes they recurred with sufficient frequency for them to be looked upon as basic features of life.

The best-known illustration of the latter view comes in Ecclesiastes 3:1–8:

> For everything there is a season, and a time for every matter under heaven:
> a time to be born, and a time to die;
> a time to plant, and a time to pluck up what is planted;
> a time to kill, and a time to heal;
> a time to break down, and a time to build up;
> a time to weep, and a time to laugh;
> a time to mourn, and a time to dance;
> a time to cast away stones, and a time to gather stones together;
> a time to embrace, and a time to refrain from embracing;

> a time to seek, and a time to lose;
> a time to keep, and a time to cast away;
> a time to rend, and a time to sew;
> a time to keep silence, and a time to speak;
> a time to love, and a time to hate;
> a time for war, and a time for peace.

In short, the writer of Ecclesiastes says all aspects of life have their appropriate times. Some of these come only once, others will recur again and again. It is important to recognise when something is having its particular time and to allow the full interval appropriate to it. The character of the event, experience, stage in life or relationship will determine the type and length of time that should be placed at its disposal.

Unfortunately, it is not always easy to recognise the significance of a particular point in time. Along with Paul we may be 'perplexed' on some occasions, but we need not be 'driven to despair' (2 Cor. 4:8). We do not always recognise the significance of large blocks of time. As the author of Ecclesiastes says, we cannot always 'find out what God has done from the beginning to the end' (Eccl. 3:11). Yet we can still echo the Psalmist's affirmation:

> But I trust in thee, O Lord,
> I say, 'Thou art my God'.
> My times are in thy hand ... (Psalm 31:14–15a)

In many other places apart from the third chapter of Ecclesiastes, we read about appropriate times for carrying out various domestic or work related responsibilities (eg, Gen. 29:7 and Is. 28:24–25). So too for various activities of an everyday kind, eg, travelling and residing (Deut. 2:14), coming out of or being in a certain place (Mic. 7:15), feasting or going hungry (Judg. 14:12; Ps. 37:19), working and resting (cf. John 9:4), beautifying oneself or embalming another (Esth. 2:12; Gen. 50:3), remaining indoors or wandering around outside (Cant. 2:10–14).

There are also apposite times for worship of God (Ps. 122:1–4) and for the healing of men (Jer. 8:15). Then there are the times related to the basic rites of passage, viz: birth (Eccl. 7:1), youth (Ez. 16:22), menstruation (Lev. 15:25), marriage (1 Sam.

18:19), maturity (Ps. 1:3), old age (Job 5:26) and death (Gen. 50:4).
In relation to God there can be times of temptation (Lk. 8:13),
refreshment (Acts 3:19), distress (Nah. 1:7), appeal (Ps. 50:15),
disgrace (2 Kings 19:3), vengeance (Is. 61:2), rebuke (Is. 13:13),
rest (Jer. 27:22), affliction (Lam. 1:7), cleansing (Ez. 36:33),
destruction (Jer. 47:4), wrath (Is. 13:13), and salvation (Is. 49:8). In
the biblical scheme of things, notice also how 'good' and 'bad',
'high' and 'low', 'happy' and 'unhappy' times all have their place.
There is no attempt to deliberately circumvent the so-called dark
side of life, or the emotions that accompany it, in favour of a
single-minded quest for spiritual or earthly pleasure, goals which
in any case are full of pride and vanity (1 Cor. 4:8–13 and Eccles.
2:1–11).

Conclusion

In summary, both the measurement and significance of time were
important in the Judaeo-Christian outlook.[13] Today we are so
preoccupied with measuring time down to the smallest unit that
we forget that generally it is the content that should determine
when and how long we should engage in something, not the other
way round. We preserve reminders of the qualitative approach in
expressions like 'lunchtime', 'holidays', 'exam time', though often
these are strictly regulated for us by the clock, diary and timetable.
We need to approach many other activities, relationships and life
stages in terms of their intrinsic time requirements rather than
fitting them in where and when we have time and determining
their length purely by the watch on the wrist or clock on the wall.

On the other hand, the biblical writings offer no encouragement to those who suggest that all measurement of time by other
than natural rhythms is wrong. Life could not proceed for any
individual or community within a larger society unless a
certain degree of personal organisation and social co-ordination
can take place. Natural indicators are not sufficient for this.
Therefore the Bible does not support the outlook so humorously
proposed in the King's Singers' clever song 'Timepiece':

> Imagine paradise full of clocks
> Full of the sound of ticks and tocks.

'Stop!' said God, holding his head,
'Clocks are bad news!
There shall be no more ticking, nor
striking, nor chiming'.

In other words, the watch and the clock have their uses. They just need to be put in their place! The difficulty with the counter culture and time management approaches is that they tend to give too little or too much place for them. We need a balance between the two. Given our present inclinations, however, this requires us to give special attention to the quality of time involved in our actions, relationships and experiences and to worry much less about its quantity or reckoning.

Footnotes

1. I have been unable to trace the source of this poem. Though part of the folklore of that Christian generation now in middle-age, declining Sunday School attendances and ever younger Sunday School teachers have led to its having a less wide distribution among the younger Christian population.

2. The influence of a nomadic existence upon teachings in the Old and New Testaments respectively has been explored by Morris S. Seale, *The Desert Bible: Nomadic Tribal Culture and Old Testament Interpretation* (New York: St. Martin's, 1974) and Gerd Theissen, *The First Followers of Jesus: A Sociological Analysis of the Earliest Christianity* (London: SCM, 1978) esp. chapter 2.

3. S. de Vries, *Yesterday, Today and Tomorrow: Time and History in the Old Testament* (London: SPCK, 1975) p. 31 and T.F. Torrance, *Space, Time and Incarnation* (London: Oxford University, 1969) p. 56. The latter, together with its complement *Space, Time and Resurrection* (Grand Rapids: Eerdmans, 1976) provide an interesting starting point for a philosophical theology of time, along with E. Bevan, *Symbolism and Belief* (London: Allen and Unwin, 1938) pp. 82–124.

4. On this see further L. Edelstein, *The Idea of Progress in Classical Antiquity* (Baltimore: Johns Hopkins, 1967).

5. In differing ways this is the theme of B. Ladner, *The Idea of Reform: Its Impact on Christian Thought and Action in the Age of the Fathers* (New York: Harper, 1967); C. Dawson, *Progress and Religion: An Historical Enquiry* (London: Sheed and Ward, 1945); J. Baillie, *The Idea of Progress* (London: Oxford University Press, 1950); A. Th. van Leeuwen, *Christianity in World History: The Meeting of the Faiths of East and West* (London: Edinburgh House, 1964); G. Grant, *Time as History* (Toronto: CBC, 1969).

6. The fullest treatment of this may be found in G. Trompf, *The Idea of Historical Recurrence in Western Thought: From Antiquity to the Reformation* (Berkeley: University of

California, 1979); M. Eliade, *Cosmos and History: the Myth of Eternal Return* (New York: Harper and Row, 1959) goes too far, however, in seeing the final thrust of biblical history in cyclical terms.

7. Over-simplified views of the difference between biblical and Greek approaches to time occur in O. Cullmann, *Christ and Time: The Primitive Christian Conception of Time and History* (London: SCM, 1951) and J. Marsh, *The Fullness of Time* (London: Nisbet, 1952). For criticisms of this see Th. Boman, *Hebrew Thought Compared with Greek* (London: SCM, 1960) pp. 123–153, though in other ways he tends to distinguish too sharply between Hebrew and Greek views; and J. Barr who, in his *Semantics of Biblical Language* (Oxford: Oxford University, 1961) pp. 46–88, rightly takes Boman also to task. Unhappily, an oversimplified view persists in more recent discussions, eg, H.M. Yaker, 'Time in the Biblical and Greek Worlds', *The Future of Time*.

8. In all this I am trying to bear in mind the strictures of J. Barr, *Biblical Words for Time* (London: SCM, 1962).

9. See N. Snaith, 'Time in the Old Testament', *Promise and Fulfilment*, ed. S. Hooke (Edinburgh: T. & T. Clark, 1963) pp. 178–181, for an analysis of vocabulary for time in both Old and New Testaments. An exhaustive study of the Hebrew term ''eth' and other temporal expressions has been carried out by J.R. Wilch, *Time and Event: An Exegetical Study of the Use of 'eth in the OT in Relation to the Temporal Expressions in Clarification of the Concept of Time* (Leiden: Brill, 1969). For a discussion of divisions of time in the Old Testament see H. Wheeler Robinson, *Inspiration and Revelation in the Old Testament* (Oxford: Clarendon, 1946) pp. 109–112 but especially S. de Vries, *op.cit.*, pp. 39–44 and R. de Vaux, *op.cit.*, pp. 180–190. I have not found any comparable discussion of terms used in the New Testament. See, however, J. Barr, *Biblical Words for Time*, pp. 120–121.

10. So de Vries, *op.cit.*, p. 42.

11. J. Barr, *op.cit.*, p. 31, makes this point. He criticises not only von Rad (G. von Rad, *Old Testament Theology: Vol. II—The Theology of Israel's Prophetic Traditions* (Edinburgh: Oliver and Boyd, 1965) p. 98) but also Marsh, *op.cit.*, pp. 19–20, and Robinson, *op.cit.*, p. 47. Supporting Barr in this is N. Snaith, *op.cit.*, pp. 179–181. The chronological approach to time occurs most noticeably in the annals of the Divided Kingdom, the priestly writer's history and in apocalyptic material.

12. Greek views on this are discussed in R.B. Onian, *The Origin of European Thought About the Body, Mind, the Soul, the World, Time and Fate* (London: Cambridge University Press, 1954) pp. 343–348, 411–415. For an excellent treatment of the Hebrew approach to time as a qualitative affair see further G. von Rad, *Wisdom in Israel* (London: SCM, 1972) pp. 138–143.

13. S. de Vries, *op.cit.*, pp. 349–350, contradicting the views of E.W. Heaton, *Everyday Life in Old Testament Times* (London: Batsford, 1976) pp. 187–188.

17

The Outlook of the Biblical Writings

We have seen that there was a two-sided approach to time in biblical days. The Hebrews were aware of the passing of time and developed various ways of measuring it. They were also shown the significance of particular times and were encouraged to give them as much time as they required. Within this general approach to time, they came to see that there were other characteristics of time that they had to take seriously. But when we examine the biblical writings we find no simple set of directions with respect to time. Rather we find a series of polarities. It is in the interplay of these that some of the clues we are searching for are to be found. We find these same polarities in what the early modern scientists referred to as God's 'other book', ie, the created order. Both the world he has made and the writings he has given us exhibit a similar pattern.

Slowness vs suddenness
There is both extraordinary slowness and intermittent suddenness in God's way of working. Think about God's creative activity. From scientific studies we know that the evolutionary process through which God brings everything into being is a slow affair which is still unfolding. Changes in the inorganic, animal and human world over a period of six thousand million years were mostly infinitesimal.[1] Yet every so often explosions of biological

novelty took place. These surprising bursts of evolutionary activity followed protracted development within species, and occurred, biologically speaking, with unexpected rapidity. Is it improper to read from this something about the way God approaches his work? The account in Genesis 2 reflects something of this in the way it describes the creative process, though neither it nor the Genesis 1 narrative provides us with a chronologically accurate picture.

For a further example think of the biblical portrayal of God's educational activity. His instruction of Israel was a painstakingly slow process. The Israelites' experiences in the wilderness after their disobedience at Sinai testify to this, as do Moses' experiences after his first abortive attempt to do something about his country-men's oppression by the Egyptians. Both had to learn fundamental lessons before God could further use them for his purposes. He spent 'forty years'—an expression which should not be taken literally but which denotes a substantial period of time—teaching them. As Kosuke Koyama comments in his useful book *The Three Mile An Hour God*:

> Forty years for one lesson! How slow, and how patient. No university can run on this basis ... God goes slowly in his educational process of man. 'Forty years in the wilderness' points to his basic educational philosophy.[2]

Koyama goes on to suggest that God works at the speed at which a person walks. We, on the other hand, tend to want things to happen in a hurry. The unusual title of his book has its origin in the notion of God's pace. Is this pattern not true of the whole process of Israel's education, between the initial call of Abraham and the eventual appearance of the Messiah? Israel's wanderings in the wilderness stand as a symbol of her subsequent history. Yet within that long, circuitous, often delayed progress in understanding there were sudden explosions of saving activity. The Exodus was one such occasion, the reign of David as well, the return from exile another.[3] It is to the prophets that God reveals the coming and meaning of such times: indeed from one point of view the prophet may be described as the person who, more than anyone else, knows what time it is.

Reflecting on what all this tells us about God's way of working, the philosopher/theologian Kierkegaard talks about 'the man after God's own heart', 'the right man' for a particular task or responsibility. Such a man, he says, is generally 'early selected and slowly educated for the task'.[4] Since the things the chosen man has to learn are of the most fundamental and personal kind, 'speed is of no value whatever in connection with a form of understanding in which inwardness is the understanding'.[5] Any attempt to short-circuit this process leaves the man without the knowledge and experience he requires for the tasks that lie ahead. It is because God cares about the quality of what is undertaken, and about the people who will be affected, that he proceeds in this way. To quote Koyama again:

> God walks slowly because he is love. If he is not love he would have gone much faster. Love has its speed ... and it is a different speed from the technological speed to which we are accustomed.[6]

Yet, when the chosen man or woman is at last ready for the task, events frequently move with the most astonishing rapidity, and with breathtaking consequences:

> Every valley is lifted up, and every mountain and hill made low; the uneven ground ... becomes level and rough places a plain. (Isaiah 40:4)

New things happen at such a time, things which have only been glimpsed or hinted at before.

The appearance of Jesus in what the Bible calls 'the fulfilment [fulness] of time is the supreme example of this. Patiently prepared for over many centuries, and long promised by a variety of prophets, the climactic event in God's drama of salvation took place. In one of his choruses from *The Rock*, T.S. Eliot captures the critical nature of this occurrence so far as time itself is concerned:

> Then came, at a predetermined moment,
> a moment in time and of time,
> a moment not out of time but in time,
> in what we call history; tearing,
> bisecting the world of time,

> a moment in time, but not like
> a moment of time,
> a moment in time but time was made
> through that moment: for without the
> meaning there is no time,
> and that moment of time gave the meaning.[7]

Eliot relates this special event to what had gone on before it, seeing it not only as a momentary interruption of the ongoing process of history, but also as something which gives ultimate meaning and significance to history.

Decisive moments in time in the biblical writings (moments where the emphasis is on God's revelation rather than human intuition) are often denoted by the Greek term *kairos*.[8] (This term is sometimes contrasted with *kronos*, sometimes with *aion*, denoting measured and extended time respectively.) The word has passed into general theological use to refer to any point in time which was specially ripe for God to manifest himself. While the term does not inherently carry this meaning, and is not always used in this way, there can be no doubt that the concept of decisive moments of time is reflected within Jesus' life itself. Jesus' insistence that his hearers respond directly to his preaching of the Kingdom of God and to his call to discipleship offers a vivid illustration of this. So does his forecast of the coming 'hour' of his suffering and vindication, and the coming 'day' of the Kingdom of God's universal appearance. In other places we find mention of both the slowness and suddenness of God's activity. Some of Jesus' parables, for example, speak of both crisis and growth, of God's rule breaking in now to confront people, yet also of its gradual development in time.

We must keep both poles of God's activity—slowness and suddenness—in view. We live now in one kind of time, now in another. If we are to move purposefully between the two, we must seek to understand in what type of time we are living at any particular moment. This applies not only to us as individuals but as members of church and society. Only so can we shape our attitudes and actions to suit the occasion, and only so can we grasp some understanding of all that is happening to us.

Regularity vs flexibility

We cannot fail to note that, both inside and outside the Bible, regulations are built into the structure of things. For instance, there are diurnal, lunar, seasonal and annual cycles. The Bible writers talk about some of these (eg, Ps. 74:16–17; Gen. 1:14; Jer. 33:20) and clearly regard them as a divine gift (Gen. 8:22). Since our own lives are inextricably bound up with them, we have to respect them and work within, not against, them. As Psalm 127:2 tells us: 'It is in vain that you rise up early and go late to rest, eating the bread of anxious toil, for he gives to his beloved sleep'. Good sleep is one mark of the person who lives in the rhythm of Yahweh's giving and calling.[9] Transgressing the limits of environmental rhythms can be an act of unbelief, a reliance upon human works rather than on God's provision.

Sometimes God's demands cut across the natural regularities he has established, just as they sometimes take priority over social and family relationships (see Matt. 14:23–25, 26:36–47; Acts 16:25, 2 Cor. 11:27). And there is also an exhaustion that stems from obedience as much as a fatigue that stems from disobedience. However, God gives special attention to his servants' physical and emotional needs (eg, in 1 Kings 19:1–8), and Jesus took care to rest and regain strength even in the most unusual circumstances (Matt. 8:23–27).

The Old Testament encouraged regularity in religious observance. The main celebrations, eg, the Feasts of Unleavened Bread, Harvest and Ingathering, had their basis in natural rhythms connected with agriculture and were linked to historical events that held particular significance for Israel. The Passover was held in conjunction with the Feast of Unleavened Bread and was based on Israel's liberation from Egypt.[10]

In addition to these feasts was the Sabbath. Lacking any agricultural or historical basis, it was fixed independently of the phases of the moon and sequence of months. Since its purpose was to celebrate time,[11] of all Israel's festivals it merits our closest attention. The Sabbath was primarily intended to give people rest, to free them from work (Deut. 5:14b–15). Their animals were to be rested also, for God's concern extended to animals as well as

people (see esp. Ex. 23:12–13). As God rested from his labour
on the seventh day, so they were to rest from theirs (Ex.
20:8–11). In so doing, the Israelites fulfilled their obligation to
'sanctify' the Sabbath, or keep it 'holy'. They were also to
remember how God had given them rest from the oppression of
Egypt (Deut. 5:12–15). But the translation of this remembrance
from a family occasion into a cultic happening, and its expression
in centralised worship, only took place late in Israel's history.[12]

The various feasts were 'structured times' in which God's
activities and redemptive benefits could be acknowledged and
savoured. God was also recognised in the regular daily sacrifices
and special offerings marking outstanding occasions and rites of
passage.[13] On the other hand, the Sabbath showed that Israel's life
also possessed the element of 'free time'. The Sabbath was a
rejection of greedy snatching at the whole of time.[14] Even in busy
periods (ploughing, harvest) the Sabbath was to be observed (cf.
Ex. 34:21). The Sabbath, not work, was fundamental. Rather
than being simply an interlude between periods of work, it was
the climax of the week. Unfortunately, the Sabbath's restful and
fundamental characteristics were obscured by the Pharisees'
pedantry in New Testament times. Ensuring that no 'work' took
place on the Sabbath became very hard work, and celebrating the
delights of freedom began to feel like a duty. The original flavour
of the Sabbath lives on in the attitudes of modern Jews like
Abraham Heschel. For Heschel the Sabbath is 'not a date but an
atmosphere'; it is a day for 'praise not petitions', a time to learn the
art of surpassing civilisation, an occasion for 'a profound conscious harmony of man, and the world', indeed 'a taste of
eternity—the world to come'.[15]

Neither the 'structured time' of the daily, weekly and seasonal festivals, nor the 'free time' of the Sabbath, passed into
Christianity without radical change. The principle of regular
weekly gatherings for religious purposes was carried over into
Christian practice.[16] These gatherings, however, were held at
various times, eg, daily in the early Jerusalem Christian community (Acts 2:46). Occasional references to the 'first day of the
week' are not proof that this was the regular day for meeting (the

reference in 1 Cor. 16:1–2 being to what people should do privately in their homes, and that in Acts 20:7 to a special 'one-off' occasion). The Passover had also been fulfilled in Christ and now was celebrated as an ongoing spiritual reality (1 Cor. 5:7–8). While Christians were no longer obliged to relax on a set day each week (cf. Rom. 14:5, Col. 2:16–17), and believed that they had already begun to enter into an eternal Sabbath (cf. Heb. 4:3), the principle of taking proper physical and spiritual rest remained important. This was now taken, apparently, whenever the need or opportunity for it arose, rather than on a specified day (eg, Mk. 4:35 ff; 6:30 ff). As well, the structured liturgical time of cultic worship gave way to a more fluid, though still orderly, charismatic arrangement (1 Cor. 14:26–40).[17]

In these different ways the predetermined Law-based character of both the timing and content of Old Testament services and festivals was set aside in favour of a more flexible Spirit-led approach to celebrating God's goodness and to relaxing from the effort expended in work. Regularities of a kind do continue, but these do not have the same fixed character as their Old Testament counterparts. This means that for us any day can become an opportunity for a religious gathering, any time an occasion for rest from one's labours, any orderly pattern of worship a valid expression of our fellowship with God and with one another.

Casualness vs consistency

The best illustration of this polarity is provided by Jesus' teaching and way of life. Jesus directed his parables not only against the idolatry of works but also against the idolatry of time. For the person who plans his own future, even if he camouflages this by alleging that God has disclosed his purposes to him, commits idolatry by virtue of his seeking to determine and control his life irrespective of God's intentions. J.D. Crossan comments:

> It is the view of time as man's future that Jesus opposed in the name of time as God's present. Jesus simply took the third commandment seriously: 'keep time holy!'[18]

Some parables represent the coming of the Kingdom as a gift which reverses human plans and expectations and empowers people to lead a new kind of life. Others warn against assuming that control of the future lies in human hands, and they depict the shock this realisation brings to someone who is unprepared for it. A good example is the parable of the Rich Fool (Lk. 12:16–20). There is clear conflict between the rich man's assumption that he can plan the future as he likes (by building bigger and better storehouses) and God's unexpected intervention (which brings the man's life to a sudden close). The parable demonstrates that all time is actually in God's hands. Similarly Proverbs reminds us: 'Many are the plans in the mind of a man, but it is the purpose of the Lord that will be established' (Prov. 19:21). And James says: 'Come now, you who say, "Today or tomorrow we will go into such and such a town and spend a year there and trade and get gain"; whereas you do not know about tomorrow ... Instead you ought to say, "If the Lord lives we shall live and we shall do this or that". As it is, you boast in your arrogance.' (4:13–16).

Even when a person places his life under God's general control, difficulties can arise:

> [W]e do not want parables. We want precepts and we want programs. We want *good* precepts and we want *sensible* programs. We are frightened by the lonely silences within the parables ... We want them to tell us exactly what to do, and they refuse to answer.[19]

We not only want to know what to do but when to do it. We want schedules as well as programmes. The disciples demanded: 'Tell us, *when* will these things be?' (Matt. 24:3) and again: 'Lord, will you *at this time* restore the kingdom to Israel?' (Acts 1:6–7) Jesus' answer: the times of events to come are not for them to know; their job is simply to get on with the immediate tasks that God lays before them and empowers them to do.

Jesus' way of life corroborated his teaching in this matter. He eschewed scheduling his activities in favour of a more casual approach. In part this was a product of the age in which he lived. The notion of a purposively followed career and planned daily and weekly activities was unfamiliar to first-century Jews. Trades and professions were less structured than their modern counterparts. Jesus and his disciples managed to get by without earning their living in the normal way, and apparently this was not difficult in the economic climate of first-century Palestine. As H.J. Cadbury comments: 'We can hardly make a picture of Jesus' life and that of his contemporaries that will be too casual for the facts'.[20] Jesus had an intermittent, unregulated pattern of activity and withdrawal. He moved frequently from one place to the next, but his moves were rarely predetermined. His style of life was decidedly fluid. But in doing this Jesus was not merely following first-century practice. His reasons were rooted in his personal needs and understanding of his mission (Mk. 1:38, 6:31); this shows that his actions were not shaped purely by cultural influences.

To get some feeling for the way Jesus actually went about his business, let us consider Cadbury's picture of a typical day in his life:

> It was not lived by schedule ... his social contacts ... were of the most accidental sort. He was neither a systematic teacher of his disciples, nor careful in his evangelistic planning. He wandered hither and thither in Galilee. He sowed his seed largely at random and left results to God ... Probably much that is commonly said about the general purpose of Jesus' life and the specific place in that purpose of detailed incidents is modern superimposition upon a nearly patternless life ... My impression is that Jesus was largely casual. He reacted to situations as they arose but probably he had hardly a program or plan.[21]

Certain features of Jesus' life do have a more purposeful and farsighted look about them, eg, his determination to go to Jerusalem from about the mid-way point in his travels (Lk. 9:51), and his predictions of his approaching capture, execution and vindication (Mk. 8). But his behaviour did not stem from the sort of rational calculation and careful scheduling that we are familiar with today. The casualness of Jesus' approach is summed up in his words to those who were trying to hurry him along: 'I go my way today and tomorrow and the third day I am perfected' (Lk. 13:33).

None of this means that Jesus' life lacked consistency. He possessed an inner co-ordination based on his consciousness of his priorities and how they should be fulfilled. Cadbury remarks:

> There is perhaps no better description of Jesus' career than those phrases in the book of Acts which describe its spontaneous consistency and casualness. It was 'all the days that he went in and out among us', says the apostles, or 'he went about doing good'. Such a life gets its unity neither from its goal nor from any standard of action, but from an unphrased inner quality and temperament.[22]

I am not advocating here some Catholic 'imitation of Christ' or Protestant 'what would Jesus do?' approach. We cannot and should not attempt to imitate him or ask what he would do in our place in any simplistic fashion. But, insofar as Jesus' attitude to time sprang from his understanding of the way in which God carries out his purposes, this feature of Jesus' way of life still has something to say to us.

Conclusion

I have drawn attention to three characteristics of God's way of looking at, and working in, time. These characteristics carry over into the way in which he expected his followers to view and use time, first of all among the people of Israel, then with certain changes among the followers of Christ. Rather than marking out certain fixed directions which would act as guideposts, he indicates that there are a number of broad polarities within which we are to find our way. Sometimes it will be appropriate for us to incline more to one side of the polarity, sometimes more towards the other. At some points progress will seem slow, life will proceed in a regular way, and our day-to-day behaviour patterns will be largely the same. At other points everything will seem to happen at once, we will need to allow for great flexibility and everyday life will take on a casual air. Other combinations of these polarities are also possible. The key requirement is to discern 'the signs of the times', to know what phase we are in and to sense when a change is appropriate.

Footnotes

1. Even if we take up the suggestion that we view such expanses of time on a logarithmic rather than linear arithmetic system and so vastly reduce the 'length' of time involved, this point still has force. See on this Roger Pilkington, *World Without End* (London: Collins, 1961) pp. 40–42.
2. K. Koyama, *The Three Mile an Hour God* (London: SCM, 1979) pp. 3, 6–7.
3. On these see further G. Ernest Wright, *God Who Acts: Biblical Theology as Recital* (London: SCM, 1952) esp. chapter 3, and N.H. Snaith, *op.cit.*, p. 175.
4. S. Kierkegaard, *Attack Upon Christendom* (Princeton: Princeton University Press, 1968) p. 195.
5. S. Kierkegaard, *Concluding Unscientific Postscript* (Princeton: Princeton University Press, 1968) p. 247.
6. K. Koyama, *op.cit.*, p. 7.
7. T.S. Eliot, 'The Rock', in *T.S. Eliot: Selected Poems* (London: Faber and Faber, 1954) p. 119.
8. G. Delling, 'Kairos', *TDNT*, Vol. III (1965) p. 461, lists a number of passages relevant to this.
9. Cf. H.W. Wolff, *Anthropology of the Old Testament* (London: SCM, 1974) pp. 134–135.
10. For a full discussion of these festivals see R. de Vaux, *op.cit.*, pp. 484–506. Later feasts such as Atonement, Hannukah and Purim are treated on pp. 597–617.
11. Cf. A.J. Heschel, *The Sabbath: Its Meaning for Modern Man* (New York: Farrar, Straus and Co., 1951) p. 10.
12. See H.W. Wolff, *op.cit.*, p. 136.
13. On these, see R. de Vaux, *op.cit.*, pp. 468–469.
14. H.W. Wolff, *op.cit.*, p. 137.
15. A.J. Heschel, *op.cit.*, pp. 21, 28, 30, 31–32. For an attempt to interpret post-biblical Jewish attitudes to the Sabbath in similar terms, see G.F. Moore, *Judaism in the First Three Centuries of the Christian Era* (New York: Schocken, 1971) Vol. 2, pp. 26–39.
16. Early Christian practice is fully investigated by W. Rordorf, *Sunday: The History of the Day of Rest and Worship in the Earliest Centuries of the Christian Church* (London: SCM, 1968). On Jesus' attitude, see the discussion in R. Banks, *Jesus and the Law in the Synoptic Tradition* (London: Cambridge University Press, 1975) pp. 113–131.
17. S. Bacchiochi, *From Sabbath to Sunday: An Historical Investigation of the Rise of Sunday Observance in Early Christianity* (Rome: Gregorian University, 1977) pp. 90–131 demonstrates that 1 Cor. 16:1–2; Acts 20:7–11; Rev. 1:10 do not imply a fixed Sunday meeting. See also R. Banks, *Paul's Idea of Community: The Early House Churches in Their Historical Setting* (Sydney: Anzea, 1979; Exeter: Paternoster, Grand Rapids: Eerdmans, 1980) pp. 122–124.
18. J.D. Crossan, *In Parables: The Challenge of the Historical Jesus* (New York: Harper and Row, 1973) p. 35. Jesus' view of time as revealed in the parables is also discussed by E. Fuchs, 'Jesus' Understanding of Time', *Studies in the Historical Jesus* (London: SCM, 1964) esp. pp. 130–143.
19. *Ibid.*, p. 82.
20. H.J. Cadbury, *The Peril of Modernising Jesus* (London: SPCK, 1962) p. 124.
21. *Ibid.*, pp. 140–141. Some specific examples of this are discussed in J. McInnes, *The New Pilgrims: Living as Christians in a Technological Society* (Sydney: Albatross, 1980) pp. 19–20. Following Marsh, he tends to set up too great a contrast between the quantitative and qualitative approach to time.
22. *Op.cit.*, pp. 148–149.

18

The Contours of a
Christian Attitude

It is by living within the polarities discussed in the previous
chapter—the slowness and suddenness, regularity and flexibility,
and casualness and consistency of God's time—that proper use of
time can be achieved. This should prevent us from adopting a
one-sided attitude to time, as both the counter culture and time
management approaches tend to do. A genuinely Christian
perspective endorses neither a laid-back outlook nor a fast pace,
developing instead a measure of each in a fully integrated life. It
idolises neither spontaneity nor organisation, but allows room
for expression of both when appropriate. It frees us from our
enslavement to the clock, but does not ignore the need to
sensibly measure time. It encourages a freer, more flexible
approach to life, but not at the expense of inner consistency or
public relevance.

   We need to draw these insights into a more systematic account
of a Christian approach to time. There are two different ways in
which we can do this. First, we can look at the way a particular
Christian, in this case Paul, shaped his life in the light of these
polarities. This shows us how they work out in practice. Second,
we can identify certain wider polarities which impinge upon the
time question. This reminds us that we need more than a biblical
view of time to construct a fully rounded Christian attitude to

A personal example

Paul is an excellent person to choose for such an exercise. He is a major Christian figure and his writings are normative for those who come after. His life's work is also described by some as a campaign that was carefully thought out and methodically implemented. He is also regarded as having a highly organised and well structured approach to church life. Many find both his style and convictions inflexible in the extreme. I do not wish to discuss the misconceptions involved in these views of Paul. It is his attitude towards time that alone concerns us here![1]

There can be no doubt that Paul fits the pattern of slowness and suddenness in God's education of him for his missionary task. His call on the Damascus Road (Acts 9:1 ff) was a dramatic intervention in his life. After a small flurry of activity he retired to Arabia where we hear nothing of his activities for three years (Gal. 1:17). Despite his call to take the gospel to the Gentiles, he spent the next 11 years in Cilicia, his home region (Gal. 1:21). Following a spell in Antioch (Acts 11:25–26), his call was renewed and he began the first of his great missionary journeys (Acts 13:1 ff).[2] These were marked by periods of patient sowing of the word, periodic hindrances and reversals, and occasional sudden advances. Sometimes he moved on rapidly from one place to the next. At other times he settled down for two or three years in the one city. At various points where he was imprisoned, he was forced to withdraw from his journeyings. While this did not prevent him having some ministry, many of his plans were held in abeyance until his release.

Paul's activities sometimes follow a regular pattern, sometimes display considerable flexibility. His practice of visiting the synagogue, on the first day each week, in the early part of his missionary travels shows a consistent method of attack (Acts 17:2). He also made a point of attending great festivals in Jerusalem when he was in a position to do so. But the synagogue pattern was overtaken by the more flexible household approach once he crossed the Aegean into Macedonia.[3] And frequently his commitments did not allow him to do such things as go to Jerusalem for the Feast of Pentecost (Acts 20:16). Overall his

missionary life exhibits a similar rhythm of activity and withdrawal as Jesus' did before him. Both within and between his
evangelistic engagements there were periods of lesser activity.
And what of Paul's personal lifestyle. How organised or
casual were his day-to-day, week-to-week or month-to-month
arrangements? We know that some people considered him a
vacillator whose statements of intention were not to be trusted (2
Cor. 1:17–18). Paul's writings show that his travel plans were
mostly provisional as to both destination and duration. His desire
to go to certain places and visit certain people was often frustrated
(Rom. 15:22, 1 Thess. 2:18). When he told his readers he
proposed to see them, he put it in terms of his 'hope' that this
would happen (Rom. 15:24). He could only talk about the
duration of his stay in inexact terms: 'perhaps ... or even' (1 Cor.
16:6). Sudden changes in plan occurred, owing to external circumstances, personal anxieties, an uncertain reception or God's
guidance (Acts 13:49–51, 2 Cor. 2:12–13, 2 Cor. 1:23–2:1, Acts
16:6–8). When one of his longest-standing ambitions, viz, to visit
Rome, was eventually realised, it was by the most circuitous of
routes and after a considerable lapse in time (Acts 26:32–28:16).
Only when he had a clear understanding of God's purpose for him
could he make predictions of a reasonably certain and time-
specific kind (1 Cor. 16:8–9). Over all his thinking about time
stands the phrase 'if the Lord permits' (1 Cor. 16:7).

Yet there were some consistent threads in Paul's life. First,
throughout his life he demonstrably strove to remain true to the
principle of doing 'all for the sake of the gospel' (1 Cor. 9:23), and
he encouraged his colleagues to do the same (2 Tim. 4:2). It was
the demands of the gospel which determined how he arranged his
affairs and spent his time. These demands gave a pattern to his life:
temporal as well as geographical, day-to-day as well as long-term.
They gave consistency to what otherwise might appear as a
relatively random way of life.[4]

Second, Paul always worked out the limits of his activities.
He had a clear belief that there were boundaries within which he
was to operate, despite the generalist character of his calling to
take the message of Christ to the Gentiles. He believed that his

task was to go into new areas, not consolidate work others had already begun (Rom. 15:20). He concentrated his attention upon predominantly middle-class households in urban centres within the Roman sphere of influence, thus limiting his activities to the social, cultural and political contexts in which he felt most at ease.[5] There he followed his own advice to his readers, carrying out his activities within the limits of the gifts he possessed, not going beyond them (Rom. 12:3, 6).

Third, Paul did not equate the opportunity or need to do something with God's requirements. He chose not to take advantage of certain opportunities because he recognised that at the time he did not have the emotional energy to cope with them (2 Cor. 2:12–13). He was careful to proceed only in the direction God indicated, though this sometimes meant bypassing whole fields in which he could have spent time (Acts 16:6–9). He never attempted to exploit every new opportunity or press every situation as far as it would go.

None of this means that Paul failed to exert himself strenuously (Acts 20:31; 1 Thess. 2:9; 2 Thess. 3:8) in his work. But we should be careful that we do not read into such passages notions of 'busyness' that were probably absent from Paul's way of life. We should also beware of interpreting comments about his working 'night and day' more literally than other remarks of a similar nature which we do not take that way, eg, his injunction to 'pray unceasingly'. In the passages cited, we do well to remember also that Paul is protesting against those who did too little. That was the problem he faced. He might well have had something very different to say to those who attempted too much. Jesus certainly did when he compared Martha's behaviour unfavourably with that of Mary (Lk. 10:38–41). For all his exertion, there was an underlying consistency, restraint and modesty about Paul's approach which is wanting in a good deal of Christian activity.

The wider framework

In identifying the main causes of our current problems with time, we were forced to look at a number of related issues which either overlap with, or lie beneath, the time problem itself. One such

issue was our understanding of work and leisure. Another had to
do with whether we receive justification for our lives from God's
hands or seek to justify ourselves by our own efforts. We also
examined the degree to which the process of industrialisation and
changes in worldview were responsible for our present condition
and to what extent our own greed and quest for status was to
blame. Also, how much were we bound by our own past actions
and how much freedom did we possess to shape our future life.
We must consider these broader polarities in order to round out a
Christian view of time.

The interplay between activity and rest is an important
matter. We must develop a more satisfactory understanding of
work and leisure, as some are now beginning to do.[6] Leisure is
both the source and climax of genuine work. The counter culture
has seen this with a clarity that the remainder of society has not.
But leisure is also basic to any profound experience of worship as
well as to individual and society-wide cultural achievements. This
means that we need to go beyond the present 'planning for leisure'
that time management advocates, social scientists and others talk
about. Work needs to be less all-consuming and to be dissociated
from status and identity. It must be understood as a wider
phenomenon than simply full-time paid employment. We have
come to the end of the full-time employment economy. Many
people will have to reckon with periods of time in which they
cannot obtain work. Others may find only casual employment or
part-time work. Others will be forced to accept a shorter working
week. Such trends call for a general reinterpretation of the place,
character and purpose of work in our lives. As unemployment
leaves people with large blocks of time on their hands, a re-evalua-
tion of the day-to-day nature, value and significance of non-work,
'free' or 'leisure' time is even more imperative. Without a proper
understanding of work and leisure, no satisfactory view of time
can come into its own. On the other hand, without a proper
understanding of time, no satisfactory view of work and leisure
would emerge.

The interplay between works and grace is also important. At
the root of our busyness and haste lies either a flight from

ourselves, others and God, or a desire to justify ourselves to God, others and ourselves. In other words, our activism is either idolatrous self-absorption or a self-justifying exercise.[7] In whole or in part, we are looking for something other than God to which we can devote ourselves or through which we can gain acceptance. It is one thing to look for meaningful, valuable, satisfying work. It is another to regard work as that which proves to myself, others or God that I have worth, that I am acceptable, that my existence is justified. If we depend on our work to give us worth, what happens if we are declared redundant, become invalids or retire? What message do we have for the disadvantaged, the unemployed, the aged? No, we have to *fully* embrace the gospel which we claim to believe, and not just apply it to our need for personal salvation. For it is through Christ's work *alone* that we have worth, find acceptance and know that our lives on this earth are well and truly justified and this must be reflected in our attitude to work as well as in our attitude to religious good works. For all its rightful rejection of the work-oriented society the counter culture tends towards idolatry of the natural; harmony with nature, rather than with the one who created it, is emphasised. Time management stresses the possibility of a technical or organisational solution to the problem of overwork. The gospel approach goes deeper than either of these, laying a basis for coming to grips with the problem of who we are in a way that returning to nature or relying on our reason cannot. No more than these can 'save' us in general can they free us from the tyranny of time in particular.

The interplay between *external forces and inner desires* also requires attention. More than that, a personal principle of evil is at work, and that is why our present-oriented, clock-dominated way of life exercises such a hold on us. In resisting, we fight not only against deep-rooted personal attitudes and entrenched social forces, but 'against the principalities, against the powers, against the world rulers of this present darkness, against the spiritual hosts of wickedness in the heavenly places' (Eph. 6:12).[8]

The exact ways in which evil forces exploit those psychological, cultural and structural factors which shape our use of time

are difficult to pinpoint. Yet we need be in no doubt that our
personal choices and social structures are manipulated by them.
Other approaches to the time problem do not recognise this.
Counter culture and time management solutions are both deficient
here. Only by deploying all the means which God has given us for
dealing with this outside interference (prayer, the word of God,
the Holy Spirit, faith, righteousness, and truth: Eph. 6:14–18) do
we have any chance of minimising or resisting it, whatever other
helps we may find from the whole range of human experience and
knowledge. We must sift the various challenges and situations
before us through meditation and through discussion with our
close Christian community. Only so can we identify all the ways
in which the power of evil is interfering in our lives and discover
effective means for responding.

Further, there is the dynamic relationship between the *fixed
and open character of time*. We often feel that what has happened has
happened, and there is nothing we can do to change it: the past is
fixed; it acts as a limit which hedges us in. Ahead of us lies a whole
range of possibilities, the future is 'open'. But it is not so simple,
for we are not absolutely bound by past actions nor are we
completely open to future possibilities. As Carl McIntire says:

> [A]t no moment is past entirely past, nor future merely future.
> The relationship is a dynamic one in which at any moment the
> past holds within it not only the conditions on which the future
> is based, but a variety of forthcomings which, unless something
> occurs to alter them, bear us into the future ... Memory,
> custom, habit and structures gather in elements of our past and
> induce us into the future. Similarly, plans, intentions, wishes,
> expectations and hopes project us into the future even as they
> take hold of the past and are based upon it.[9]

The trouble with the counter culture return to past values is that it
does not leave sufficient room for the novel ways in which God's
Spirit can take hold of our personal memories or habits, as well as
our collective traditions and structures, and transform them into
something more creative. The weakness in the time management
approach is its tendency to channel our hopes and plans at a more
superficial level than that of the deepest, longstanding, frequently

divinely-implanted longings or possibilities within us or the group to which we belong.

Conclusion
Overarching all these is the tension between the temporal and the *eternal*, between the 'now' and the 'not yet'. The Christian does not live only in the world of everyday time, whether that be thought of in terms of 'body-time', 'inner-time', 'clock-time' or 'social-time'. He or she already enjoys in part the heavenly time of God's coming transfigured universe. Our present experience of eternal life should call us to question the desperate busyness which marks so many Christians. To engage in frantic activity is to become enmeshed in the time patterns of a world which will one day come to an end and is even now passing away (1 Cor. 7:29–30). It is no more commendable to be frantically busy for evangelistic reasons than it is for materialistic ones. We do not need to feel anxious about either evangelism or material survival, for God supplies our material needs (Matt. 6:25–34, Prov. 13:25) and blesses our evangelistic efforts (Is. 55:10–11, Eccl. 11:1) in *his* good time. Our responsibility is to recognise the opportune time for evangelism when it comes, not try to turn every moment into an opportunity. The latter approach smacks of a finite, earthbound perspective on time and is an attempt to take time into our own hands.[10] When the Psalmist prays, as we should pray ourselves, 'Teach us to number our days', he does not go on to add 'so that we can hasten to do as much as we can but rather 'so that we can gain wisdom of heart' (Ps. 90:12). That is what the shortness of our time should encourage us to seek.

The Christian view of hope involves not only looking towards the future but acting now in the present. Though it is something that a person can never bring under his control by his own planning, yet it can shape our personal lives, social structures and cultural activities. The mystical kind of time which so many people seek to experience in counter culture circles only helps them to escape from the world for a while; or at best helps them to withdraw. The divine time which the Christian inhabits is not an escape from reality. Nor is it merely an aid to handling reality. It confronts reality, forcing us to engage with it wholeheartedly. As well it introduces fresh possibilities for action. This capacity for generating new input distinguishes the Christian attitude from the time management approach which seeks only the re-ordering of existing activities. Through the work of the Spirit, the new possibilities God has in store for us can enter into our present experience and into current events.

> As it is written, 'What no eye has seen, nor ear heard, nor the heart of man conceived, what God has prepared for those who love him', God has revealed to us through the Spirit. (1 Cor. 2:9)

Only as these new possibilities emerge, says Jacques Ellul, will there be a renewal of time. If Christians learn what it means to live through hope, time will come to possess genuine value and meaning again.[11]

Footnotes

1. Oddly enough Paul's attitude to time in the everyday sense that we are investigating does not directly come up for discussion in the standard works. His view of time in the broader historical or metaphysical sense has been quite fully discussed. See, for example, the discussion and literature cited in O. Cullmann, *Salvation in History* (London: SCM, 1967) pp. 248–267.

2. On the chronology of Paul's life see particularly G. Ogg, *Chronology of the Life of Paul* (London: Heinemann, 1968) and J.J. Gunther, *Paul: Messenger and Exile—A Study in the Chronology of His Life and Letters* (Valley Forge: Judson, 1972).

3. The change in pattern is documented by E.A. Judge, 'The Early Christians as a Scholastic Community', *Journal of Religious History*, 2 (1961) pp. 125–137.

4. Further implications of the passage in 1 Corinthians 9 are explored in S. Barton, 'Was Paul a Relativist?', *Interchange*, 19 (1976) pp. 164–192.

5. See the seminal work of W.M. Ramsay, *Paul the Traveller and Roman Citizen* (Grand Rapids: Baker, 1962). Also E.A. Judge, *The Social Pattern of Christian Groups in the First Century* (London: Tyndale, 1960) pp. 49–61.

6. Cf. S. Hiltner, 'Needed: A New Theology for Work', *Theology Today* (October, 1974) pp. 243–247; and J. Pieper, *Leisure: the Basis of Culture* (London: Faber and Faber, 1952).

7. Cf. J. Moltmann, *Theology and Joy* (London: SCM, 1973) p. 69.

8. Unfortunately, interpretation of the relevant passages hovers between too great an emphasis on their being simply social and political structures without any supernatural

dimension or, where a supernatural dimension is affirmed, too restricted a view of their operations which are seen as affecting individuals alone. Both views contain truth. More thoughtful representatives of these two approaches are H. Berkhof, *Christ and the Powers* (Scottdale, PA: Herald Press, 1962), (who has been very influential in the subsequent debate) and P.T. O'Brien, 'Principalities and Powers and Their Relationship to Structures', *Reformed Theological Review*, 40 (1981) pp. 1–10, respectively.

9. C.T. McIntire and R. Wells (eds.), *History and Historical Understanding: Some Christian Reflections* (forthcoming). I am indebted to Dr McIntire for allowing me to quote this passage.

10. K. Rahner, *Theological Investigations*, Vol. XI (London: Dart on Longman and Todd, 1974) p. 290.

11. J. Ellul, *Hope in a Time of Abandonment* (New York: Seabury, 1973) p. 232. On the subject of hope we have the stimulating theological exposition of J. Moltmann, *Theology of Hope: On the Ground and Implications of a Christian Eschatology* (London: SCM, 1967) and the suggestive, if brief, philosophical treatment of J. Pieper, *Hope and History* (London: Burns and Oates, 1969).

A Prayer about Time

God our Father
you are the Maker of everything that exists,
the Author of the world of nature
and of all living things,
the Creator of both space
and time.

Without you there would be no past,
present or
future;
no summer or winter,
spring or autumn,
seedtime or harvest;
no morning or evening,
months or years.

Because you give us the gift of time we have the opportunity
to think and to act,
to plan and to pray,
to give and to receive,
to create and to relate,
to work and to rest,
to strive and to play,
to love and to worship.

Too often we forget this and fail to appreciate your generosity:
we take time for granted and fail to thank you for it,
we view it as a commodity and ruthlessly exploit it,
we cram it too full or waste it, learn too little from
the past or mortgage it off in advance,
we refuse to give priority to those people and things
which should have chief claim upon our time.

Help us to view time more as you view it,
and to use it more as you intend:
> *to distinguish between what is central and what is peripheral,*
>> *between what is merely pressing and what is really*
>> *important,*
>> *between what is our responsibility and what can be*
>> *left to others,*
>> *between what is appropriate now and what will be*
>> *more relevant later.*

Guard us against attempting too much because of
> *a false sense of our indispensability,*
> *a false sense of ambition,*
> *a false sense of rivalry,*
> *a false sense of guilt,*
> *or a false sense of inferiority:*
> *yet do not let us mistake our responsibilities,*
>> *underestimate ourselves,*
>> *fail to be stimulated by others,*
>> *overlook our weaknesses,*
>> *or know our proper limits.*

Enable us also to realise
> *that important though this life is, it is not all,*
> *that we should view what we do in the light of eternity,*
>> *not just our limited horizons,*
> *that we ourselves have eternal life now.*

God our Father,
> *you are not so much timeless as timeful,*
> *you do not live above time so much as hold*
>> *'all times . . . in your hand',*
> *you have prepared for us a time when we will have leisure*
>> *to enjoy each other and you to the full,*
> *and we thank you, appreciate you and applaud you for it.*

Amen

Part 7
Putting Time in Its Proper Place

What will free us from this
bondage to the ever spiralling
demands that are placed
upon us? The answer is
found in the grace of Christian simplicity.
R. Foster, Freedom of Simplicity

19

The Primacy of Becoming over Doing

In the remainder of this book, we will be looking at practical ways in which we can do something about our time problem. The biblical writings have provided a general framework within which we should operate with respect to time and have given us a set of perspectives from which to approach it. They have also yielded some basic guidelines for day-to-day guidance. The counter culture and time management solutions also contain some valuable orientations which must be taken into account. What follows will contain a blend of all these, mixed together with a measure of personal experiences. Some of these experiences are my own and have been tested out over a period of years. I have also drawn on the experiences of others, both written and oral, wherever they have had something to contribute.

The danger of simplifying
In no sense are these suggestions intended to dictate to others what they should do about their time pressures. They are suggestive not prescriptive. They are designed to stimulate a response not regulate it. There is a simple reason for this: there is no single answer to our time problems. There are as many solutions as there are individuals in search of them. Both the nature of the problem and our response depend upon a variety of personal and social factors. For example, the pressures on couples in their mid-

twenties to mid-thirties—when family demands are greatest—differ from those on people in adolescence, middle-age and retirement. Then there is the effect of the life cycle; time pressures vary depending on which stage one is passing through. They can be greatest when a person is moving from one stage of development to another. As people grow older they sense time differently: it seems to pass more quickly. Class upbringing shapes people's attitudes to time, and it is difficult to transfer from the viewpoint of one class to that of another. Ethnic background is also significant: there are considerable time-attitude divergences between people of Anglo-Saxon, Asian, West Indian and Mediterranean background for instance, even in multi-racial, advanced industrial societies like Australia, England and the United States. Much also depends on one's marital status, household arrangements (eg, institutional, community, family), urban, suburban or rural setting, and employment status (employee, employer, self-employed, part-employed, unemployed). Temperament must also be taken into account. People speak at different speeds, are more (or less) outgoing and gregarious, prefer unstructured or structured frameworks within which to work. Personality differences also affect our attitude. 'Feeling' types tend to relate to the past, 'sensitive' types care about the present, 'intuitive' types look to the future, and 'thinking' types relate to past, present and future in a relatively detached way.[1]

These factors occur in people in differing combinations and in varying degrees, making it impossible to produce a uniform set of recommendations. Yet there are enough broad similarities between sufficiently large numbers of people to allow us to make some practical suggestions about the time question. Others have certainly felt this to be the case. Proponents of the time management solution claim that the basic principles are applicable to people in virtually every walk of life. Voices from the counter culture believe that their course of action is available to anyone who wishes to take it up, despite the fact that only a minority have so far done this. Christian tradition has always recognised that to some extent people's backgrounds and circumstances affect the way in which they order their lives. Yet it also insists that there are certain constants in human nature and certain consistencies in God's will for us.

In considering practical steps we can take to deal with the problem of time, there is a further danger we must avoid: simplifying can take place in another way than by prescribing one solution for all—it can take the form of a one-dimensional approach to our difficulties. This is precisely what happens in many Christian books dealing with time. They treat the subject as a purely personal concern. Even the responsibility of other members of our families or our churches in helping us to work our way through the question does not come into view. But there are still other dimensions to the time problem. In fact there are three planes of action that require attention.

The first is the individual's attitudes. To some extent the power to alter our way of life is in our own hands. It is a matter of personal decision, aided by the encouragement and assistance of others, whether we will do what is necessary. The second level is that of structural change. Many time problems stem from patterns established by the groups and institutions in our society. We must join together with others to bring out corporate and structural alterations. The third level is that of demonic activity. Many of the personal and social pressures on our time are being manipulated by evil forces. Struggle against these forces, using all the means God has placed at our disposal, is essential. These three planes of action interpenetrate. To operate only on a single level is like fighting an opponent with one hand tied behind one's back. It is possible to achieve something by doing this. But this is only up to a point and only at considerable psychological cost. For some the effort proves too much and they find it easier to bow to the prevailing pressures. We have to strive on all three levels to achieve substantial, lasting success, and we must pay attention to each of the areas of life where time is an issue.

The inadequacy of being
We begin with a fundamental observation. It is one alien to our whole Western way of thinking and is no less alien to Christians than to other people in our society. Our temptation is always to

ask what we should 'do' about something. Our approach to the problem of time is generally along this line. We want action. We want a programme. We want a manual of do's and don'ts to help us shift into a different lifestyle. Unfortunately this is not the way to go about it. Our difficulties will not dissolve simply by substituting one set of actions for another, eg, handling our responsibilities better, or reducing our commitments. The time management approach tends to look at the question in this way and that is why it fails to offer a satisfactory solution. Our Christian tradition should have made us wary of its proposals, for there are many warnings against attempts to overcome problems by sheer effort. It does not encourage us to resolve the time issue—in the first instance—by 'doing' something or other.

At first sight the counter culture approach comes closer to the truth here. It asks us to forsake 'doing' in favour of 'being'. This emphasis comes from the influence of Eastern religions and from certain types of Western psychology. The first tends to encourage its followers to lose themselves in the all-pervading cosmic 'Being', the latter stresses their need to get in touch with their own 'being'. Both criticise the restless striving characteristic of our society as a whole, as well as of institutions like the church within it. Only by turning inwards, they suggest, will we find the answers we are so busily seeking. Only by contemplating our inner selves will we learn how to live in a peaceful way. Only by knowing ourselves will we have any contribution to make to the world at all.

There is a good deal of truth in this. The retreat into 'being' certainly helps hyper-active Westerners to establish a closer harmony between our outer and inner selves. Carried out in the right way it should also bring us into greater accord with the natural world about us. Both of these enable us to sense more clearly our biological rhythms and the rhythms of our environment. We may also find certain long suppressed desires begining to come to the surface, desires which may suggest a change of lifestyle to the one we have been following.

All this is to the good. For the trouble with a life centred around 'doing' is that what is done often fails to express the inner life and real potential of the doer. Too much 'doing' arises simply in imitation of what others are doing. Or it stems from pressure —parental, societal or religious—to engage in certain activities. This leaves too little time for our private self to come to the surface and for our full potential to mature. Our actions become mere shadows of the hidden person within us, lacking substance, lacking sharp definition, lacking personal or social force. The shift over from 'doing' to 'being' makes us aware of some of these things and opens up possibilities for us.

But a concentration on 'being' has its limits too. The trouble is that what we discover when we begin to make contact with our inner selves, and start to live in harmony with them, is a nest of contradictions, weaknesses and uncertainties. The less people have felt the impact of the gospel upon them, the more is this the case. Even where the gospel has left its mark, the superficial nature of the preaching frequently results in only a limited exploration of a person's real nature and potential. As much as the attempt to solve our life or time problems by doing, placing our hopes upon the quality of our 'being' refuses to face up to the basic issue, that is, our need to change, not just exert ourselves or be more ourselves.

Our time problem, we saw, has its roots deep inside ourselves. It is not enough for people to get in touch with the genuine core of their being, for that core is itself a part of their problem.[2] Only a radical change in that core brings hope of a radical transformation of life. This takes place through a process of dying and rising in our inmost selves, a process that only the gospel can bring to pass. Where that has already happened, in a general way, what is required is for the ongoing implications of that to have their effect upon specific areas of our lives. One of these has to do with our approach to time.

The vitality of becoming

So, from a Christian point of view, the most important thing is not that we are 'doing' or 'being' but that we are 'becoming'.[3] The process of 'becoming' has a dynamism which merely 'being' lacks, and a depth which mainly 'doing' lacks. Not only individuals but also groups (eg, families, churches, organisations) also need to focus more on becoming what God wishes them to be. In 'becoming' I gain a real centre to my life and arrive at a clearer understanding of my direction in life. This is the consistent thrust of the biblical writings. The right sort of 'doing' inevitably follows. In becoming 'like God' or 'like Christ', we develop gifts and qualities of character which fit us for whatever tasks God has in view (cf. Matt. 5:21–48, Col. 2:20–3:17). While we are constantly preoccupied with what it is God wants us to *do*, he is far more concerned most of the time with who or what he wants us to *become*. He wants to fashion the right kind of person or group for particular tasks, not rush us prematurely into a busy round of activities. As one writer has suggested: 'The content of the action [is] less important than the internal orientation with which it is carried out'.[4]

When it comes to actions, those which contribute to a genuinely alternative way of life, individual, communal or societal, are the most important. Jacques Ellul has written eloquently about this, with an eye to the biblical emphasis. What the world needs, he says, is not just alterations in its social, economic and political arrangements or in its intellectual and cultural character, but nothing less than a new kind of civilization:

> It is not [our] primary task to think out plans, programs, methods of action and achievement. When Christians do this it is simply an imitation of the world, which is doomed to defeat. The central problem which today confronts a Christian is *not* to know how to act ... [The Church's] first objective should be the creation of a style of life ...[5]

So then, the first step we can take towards solving our time problems is to reject the activism which permeates our thinking. We must also reject the emphasis on being which is commonly regarded as the only alternative to activism. We need a transformation of character and lifestyle, both in ourselves and in the groups to which we belong. This transformation must include commitment to a less hurried, less harried existence, one that reflects the 'peace' which Paul lists as one of the fruits of the Spirit (cf. Gal. 5:22). In our agitated, frantic society, it has become

imperative for a differently paced style of living to appear. There
were times in the past when a flurry of activity was the very thing
society required. The early Christian era was one such period. A
static order prevailed, and some people had to demonstrate the
alternatives that lay only an arm's length away. Our post-
industrial age is not such a period. We live in a time when too
many people are attempting too much. Some should be demonstrating the creative possibilities that lie in doing less, living at a
more measured pace, and acting in a less regulated way. As
Christians, we must recover our equilibrium and discover for our
contemporaries a different way of life. As Paul Tournier says:

> The yield of our life does not depend so much on the number of
> things that we do, but more on the quality of the self-giving we
> put into each thing. In order to add this quality, we must depart
> from the atmosphere of the modern world which is completely
> obsessed with activism, even in the church: do, do, do always
> more. Let us rather, once again, become inspired and tranquil
> men.[6]

Is this asking too much? Surely differences in temperament and
calling should allow a place for some busy people? Individual
differences are undoubtedly important, but they do not absolve us
from the responsibility to change.[7] Karl Barth points out that, far
from ushering in the leisured society, all the new technical
possibilities of our Western (and Communist) society have created
a mounting fever of work and accelerating tempo of life, symptoms of the approaching collapse of our civilization. Preaching
against this trend is insufficient, for many are trapped by the
present economic conditions and cannot aspire to an alternative
way of life. Helping to create opportunities for rest through
initiating social changes has more to commend it. But since most
people cannot understand what this different style of life entails,
they need a practical example.

> One quiet man can accomplish wonders in a whole room or
> hall full of excited people ... There is no avoiding the fact that if
> we exhort others to be quiet in their work, as we ought to do,
> then we must first have exhorted ourselves, so that in our own
> existence we can at least give some indication that there is such
> a rest among men and that it may really be expected. Perhaps

one of the most important contributions which Christianity has to make towards the conquest or at least the mitigation of the unrest of work which threatens the world and the Church today is to produce here and there a few quiet people who by their existence can give others the chance also to find rest.[8]

Conclusion

Those who set an example in this way make a social contribution far more significant than the relieving of specific time pressures in our society, important though that may be. They make a major evangelistic contribution as well. As a result of their influence, other people begin to experience the rest which is necessary for God's Spirit to alert them to their true condition. Such would also have time to actually hear the Christian message, a possibility denied to many by their present lifestyle.

As Helmut Thielicke once commented:

> Modern urban man's lack of time and overcrowded housing conditions provide the devil with more welcome opportunities than all the Feuerbachians, Nietzcheans and anti-Christian propagandists put together.[9]

Eugen Rosenstock-Huessy argued similarly that only *between* his various commitments and appointments does modern man have any hope of hearing the gospel.[10]

But how do the 'few quiet people' come into existence in the first place? What practical steps can you take to become one of them? Where does a commitment to 'becoming' lead for the one who wishes to become a more 'timeful' person?

Footnotes

1. Robert J. Maxwell, 'Anthropological Perspectives', *The Future of Time*, p. 55.
2. R. Hudnut, *The Bootstrap Fallacy: What the Self-Help Books Don't Tell You* (London: Collins, 1979).
3. See the discerningly chosen title of K. Miller, *The Becomers* (Waco: Word, 1977).
4. P. Slater, *Earthwalk* (New York: Anchor, 1974) p. 193.

5. J. Ellul, *The Presence of the Kingdom* (London: SCM, 1951) pp. 43, 60, 80, 92, 146.
6. P. Tournier, *op.cit.*, p. 27.
7. S. Kierkegaard, *Purity of Heart*, p. 107.
8. K. Barth, *op.cit.*, pp. 555, 559.
9. Helmut Thielicke, 'Talking About God or With God', *Leadership*, I, 3 (1980) p. 53.
10. E. Rosenstock-Huessy, *The Christian Future* (New York: Harper and Row, 1966) p. 204.

20

A Singleminded
Approach to Life

It takes time to do something about time! This is true even if you
make a radical break with your present lifestyle. It takes our
bodies, nerves and spirits a long time to adjust to a new way of
life. We may experience 'withdrawal symptoms' as we make the
transition from a high speed lifestyle to a steadier pace. If you
choose not to make a radical break with your present lifestyle,
then it will only be possible to begin making changes at a few
points, not everywhere at once. It is better to make a handful of
changes well than to make many halfheartedly. One of the
dangers in attempting to do something about our pace of life is
forcing the pace of change! We should not try to enter into a less
hurried life too hurriedly. When we have drawn up some general
guidelines for change, we will require time to apply them to our
own circumstances. Then, since we ultimately learn only through
experience, we need more time to put things to the test, to get
feedback and to evaluate our attempts at change. This is the only
route through to a different tempo of life. There is no short cut
round, under or over.

Singleness of purpose
The first step is to become clear about the main path in life God
requires us to follow. We can be quite sure that whatever God
wishes us to devote ourselves to he will grant us time enough in

which to do it. Our responsibility is to find out exactly what he wants and hold resolutely to that. One of our greatest problems is that we misunderstand what God asks of us, either by adding all kinds of extra responsibilities or by possessing only a hazy idea of what he wishes. We will gain more time by properly understanding his will for us than by all the time-saving suggestions put together. No amount of re-ordering and scheduling our affairs, no amount of trimming and delegating our responsibilities, no amount of organising or managing our time, will achieve the same result. It is a matter of taking Jesus' words seriously and applying them to this particular issue: 'Seek first his Kingdom ... and all these things shall be yours as well' (Matt. 6:33). That is, discover what God's will is for you and all the time you need to fulfil it will come your way. In fact, the greater sense of satisfaction that you will feel means that the amount of time involved in doing this or that will not matter anywhere near as much. While the measurement of time will remain necessary to some degree, your awareness of the quality of particular times will become heightened.

More than any other Christian writer, Sören Kierkegaard insisted upon the importance of a singleminded approach to life. In one sense the whole of his remarkable book *Purity of Heart is to Will One Thing* is an exploration of it. He states:

> [That] which absorbs men's time when they complain about lack of time is irresoluteness, distraction, half thoughts, half revelations, indecisiveness ... The person who in decisiveness wills to be and to remain loyal to the Good, can find time for all possible things. No, he cannot do that. But neither does he need to do that, for he wills only one thing, and just on that account he will not have to do all possible things, and so he finds ample time for the Good. Moreover, such a person does not have the task of changing the Good into a thing of the moment, into something that shall be voted upon in a noisy gathering ... the one, who in truth wills the Good, must not be busy. In quiet patience he must leave it to the Good itself, what reward he shall have, and what he shall accomplish.[1]

Kierkegaard puts the issue before us with characteristic force and clarity. It would be as hard to improve upon his statement here as to evade the challenge in it. He puts his finger unerringly upon the obstacles to the singleminded life and accurately pinpoints its advantages. With great perception he finds its source in faithfulness to God and in a willingness to trust him for its results. The failure to be singleminded, then, arises from disloyalty and self-confidence.

How can we discover the parameters of God's will for us in this area? How can we discern the basic purposes or plans that God has for each of us, and how are we to realise them? It takes a long time to fully discover one's vocation or basic direction. If we begin to seek it early in life, we will probably have gained a preliminary understanding of what is involved by the time we are in our late teens or early twenties. Our thinking may be further clarified in early adulthood. Then in mid-life—when (for the first time, Jung would say) we become fully aware of our basic desire, gifts and limitations—it should come to maturity. There may be further refinement at the onset of old age, when consolidation and crystallisation of thought and efforts tend to occur.

At such critical points in life we should allow time to discern what God is saying. There needs to be extended self-appraisal, reflection upon possibilities, conversation with God, discussion with others, consolidation of what has been learnt from experience, and testing of principles in practice. Ideally, we should take time away from our usual round of activities, or at least withdraw from many long-standing church and community responsibilities. If we do not do this, the process of discovery is disrupted by constant distractions. A brief 'sabbatical' (something that long-service-leave often makes possible) has become a virtual necessity in mid-life.[2] A year 'off' for experiment in early adulthood (something that tertiary institutions allow and unemployment might make mandatory) has also a great deal to commend it.

When this kind of evaluation takes place it must be thorough. We need to reconsider everything we have aimed at and engaged in up to that point. We should make no exceptions, not even for deeply felt commitments, eg, to one's local church, some Christian organisations, or a social, charitable or educational institution. For often it is these commitments which are a major cause of our time problem. Viewed unsentimentally, some can be seen to be irrelevant to God's purposes: they should be terminated without loss. As for other commitments, more can often be achieved if they are undertaken in different ways or carried out in different contexts or less time is devoted to them. The occupation in which we are engaged, the type of accommodation in which we live, the place where we work—all have to be looked at. The singleminded pursuit of God's vocation for us may necessitate change in one or more of these areas. Many people find it hard to work through these issues by themselves. There is a need for others to be available to help, and for suitable environments where they can spend time thinking.

We must look behind our commitments and responsibilities to the priorities which inform them. These may require more than simply re-ordering. Our time problems may well be based on poor priorities. Only a radical reappraisal will reveal where we have gone astray and where God now wishes to lead us. Between our fundamental priorities and ongoing commitments lie working principles (or style of life). These principles dictate much of what we strive after and where our time goes. They influence, for example, the standard of living we aspire to (possessions owned, services utilised, attainments sought, groups joined). In view of the link between these and the busy life, we have some hard decisions to make in this area if we are to lessen our time problems.

Keeping on track

In between making critical decisions, we should allow time for monitoring our activities so that we do not lose our sense of direction or take on more than God asks us to do. Various criteria can help us here. Two in particular are of basic importance.

We must draw a distinction between the *central* and *peripheral* in our lives. Like Paul, we need to know where our main responsibilities lie, and we must leave everything else to one side, no matter how worthwhile or legitimate these concerns may be. Clearheaded, consistent choices are needed. For the choice-maker:

> [N]ot anything or everything can or should lay claim to him;
> not anything or everything can or should pull and tug and

> gnaw at him ... He has no time at all to lose, ie, none of the time which he needs to do what is required. Indeed to do what is required he must make time. With all the demands that crowd in upon him he must know how to give preference to one thing and set aside another.[3]

If we have a bad conscience about what we cannot undertake for lack of time, or if we allow sideglances at it to distract us from what we can and should do, it is a sign of a wrong decision. In other words, once we have decided upon our course of action, we need to feel at peace, indeed justified, in our new use of time, no matter what others may think of us or choose to do themselves.

One person I know has applied this principle in an unusual way. Alongside the list of books he plans to read he compiles a list of books which he would like, but feels he does not have time, to read. He keeps this second list as a reminder lest he stray into temptation. Another person suggests learning to read at the rate of 50,000 words a minute—all you have to do is recognise within one minute that a 50,000 word book has no relevance to your present needs and decide to leave it unread![4] This method works well with reports, newspaper articles, magazines and journals; with meetings, functions and committees; with television and radio programmes, and any number of other activities. It is one of the most effective ways of preventing busyness and creating usable time. (So far as reading matter is concerned, it is simple to keep a record of materials you have chosen not to read just now. This record can be consulted if and when some free time is found.) Many Christians are now coming out of their isolation from the world and, in their endeavour to understand what is going on about them, are attempting to read, hear and see too much all at once. Such people should concentrate on those things which are most significant for them and their 'vocation' and not feel under an obligation to keep up with all that is happening about them.

We also need to distinguish between the *important* and the *urgent*. According to one Christian writer, Charles Hummel, the greatest danger in Christian work today is to allow pressing matters to crowd out more important ones:

> [T]he important task rarely must be done today, or even this week ... But the urgent tasks call for instant action ... endless

demands pressure every hour and day ... The momentary appeal of these tasks seems irresistible and important and they devour our energy. But in the light of time's perspective their deceptive prominence fades; with a sense of loss we recall the important tasks pushed aside. We realise we've become slaves to the tyranny of the urgent ...[5]

Is there any escape from this tyranny of the urgent? Hummel finds the solution in Jesus' practice of daily seeking of God's will:

By this means he warded off the urgent and accomplished the important. It gave him a sense of direction, set a steady pace, and enabled him to do every task God assigned. As we wait for directions, the Lord frees us from the tyranny of the urgent. He shows us the truth about Himself, ourselves and our tasks. He impresses on our minds the assignments he wants us to undertake. The need itself is not the call; the call must come from the God who knows our limitations. If the Christian is too busy to stay, take spiritual inventory, and receive his assignments from God, he becomes a slave to the tyranny of the urgent. He may work day and night to achieve much that seems significant to himself and others, but he will not finish the work God has for him to do ...[6]

Jesus did not finish all the urgent tasks in Palestine, nor all the things he would have liked to do. But he did finish the work God gave him to do. So can we.

All this underlines the importance of giving time to meditation in any attempt to live a singleminded life. As Paul Tournier says, 'meditation remains the source of every great reform of life'.[7] This involves something more than prayer to God concerning these matters. It means waiting upon him to see what he has to say about them. Unhappily, we have almost lost the capacity to meditate. We do not have the time for it and, even if we did, many of us would not know how to use it. Yet it is imperative that we spend time regularly opening ourselves up to God in this way.

For this to take place we have to get clear of both the external distractions of our everyday activities and the internal distractions of our ever-planning minds. Only if we are quiet and receptive can God communicate with us as fully as he wishes. 'I wait for the Lord', says Psalm 130:5, 6, 'my soul does wait, and in his word

I hope; my soul waits for the Lord more than watchmen for the morning.' Or as Psalm 46:10 says (in Joseph Pieper's lovely translation), 'Have leisure and know that I am God'. The way in which each person finds this time will vary greatly. We each have to discover what is most apposite for us. Our varying personalities, circumstances and obligations will lead us in different directions. This does not matter so long as each of us finds the times, the places and the means which are most conducive. The patterns and rhythms we establish must bear our individual stamp.

This kind of meditation should have a regular place in our day-to-day activities.[8] There is also much to be said for giving an extended period of time to it weekly or fortnightly. We need to look beyond our immediate concerns to ensure that we are keeping our lives 'on target' and everything in the right perspective. Once a year we should spend a few days alone re-evaluating ourselves, our relationships and our responsibilities. Breakthroughs in our awareness of what God wants for us, and shifts of gravity in the way we look at life generally, tend to occur during such periods. There is value in keeping a written record of such times alone. This practice brings greater precision to our thinking at the time. And later we can bring our past and present experiences closer together, by re-reading what we have written.

However, it is not only during these quiet times that we gain a clearer understanding of who we are and where we are heading. Sudden insights can be gained at odd moments during the day. As Michel Quoist advises, when these reflective moments crop up, do not hurry off to fill them with noise, or with the newspaper, or with a conversation, or with the mere presence of another person:

> While you are waiting for the hairdresser, don't grab the first magazine you see! Stop for a moment! You find yourself packed like a sardine in the bus, lulled by the sense of the anonymous crowd. Stop your day-dreaming! Lunch isn't ready yet?—don't run out just for a minute to see a friend down the street. Stop for a moment! You have a few moments, don't put a record on. Stop![9]

Conclusion

There are creative 'moments' of time. Such moments are the
hidden source of singlemindedness. William Wordsworth spoke of
them in his great autobiographical poem 'The Prelude'.

> There are in our existence spots of time,
> That with distinct pre-eminence retain
> A renovating virtue, hence ...
> in trivial occupation and the round
> of ordinary intercourse, our minds
> Are nourished and invisibly repaired.[10]

Sometimes these occur during a period of reflection. Sometimes
they surface in dreams and have to be interpreted. Sometimes they
flash upon the mind, unforeseen and unsought.[11] However they
come, it is the quest for singleness of purpose that creates the
conditions for their appearing, and the setting aside of time for
meditation that is the seedbed from which they grow.

Such moments may come and go but in small ways they
should be part of our everyday activities. Attention to God enables
us to become inwardly acquainted with his voice at all times.

> We are increasingly able to discern the true Spirit from the
> clatter and clamor of human voices, and even the hollow voice
> of the enemy who comes under the guise of an angel of light.
> We begin to live in guidance. Inward promptings give unity to
> our decisions. All the demands for service are somehow filtered
> through the Light. Our lives are being simplified because we
> are giving attention to only one voice, and our Yes and No arise
> from that Center. We no longer rush puffing and panting
> through our jam-packed day, yet somehow we accomplish
> more.[12]

Footnotes

1. S. Kierkegaard, *Purity of Heart*, pp. 123–124, 145–146.
2. Compare the related suggestion of E. Rosenstock-Huessy, *op.cit.*, p. 204. On the
   question of 'time' at this point in life see P. O'Connor, *Understanding the Mid-Life Crisis*
   (Melbourne: Sun, 1981) pp. 16–17, 49, 120–121.

3. K. Barth, *op.cit.*, pp. 587–588.
4. J.C. McKay, *The Management of Time* (New York: Prentice Hall, 1959) p. 142.
5. C.E. Hummel, *The Tyranny of the Urgent* (London: Inter-Varsity, 1967) pp. 4–5.
6. *Ibid.*, p. 5.
7. P. Tournier, *op.cit.*, p. 32.
8. Further on all this, see the helpful discussion by M. Kelsey, *The Other Side of Silence: A Guide to Christian Meditation* (New York: Paulist, 1976) and, more briefly, L.D. Weatherhead, *The Significance of Silence* (London: Epworth, 1945) esp. pp. 7–16 or Henri Nouwen, *Reaching Out: The Three Movements of the Spiritual Life* (New York: Doubleday, 1975) pp. 13–44.
9. M. Quoist, *op.cit.*, p. 77.
10. W. Wordsworth, *op.cit.*, Book XII, lines 208 ff.
11. See the experience of A. Schweitzer, *Out of My Life and Thought* (New York: Henry Holte, 1933) pp. 185–186.
12. R. Foster, *Freedom of Simplicity* (London: SPCK, 1981) p. 86.

21

A Developing Sense of
Personal and Social Rhythms

A few years ago Gail Sheehy's book *Passages: Predictable Crises of Adult Life* reached the top of the bestseller lists around the world.[1] The book drew the public's attention to something that was already well known in psychological circles. This was the idea of the life cycle. Carl Gustav Jung had earlier concluded that every person passes through clearly recognisable stages.[2] In the fifties, Erik Erikson enlarged the number of stages to eight, though five of them occurred during childhood.[3] Sheehy modified this pattern by speaking of our adult phases. After late adolescence, which is characterised by a desire to pull up roots, there comes what she calls 'the trying twenties'. These confront us with the question of how to find our personal, vocational and relational place in the world. In 'the catch thirties' people seek to move beyond their early illusions about life towards fresh or deeper commitments at all levels of their personality. In the mid- to late-thirties 'the deadline decade' begins, when everything is reassessed and new directions become possible. The equilibrium gained at the end of this period of mid-life crisis leads into 'the refreshed (or resigned) fifties'.

Though the analysis may sometimes be too slick, books like Sheehy's remind of the larger rhythms which make our lives. They assure us that the experiences we are undergoing at a particular stage are not unique. This should help us to recognise such stages more easily and negotiate them less traumatically. We are able to understand better what 'time' we are in and let it have its way. These stages affect our spiritual development as well and enable us to chart its tensions and possibilities more discerningly. But there are many other cycles we pass through, or rhythms that influence us. All these have a place in the balanced and obedient life.

Attuning ourselves to an inner tempo

It is important to discern our natural rhythms and to adjust our behaviour accordingly. Only so can we experience a more organic sense of time that is less dominated by the clock. These rhythms differ from one person to another, and we vary in our ability to deal with disturbances to our natural patterns.[4] Each person must learn to sense his or her own rhythms and to heed their counsel. Only when there is some overriding exigency—something important, not just urgent—should these natural structures of life be transgressed. Rhythms are implanted by God for our proper functioning and protection. Refusal to heed them undermines that 'temple of the Holy Spirit' (1 Cor. 6:19) which is the body.

Our rhythms range from small 'ninety minute ones' through which our bodies move during the day and to which we should adjust our work and leisure patterns, to longer annual cycles which we should mark by holidays and times of personal reorientation. Between these are daily, weekly, monthly and seasonal cycles, all of which we should take into consideration. We should maintain regular sleep patterns (consciously making up for disruptions, late nights and changes of time zone). Men as well as women should identify and make allowances for their monthly cycles. We ought to lower our expectations of what we can achieve when the weather is extremely hot or cold. And the leisure we enjoy should be adapted to take account of seasonal changes.[5]

There are other physical patterns. One is the interplay of activity and sleep. A balance has to be struck between these, one that will differ from person to person. Then there is the relationship between eating and fasting. Naturopaths tell us there are times when fasting has its place and the Bible suggests it for certain occasions. We oscillate between health and sickness and we should recognise the behaviour appropriate to each condition. Illness needs to be given its time so that we return to full health. Travelling and staying put also need to find their proper levels. Too much travelling puts stress upon us.

There are also various psychological rhythms. For example, our own needs require attention as much as those of others, and we should allow time for privacy as well as for enjoying company. A balance should be struck between large gatherings and smaller ones, between times devoted to strangers and time with friends, between demanding, time-intensive, people-oriented periods and relaxed, time-expansive, self-regarding ones. Relaxation, friendship and time alone are particularly important for those engaged in counselling or pastoring others. Such people should arrange their time so that they have periods for recovering from their work. Otherwise they are soon likely to be in need of a counsellor or pastor themselves! Periods of high emotional energy should be compensated for by periods of low emotional demand. It is also important to ensure that time spent directly with God is balanced by time spent simply with ourselves: and time given to appreciating the world is needed alongside time spent consuming its benefits.

A friend captured the essence of one such time in a delightful little poem entitled *Time For Me*:

> Looking through my window
> nature lies secure, untroubled, unpressured, calm.
> Deeply rooted trees standing upright
> rustle in the breeze graceful, quietly being.
>
> Today I feel one with them
> no pressure, no people, no distractions, just time.
> Time to sit, to think,
> to let thoughts drift by
> pausing on one here or there sifting, sorting, weighing.
>
> In the quietness I see clearly,
> make decisions, reach conclusions.
> I feel more complete, sense of satisfaction in having time for me.[6]

At such times we should leave our watches far behind. Clock-time has no place here, except perhaps as forming the boundaries of such a time if we have other responsibilities to fulfil. But we can leave our watches behind at other times as well. Most of the time this is not difficult during periods of leisure. Despite what people think, it is not even so difficult for many people at work. I know of one director of several companies who does not wear a watch. He finds there are ample other ways of finding out what time it is when it is necessary for him to do so. Anyone who has reduced his or her dependence on the watch in this way will testify to the sense of liberation this brings. Also to the heightened sense of awareness it gives them of their own natural rhythms.

There are also spiritual rhythms we should be able to identify and observe. Am I in a period of slow consolidation, for instance, or poised for a sudden forward movement? Is this a time for quiet reflection or for strenuous activity? Am I in a transitional stage of uncertainty and doubt, feeling God is absent, or am I reacting against a constricting form of religious practice? If we are in a period of slow growth, we should not become impatient because so little seems to be happening. Things are happening but just need time to mature so that they can have their full effect. At the right time we will begin to move in a more noticeable way. But after that has happened for a while we feel the need to slow up once again.

In his book *Freedom of Simplicity*, Richard Foster talks about the balance between quiet reflection and strenuous activity. He comments on the great relief he experienced in discovering his own cycle.

> I function best when I alternate between periods of intense activity and of comparative solitude. When I understand this about myself I can order my life accordingly. After a certain amount of immersion in public life, I begin to burn out. And I have noticed that I burn out inwardly long before I do outwardly. Hence, I must be careful not to become a frantic bundle of hollow energy, busy among people but devoid of life. I must learn when to retreat, like Jesus, and experience the recreating power of God.[7]

He comments on how liberating this discovery was. He no longer castigates himself for giving insufficient attention to study or meditation during periods of activity. Nor does he rebuke himself for lack of activity in times of quiet reflection or vacation.

Sometimes we find ourselves in a stage of uncertainty or doubt. When this happens many Christians are inclined, or advised, to move out of it as quickly as they can. But it is not always so simple. The stage we are in may have its roots in very deep and long-term factors. These cannot be eradicated in a moment. They take time to work through. Again, the stage we are in may have its source in God's purpose for us. Jesus' temptations in the wilderness are a prime example (Matt. 4:1 ff.). There is no way of hurrying such a process. We have to see it through to its end. Only when our period of trial is complete will we regain our spiritual equilibrium.

Developing a social sense of time
Social organisation and environmental rhythms affect each other. We have begun to learn that we cannot disregard the effects of our industrial and commercial way of life upon the world in which we live. We are developing a concern for preserving the natural and historical legacy of earlier generations; a great deal more could be done in this area, and everyone, not just groups of conservationists and preservationists, should contribute.

A concern for the historical legacy has long been part of English national consciousness, and for some time part of Northern American thinking as well. On the Australian scene it is a relatively recent phenomenon. Through the work of the National Trust, local councils and civic-minded individuals, we now have well preserved houses and estates, restored townships and diggings, and replicas of earlier times and places. All are popular and well patronised because they offer us a glimpse of times past and the more stable rhythms of social life that accompanied them.

Life in a small city, a country town, or on the farm moved to a different rhythm to ones with which we are familiar. Various kinds of work were taken up or laid down according to need, labour or the seasons and work tended to be a more social and sociable affair. Social life was more integrated with the rhythms of work or religious occasions—before and after church, for example—but sometimes had an independent existence. Some people today hark back to those times, when personal, social, religious and environmental rhythms possessed a greater unity. In part, the popularity of holiday farms for urban residents reflects this longing.

But few of us live in such circumstances today. And the social rhythms of rural or small town life do not translate easily to life in a big city. In our urban environment, however, we need to find ways of integrating personal, social and environmental rhythms more successfully. In his fascinating book *What Time is This Place?* Kenneth Lynch makes several practical suggestions.[8] We could, for example, ensure that signs of the seasons are present in our workplace and homes as well as our suburbs, towns and cities. Planting deciduous trees in places where artificiality reigns would remind us of the phases through which the year is passing. We need to counter and supplement the arid concrete zones through which so many of us pass our days. As we spend more and more of our lives in interior environments, we are deprived of many natural clues to the passage of day and season. Office and factory buildings, long corridors and subways are timeless environments.

Secondly, we could retain or restore natural environments which operate according to different rhythms from those of urban society. One way is to preserve natural tracts of land in the suburbs rather than building on every square centimetre of land or creating artificially landscaped parks. Deciduous trees and native plants play their part here. Thirdly, different areas in a town or city could be encouraged to operate at different tempos: in 'change-retarded' areas people could operate at a slow pace; 'change-speeded' environments would be for those who wish to pioneer new directions; 'present-oriented' environments would be for those who can cope with the prevailing pace. Pioneer villages and exhibition suburbs are not what Lynch has in mind, for they have an artificial museum or showpiece air, unlike truly lived-in environments. However they do have a contribution to make;

they remind us of past patterns of living and anticipate future ones, so helping us to enlarge our time sense and adjust to changes that have taken or are about to take place. A clearer signposting of less artificial, more organic, remnants from the past would be even more useful, especially in cities.[9]

In looking at ways in which we can bring our personal rhythms into harmony with natural rhythms, and social rhythms into harmony with both personal and natural rhythms, it is appropriate to say something about the car. There is no denying the many benefits mass ownership of cars has brought to individuals and society. But the personal and social costs are far greater than most people are willing to acknowledge. Among the costs are chemical and noise pollution, energy and land use, physical injury through accidents, and psychological strains.[10] The car escalates the speed at which we live and increases the number of things we attempt to do. It insulates us from the natural environment and hinders us from exercising our bodies. It isolates us from social contact with neighbours and is in large measure responsible for the deteriorating public transport systems in cities. It adds greatly to our cost of living and requires us to work harder or longer to afford it.

Though not everyone could do without a car, many would gain from doing so. Almost all car owners would benefit from using their vehicles with more discrimination. People who begin to do this soon find they have more time with the family. Travel by train or bus is less pressured. Cyclists and pedestrians have more appreciation of the natural world and are much fitter. Non-car travellers have more contact with people who live round about, and feel more part of the natural and social rhythms of the place in which they live. They are closer to these and therefore sense them more easily. Even if you are not in a position to give up your car, you can experience some of these benefits by walking and cycling more and by patronising public transport.

I recognise that there may be difficulties in doing so. The family situation of some people precludes them from doing very much about this. Their place of residence may militate against it. The adequacy or proximity of public transport systems is sometimes a problem. The nature of the local terrain is another factor. All these things have to be taken into account. They make it more or less hard to put some of these suggestions into practice. But the high mobility in industrial societies—in Australia one-fifth of the population moves house every year—provides an opportunity to improve the situation. In settling in a new locality, the possibility of its requiring less use of the car, and more of alternative forms of transport, should be a major consideration. So should the extent to which it permits a greater integration of personal, social and environmental rhythms generally.

Conclusion

In Carmen Bernos de Gasztold's collection of prayers, there is a lovely entry entitled *The Prayer of the Ox*.

> Dear God, give me time.
> Men are always so driven!
> Make them understand that I can never hurry.
> Give me time to eat.
> Give me time to plod.
> Give me time to sleep.
> Give me time to think.[11]

This reminds us how much more animals are attuned to their natural rhythms than we are. In part this is because they can do no other; one of the glories of human beings is their capacity to rise above necessity and choose other patterns for themselves. In particular they are able to create and enjoy the whole texture of social and cultural life. This also has its rhythms, both beneficial and harmful.

Our pets and other animals remind us of the need for integration of the various rhythms which make up our world. They can also teach us how to begin doing this so far as our natural rhythms are concerned. For the rest we are left to our own devices. We have the help only of anyone we meet who has found a proper balance or at least is on the way to doing so. Such people are rare. We should not let them far out of sight when we find them. One day, perhaps, we may be able to join them and provide a model for others who are on a similar search.

Footnotes

1. G. Sheehy, *Passages: Predictable Crises of Adult Life* (New York: Dutton, 1976).
2. C.G. Jung, 'Stages of Life', *The Portable Jung*, ed. J. Campbell (New York: Viking, 1971).
3. E. Erikson, *Identity and the Life Cycle* (New York: International University Press, 1967).
4. G. Hildebrandt, 'Rhythmic Processes, Health and Way of Life—Results of Medical Research', *Universitas*, 21, 4 (1979) p. 255.
5. The most helpful account of rhythms I have come across is contained in G.G. Luce, *Body Time: The Natural Rhythms of the Body* (St. Albans: Paladin, 1973). See also D. Saunders, *An Introduction to Biological Rhythms* (Glasgow: Blackie, 1977).
6. Courtesy of Freda Banks, who wrote the poem partly in response to a discussion we had about time.
7. R. Foster, *op.cit.*, p.91.
8. K. Lynch, *op.cit.*, p. 69.
9. P. Slater, *op.cit.*, p. 52. See further the comments of F. Stuart Chapin, Jnr, *Human Activity Patterns in the City: Things People Do in Time and Space* (New York: Wiley, 1974).
10. Cf. J. McInnes, *op.cit.*, pp. 186–214, chapter entitled 'The car: a symbolic case study'.
11. C.B. de Gasztold, *Prayers from the Ark* (London: Macmillan, 1963) p. 55.

Part 8
There Is a Time for Everything

Time is a gift of God and he will demand of us an exact accounting of it. But be at peace; God doesn't give us a job to do without at the same time giving us the means to accomplish it. We always have time to do what God wants us to do.

M. Quoist, The Christian Response

22

A New Quality of Family Life and Friendship

Turning to family life and friendship, our first need is simply to find time to be together. It is not enough to grab a few minutes here or there, nor to fit in occasional extended gatherings. What is required is 'quality time': regular, leisurely periods in each other's company. This is not the way quality time is always talked about. Many parents use this phrase to rationalise spending only small amounts of time with their children. It is the quality that counts, they say, not the amount. This is a dangerous half-truth, especially in today's busy society. Quality can be present in even minimal periods of time together. But over the long term there is no quality without quantity. Extended, open-ended time is one of its key characteristics. This is as true for friendships as it is for families.

Renewing family life
Within the family we can begin by reducing our expectations. Settling for a more modest standard of living frees time which otherwise has to be spent earning money, maintaining equipment or consuming goods. As Kosuke Koyama says, 'Freedom from greed is freedom from time'.[1] Settling for a more modest range of activities (eg, each family member belonging to just one outside organisation instead of several) also allows more time for family togetherness.

It is important for children to have opportunities simply to play. Since such play serves as the principal model for all later attempts to enjoy genuine leisure, this play benefits parents as well.[2] A less regulated, less busy lifestyle for our children also enables them to become more in tune with the rhythms of their own bodies:

> Children might be taught not only to 'tell time' from the clock hands but to attend to and anticipate internal rhythms, to act in harmony with them in eating, sleeping, excretion, work and play.[3]

Because of their more instinctive approach to life, children are in a much better position to get in touch with their natural rhythms. They can teach us a lot about how to get in touch with our rhythms and can help family life operate more harmoniously in accordance with them. For this reason we should be wary of giving them watches too soon: there are other sorts of time they should learn to tell and observe first.

A graphic illustration of the changes that can occur when our expectations are scaled down comes from a family which was suddenly transferred from the U.S. to Kenya. As the mother recounted later:

> When it first made news that 1979 would be the official 'Year of the Child' I was living a very ordinary middle-class American life. My thoughts immediately turned to child beating, child prostitution and pornography, unwanted children, malnutrition, and other cruel, sinful affairs that so dreadfully touch the lives of God's littlest humans. My response to those problems was the same as my response to so many problems—plan a program.
> But by the time the 'Year of the Child' began, an amazing set of events had landed me in Kenya, East Africa. Now as the special year unfolds I find my whole response changing. Here, as in the United States and other places in the world, the toil and pain of the child is being lifted up and real efforts are being made to inform and to change opinions. So it is not a confrontation with a new approach that has so changed my response; rather it is a drastic change in lifestyle which has forced me to respond in new ways to some very special children—my own.
> My children are six, nine, and eleven. My husband and I love them and have always attempted to be good parents. We have

read the child-rearing books, attended the classes, and prayed
for guidance. We have fed them well and provided them with
stimulating playthings as well as the opportunity to participate
in Scouts, sports, and music. Time was set aside for family
events, and we all participated fully in the life of the church. I
answered appeals to make play costumes and bake cookies and
many times took off from work to be a chaperone or provide
transportation.

Any uneasiness that I felt over my role as parent was easily
brushed aside, for do not all parents have those pangs of
inadequacy? And the work I was doing on the job, in the
church, and in the community certainly seemed important ...
I now realize that in the U.S. I did not have the time or at least I
did not take the time necessary to parent. And after Scouts,
sports, school, church, parties, music, and camp my children
did not have the time or energy to be parented.

Our lives are full and busy here, but the lack of pressure and
rigid schedules seems to have released an abundance of energy
and curiosity in all of us. The children are busy for hours
building a chicken house or skipping rocks, and cooking the
family's lunch or planning a family talent night gets as much
time as it needs. To learn to grind millet and make it into
porridge takes time—time my children now have ...

Time seems to be the greatest gift of this move. The children
have acquired time to be children. Other than lessons and
chores, their lives are unscheduled, and I have yet to hear that
cry, once so familiar to me, 'I'm bored! What can I do?' With
fewer options they are more content. They watch the puppy
grow, they gather tadpoles and watch them change, or they sit
and watch their Kimeru-speaking friends with their herds of
goats. We all have time to wait for the sun to heat our bath
water. And we all look forward to the time each evening when
we read aloud ...

We now stay home evenings. With no electricity and very few
private cars in this area, events are not planned for evening
hours. We read, play games, write letters, and share lives and
dreams by kerosene lamps.

We are grateful for this experience, for the simplicity that we so
awkwardly, unsuccessfully sought in the U.S. has become
reality. For me the 'Year of the Child' will continue to be a time
of examination and struggle over what is happening to children
because of progress, modernization, and development. As the
world plans its programs to emphasize the very real social ills

that are deadly to children, we dare not be blind to what we are doing to our children by the very lives we have chosen to lead.[4]

Instead of reinforcing society's pressure to clutch greedily at all the experience life has to offer, we should encourage children to catch the spirit of Eleanor Farjeon's poem *There Isn't Time*:

> There isn't time, there isn't time
> To do the things I want to do—
> With all the mountain tops to climb,
> And all the woods to wander through,
> And all the seas to sail upon,
> And everywhere there is to go,
> And all the people, every one,
> Who live upon the earth to know.
> There's only time, there's only time
> To know a few, to do a few,
> And then sit down and make a rhyme,
> About the rest I want to do.[5]

How many poems, stories and compositions have never come to life because of the activism we have encouraged in our children? How impoverished has family life become as a result?

Meals are important gatherings in family life. We should guard these gatherings strenuously against fragmentation and intrusions. In his delightful little composition 'The Breakfast Song', Australian folk-singer Peter Campbell takes up this theme. His song is a complaint about the loss of family unity around the breakfast table. In most homes breakfast is an individual affair, with each person coming and going according to his own morning routine. We must reinstate the ritual of the early morning family meal. 'Leave when you must', runs the song, 'but you must come breakfast here with us'. In European countries the long midday workbreak has traditionally allowed husband and wife to meet for lunch. It is a pity that this practice is now being sacrificed in the name of efficiency. Television is the worst intruder on the evening family meal. There is a place for the occasional meal together in front of the T.V. (in our home it is a Sunday night ritual), and it is pleasant on occasions for husband and wife to eat together while the children watch their favourite programme. But the family should generally join together at dinner: it tends to be the time important family discussions take place.

There is much to be said for not answering the telephone during family meals. Others can wait at such times; our full attention should be given to those nearest to us, those for whom we have primary responsibility. The telephone should also be ignored on other family and individual occasions: when praying or meditating, when resting, and when recovering from a surfeit of demands on our time and energy. We need to learn to master the telephone rather than remain enslaved by it. Most people feel bound to answer the telephone. When they are away from home they do not worry that it might be ringing but the moment they return it assumes command. After the watch, the telephone exercises greater tyranny over us than any other mechanism. We must resist its totalitarian tendencies. The telephone was made for man, not man for the telephone!

A regular 'family day' when no visitors are entertained and no invitations accepted has a great deal going for it. If a weekly 'family day' cannot be arranged, perhaps a monthly or bi-monthly family weekend is possible. Family walks, rather than drives, especially in parkland and bushland, also add to the quality of family life. The driver is also able to participate and there is more leisure to appreciate and enjoy the outside world. Annual family holidays are of the greatest benefit when they are not too hectic or too planned. For those who live in cities, there is much to be said for taking these in a rural or semi-rural environment.

I know several families who, exhausted by the round of church and community commitments they had sustained over many years, decided to take a 'sabbatical' year from almost all such responsibilities. Many Christian families today would do well to follow in their footsteps. There are now specially established rest places to which they can withdraw to gain the maximum benefit.

Family rituals are also important. Unfortunately these are not as frequent as they once were. Birthdays and Christmas or Thanksgiving apart, together with occasional rites of passage, family rituals have largely faded from the scene. Instead of allowing these occasions to slip even further, we could make special efforts to revitalise them. Other events in our family history of a more individual kind could also become the opportunity for new rituals. Children love rituals. They enjoy preparing for them as much as participating in them. Even the smallest weekly ritual, developed out of some happy experience or focussed upon some enjoyable pastime, enriches family life. Both children and parents learn something significant about time by taking part in such events.

Another important contribution to family life is the passing on of family history from one generation to another. Consider how important this was in biblical times, as the many genealogies in the Old and New Testaments bear witness. In previous times this task was often happily and faithfully undertaken by grandparents living with or near the family. Today the nuclear family, high mobility, and separation of the aged into caring institutions have weakened contact between generations. Also, the dislocation of work from home life and home life from an integrated community mean that most people have shallow roots and tenuous histories. According to social psychologist Ronald Conway, ignoring or repressing one's family history leaves a yawning gap in the individual and social consciousness.[6] This seems particularly true of Australians. Having little sense of our past, as members of families or as citizens of a nation, we lack the depth which only knowledge of the past gives. This makes us less than full, mature people and explains our facile preoccupation with the present and superficial hopes for the future. Parents and grandparents carry a responsibility to link up past and present for their children. Tell your children stories about your childhood in the 'good old days' and trace the family tree as far back as you can go.[7] Involve them in following up the family history; most children love to take part in checking old letters and newspapers, visiting earlier residences and graveyards, and in hunting through genealogical records.

Restoring friendship bonds

Many things have contributed to the decline of friendship in the modern world. C.S. Lewis discusses some of them in *The Four*

Loves.[8] Though he does not mention it, the pressure of time is certainly one of them. Because of the busy lives so many of us lead, large numbers of people who regard themselves as friends never really know, enjoy or benefit one another as they might. They float in and out of each other's lives in only an intermittent and superficial fashion. Realisation of this can come as a shock in mid-life, when we sense that time for relationships is growing shorter with each passing year.

We need to identify our close (or potentially) close friends and determine to give them priority time. If this means spending less time with other acquaintances, contacts, colleagues, fellow-members and the like, so be it. Then, instead of satisfying ourselves with the customary afternoon or evening together, we should share whole days or weekends in each other's company, sometimes even sharing joint holidays. Three or four hours together is only sufficient to catch up on what has been happening since we saw each other last. It is not until we move through this stage that conversation takes an exponential jump into more serious territory. Stay a few hours longer and people really begin to talk with one another about the things that matter most. Up till then discussion tends to revolve around what has been going on around us; after that it begins to centre on what has been happening inside us. Then friendship really takes off. Another way of improving friendships is to adopt a more flexible approach to time. We need to keep some time free so we can see people on the spur of the moment. Alternatively, we can have regular 'open days' when friends and others know we will be home and available to them if they care to drop in.

When a friendship comes under threat from any of the powerful forces in society, eg, the high rate of social mobility, we should take conscious steps to ensure the friendship continues and develops. If long distances are involved, this means setting aside time to write regularly—and at length—to one another. The intermittent postcard or even aerogramme will not do. Friendship depends on ongoing contact. It requires a constant flow of letters containing a leisurely flow of information, gossip, questions, advice, thoughts, experiences, problems, hopes and ramblings.

Only if this happens will the friendship flourish. There is also a place for the occasional telephone-call, however costly, for it brings friends into living contact and brings them more vividly into each other's presence. The exchange of photographs at periodic intervals also helps this along. A visit, if at all possible, cements the relationship in the way that nothing else can. It is also an irreplaceable pleasure. All this requires giving priority time to our friends. There is no substitute for this.

Experience shows that sometimes surprising ideas and creative contributions have come out of people giving priority to each other in this way. We may not all have the gifts which enable us to profit as much from each other as did C.S. Lewis, J.R. Tolkien and Charles Williams, who met together regularly over many years, but in a small way we can all experience something of the enrichment their relationship produced.[9] But friendship does not have to issue in anything like this to have real value. Ultimately friendship is its own reward. Simply being with others whom we like and enjoy, growing together in intimacy and understanding, is more than enough. We experience too little of these in our world today. Yet they are one of the main sources of our growth to maturity. And as C.S. Lewis also explains:

> It is the instrument by which God reveals to each the beauties of all the others ... by Friendship God opens our eyes to them. They are, like all beauties, derived from Him, and then, in a good Friendship, increased by Him through the Friendship itself, so that it is His instrument for creating as well as revealing ... Not that we must always partake of it solemnly. 'God who made laughter' forbid. It is one of the difficult and delightful subtleties of life that we must deeply acknowledge certain things to be serious and yet retain the power and will to treat them often as lightly as a game.[10]

We border here on the area of play. More than once we have touched on the importance of this and will give attention to it again in the concluding chapter. Friendship does contain an irreducible play element. That is one of its greatest attractions and profoundest delights. It adds something not only to the texture of the friendship but to the whole of our life. This, like all the other aspects of friendship, comes over into our other activities. Quality friendship enhances all that we do. It is a gift, and an experience, not to be missed.

Conclusion

To some people these suggestions will sound impractical, if not utopian. Young mothers trying to look after two or three young children would probably think so. Upwardly mobile middle management men might well agree. Such people find their immediate responsibilities overwhelming. Even if they had the time, they would not have the energy to live in the way outlined here. Their pessimism is not unfounded. It arises from a realistic assessment of their present situation. Unfortunately many young married people are in this position—the wife at home and the husband at work. She does not have much time for her friends. He does not have much time for his family. Neither has enough time for the other.

To some extent they cannot do a great deal about this and have to recognise the constraints they are experiencing. They are passing through a particular life stage and simply have to grit their teeth and wait for it to pass. It will pass, gradually. They can draw strength from that realisation. But sometimes they could do more to help themselves. Many husbands seek to rise too quickly to the top: they could well bide their time a little until family pressures are not so great. Some wives are too independent: play-groups apart, they do not search enough for ways to share their load with people in a similar situation. Others could also alleviate their situation. Their churches should not only demand less of them at such a time, but find practical ways of assisting them. For example, older women could take the children off the mother's hands regularly so that she could have some time to herself. At formal or casual Christian meetings, younger people could occupy the children and give their parents a rest. And now and again a whole family could take the children for a weekend so that the parents can take a complete break. In these and other ways, time could be created for some of the suggestions about family life and friendships that we have discussed.

Footnotes

1. K. Koyama, *op.cit.*, p. 14.
2. Cf. D. Riesman, *Selected Essays from Individualism Reconsidered* (New York: Anchor, 1954) p. 147.
3. K. Lynch, *op.cit.*, p. 119.
4. M. Beach, 'Leisure to Love', *Sojourners* (November, 1979) p. 16.
5. E. Farjeon, 'There Isn't Time', *Out of School* (ed.) D. Saunders (London: Evans, 1972) p. 85.
6. R. Conway, *Land of the Long Weekend*, pp. 2–5.
7. Australian readers may begin with N. Gray, *Compiling Your Family History* (Sydney: Society of Australian Genealogists, 1965) and readers from the United Kingdom with D. Iredale, *Discovering Your Family Tree* (Aylesbury, Bucks: Shire, 1973).
8. C.S. Lewis, *The Four Loves* (London: Collins, 1963) p. 55 ff.
9. It is primarily in biographies of people who belonged to such groups—biographies of groups themselves are few and far between—that the nature and value of friendship comes to light. It is symptomatic of the decline of friendship in modern life that so few books address themselves to the subject. Apart from the chapter in Lewis' book mentioned above, the only serious Christian treatments of which I am aware are: E. Holmes, *Friendship: A Guide to Problems of Human Relationship* (London: SCM, 1959) and L.L. Morris, *Testaments of Love: A Study of Love in the Bible* (Grand Rapids: Eerdmans, 1980) pp. 107–111, 117–119, 260–270. A rare biography of a group of friends has been provided by H. Carpenter, *The Inklings: C.S. Lewis, J.R.R. Tolkien, C. Williams and Their Friends* (Boston: Houghton Mifflin, 1979).
10. C.S. Lewis, *op.cit.*, pp. 83–84.

23

A Revised Shape for the
Church and Christian Organisations

The proliferation of activities in Christian circles over the past century has claimed much of individual Christians' time and energy and severely fractured family life. There are organisations for every conceivable interest that members of congregations may have, from prayer meetings to fetes to sporting clubs. There are groups to cater for all ages and both sexes. There are ecumenical and para-church endeavours. There are evangelistic, charitable, social and intellectual ventures. There are special functions for different ethnic, occupational and disadvantaged groups. Some churches boast that they have some activity on every evening of the week and encourage (pressure) people to come to as many meetings as possible. Often the spirituality and commitment of church members is judged by their level of attendance at such gatherings. If any gaps are left between local church activities, leaders pressure members to attend denominational and inter-denominational organisations.

Such attitudes and practices effectively remove Christians from the wider culture around them. They leave Christians with no time for others. Even where church activities are directed to outsiders, their quality and value are frequently questionable. As Karl Barth points out, insufficient time is given to determining content:

> We certainly cannot print and distribute too much paper for the
> Christian cause. But the question of what is written on this

paper, and whether or how far it is genuinely Christian, demands careful scrutiny, and for this rest is essential so that it might be better to print and distribute less ... The much cited and exercised claim of the Church to speak on public questions is also intrinsically good. But it is again worth considering what has really to be put before the public. Surely we cannot be content either with conventional slogans on the one side or on the other with new demands and programs which have not been scrutinised to see if they are more secular than Christian ... For this kind of examination, rest is necessary :... Conferences, meetings, retreats, weeks of work and even 'schools' are also good in themselves, but only when those who assemble both come from something definite and go towards something definite. But for this rest is needed: otherwise they will not achieve the desired result and the coming together will simply be a useless flight from the void into the void ... All in all, is there not perhaps in our Churches today too much self-encircling movement of all kinds, from which we would do far better to rest for a period ... If we were to do this, we might then work much more earnestly and productively, and in a manner far more impressively Christian. The whole advance of the Church in our day might then become much more imposing and promising than it now seems.[1]

Helmut Thielicke refers to the modern clergymen's 'flight into busywork' as one of the problems here. He also speaks of the international round of confessional and ecumenical gatherings which today catch up so many leading people and devour their energies.[2]

The need for individual discernment and care

If any reduction in activity is to take place, responsibility falls on those who wish to go ahead with time-consuming projects to justify their worth. We have to look more closely at the criteria by which we judge whether we should begin or maintain some activity on God's behalf. The fact that an idea comes into our minds is not sufficient reason for starting something new. Nor is the fact that we see a need around us.[3] To some Christians this attitude is abhorrent: they cite the parable of the Good Samaritan to justify their belief that we must act whenever we see a need. But there is a difference between individual acts of compassion and

long-term schemes set up to meet particular needs. And
remember that in the parable there were no other potential helpers
at hand when the Good Samaritan came along. When I see a need
close by, it may not be my responsibility to try to meet it—responsibility may fall on somebody else. Jesus did not help every
needy person he encountered (cf. Mk. 1:32–38).

The fact that I have the gift to carry out a particular
undertaking is not reason enough for me to initiate something.
The fact that I had good grounds for doing something in the past
is not sufficient justification for my continuing to do it in the
present. Even if the vision, the need, the capacity and the
precedent all occur together, we still need to ensure that *now* is the
time God wishes us to set to work. God is much more prepared
than we are to wait for the propitious moment before signalling us
to proceed. All aspects of a proposed move must be prayed 'into',
not just 'over', allowing God time to give direct confirmation if he
chooses. All too often we implement our own plans, or those of
others we are imitating, not those that issue out of God's mind.
Distinguishing his thoughts from ours is the only way the church
or Christian group can have the singlemindedness God desires of
it.

People invited to participate in a new or already existing
concern must test the rightness of their doing so. First of all, we
need to discern whether the group has sought and received God's
endorsement for their efforts. A rushed invitation to join in some
enterprise, particularly when a decision is required on the spot or
in a very short period of time, probably indicates that something is
astray. An indefinite proposal may also betray problems. Many
Christian organisations simply limp along without a great deal of
purpose, propped up by a few insiders who are reluctant to let
them go or by a range of outsiders who plug gaps in the
programme. Next, we must ask ourselves whether we actually
have the gift we are being invited to contribute. Even if we do,
does someone else have it in greater abundance or would it
provide the opportunity for someone at hand to gain experience?
If a talk is requested, is it on a subject we have genuinely thought
about and personally experienced? Finally, do we have the time to

do justice to the task? Time will be needed to prepare and pray for the project, to follow it through, and to unwind after it.

If all these questions were considered, fewer Christians would have difficulty in saying 'no' to requests. This is one of the greatest difficulties for the Church today. Christians do not know how to say 'no'. Indeed they feel positively guilty if they do so. But, as the abovementioned factors demonstrate, sometimes we must decline. To say 'yes' without considering these factors is as much disobedience as saying 'no' to something we know God wishes us to do!

Churches and other Christian groups need to be more discerning in the demands they make on individuals. The clergy, particularly, should be less pressured—they already have an inordinate burden to carry. Together with their congregations, the clergy should draw up some sort of understanding, perhaps even a written one, which recognises their need for time for relaxation, spiritual refreshment, sermon preparation, general reading and sustained personal reflection. The clergy would not be the only ones to gain.[4] Others involved in full-time Christian activity, eg, leaders of Christian organisations, youth workers, and missionaries would also benefit from a similar arrangement.

There are times in other people's lives when the amount of work they are asked to do should be minimal. For example, students should not be pressured to devote all their energies to congregational activities; churches should recognise that students can have a wider ministry and deeper learning experience by being more fully involved in their educational institutions. For people who have just entered into marriage, the same principle applies; following the wise biblical precedent of relieving a husband of military duty for the first year of his married life, churches should excuse a newly married couple from congregational demands so that they can adjust to their new way of life and establish a foundation for their future family. People going through mid-life problems should also be released from their church commitments so that they can properly re-orient themselves and make a more fruitful Christian contribution throughout the remainder of their lives.

Courtesy 'On Being' magazine

The principle behind these suggestions also works in reverse. Some people have plenty of time on their hands as a result of being unemployed or retired or working only part-time. The churches have a definite responsibility to them. However they should not press them into service simply to fill the gaps in their organisations' programmes. It is better to help them find the work that suits them best or that God has in store for them, whether that be inside the church or outside it. In particular the churches should be at the forefront of defining the nature of work and creating new types of work so that all such people get a better deal in the future.

The role of structural and corporate changes

Apart from making less demands upon members, local churches should reduce the plethora of organisations that meet under their auspices. They could dissolve most of the organisations which parallel or copy others outside the church. A number of previously first-rate organisations which started life on a firm Christian base, eg, the Boy Scout and Girl Guide movements, the Y.M.C.A. and Y.W.C.A., have been weakened by the withdrawal of Christians into poorer denominational imitations. Much less time and effort would have been required to strengthen the non-church groups than to set up and maintain competing ones within the church. Where legitimate church-related activities do exist members should bear in mind the possibility that their programmes will have only a limited existence. Many local church and denominational programmes, committees, organisations and buildings should be of a temporary character, fulfilling a specific purpose or channelling a particular set of gifts then quietly coming to an end. All Christian activities should come up for periodic review and be required to justify their continued existence. Indeed there are reasonable grounds for making most, if not all, church organisations provisional affairs, set up for a one to three year period, after which a full review of their value and of alternative ways of achieving the same objects would take place. There is also a strong case for the principle that a new organisation can only come into existence if an old one comes to an end. If you wish to add something, you must make room for it by subtracting something else.

Christians should consider building up alternatives to replace some existing structures.[5] For example, the introduction of house church groups into the local church in time permits the dissolution—or at least scaling down—of a large number of organisations that cluster around the average congregation.[6] One weekly, four-or-five-hour house church gathering incorporates most of what takes place in Sunday school, men's and women's fellowships, the Bible study group, prayer and charismatic meetings, and pastoral and cluster groups. It relieves the minister of much of his enormous pastoral burden. It enables members to become deeply involved, in a personal, helpful way, with one another. It permits time (at other stages of the week) with family, friends and God. It helps people work through their problems in a supportive, directive atmosphere, making them freer to help others who are in need. There are other advantages in this way of meeting. Fellow believers should be able to help each other work through their present time pressures, negotiate the various life stages that individuals enter, and cope with problems like unemployment or retirement.[7]

Churches should also help people to view time differently. Preaching and teaching a Christian understanding of time will help in a small way. Living a different style of life would go much further. Enabling people to taste a new quality of time would help even more. Christians should be experimenting with the possibilities of creative freedom. Jurgen Moltmann advises Christian congregations to arrange different activities to the educational and service-oriented ones that presently dominate:

> By this we do not mean the kinds of conversation, fellowship and games which only serve to provide the necessary relaxation from the tensions caused by the excessive demands of day-to-day living. This is also important but not yet free. But it does mean that at these points we try to ... encourage productive imagination ... bring back to light man's repressed spontaneity.[8]

One time where this should happen is during the church's 'worship' or in smaller 'fellowship' meetings. Among the branches of Christendom it is only the Orthodox Church which has preserved some understanding of this, though in part the Charismatic movement has begun to rediscover it. Orthodox worship lasts several hours, commencing only when people have gathered and concluding when it has run its leisurely course. Charismatic meetings may start according to the clock and follow a certain form but they contain some flexibility as to how long will be spent on each aspect of worship. In worship we enter into God's time, heavenly time, the time of the Kingdom of God and eternal life. What we do together should be allowed to take its own time; the commencement, length and order of the elements in our gatherings should flow as God's Spirit, not our artificial watch-time, directs. We should all take off our watches and leave them at the door for there is no need for clock-time in church.

From one point of view, church is a corporate 'holiday' with God. The leisurely fellowship which many people enjoy once a year at a Parish Weekend, Camp or Houseparty should—and could—be a weekly experience in church for all. This is certainly possible in smaller 'house church' gatherings as any who have experienced life in one will testify. In a different way it is also possible in larger meetings of the 'whole church'. But we would need to look more radically at why and how we can best fellowship with God and each other during such times for this to take place. Our present buildings and forms of worship do not allow for this as much as they should. There is no reason why sometimes we should not meet outdoors and celebrate our life together in the open air. My own church makes use of a local park now and again precisely for this purpose. We can vary the nature of our meeting as much as the place. In particular we need to find ways of celebrating our life in Christ in more spontaneous and uninhibited ways.[9]

As a final word here about the busy round of denominational and ecumenical gatherings, Helmut Thielicke has some wise things to say:

> We should not neglect the cultivation of contacts and encounters. The Body of Christ must be constantly re-experiencing its oneness in all its many members and also in its geographical dimensions. The only question is whether this

task could not be met in quite other ways. My own experiences in a fairly large number of countries have led me to the view that one should send to other churches and other parts of the world men and women who will perform under ecumenical auspices certain *tasks*, such as preaching, lecturing, helping to establish institutions. We learn to know one another only by working in a common cause.[10]

The same principle could be applied in some measure at the local level to the perennial round of conferences and committees as well.

Conclusion

So, then, churches and other Christian groups can make a significant contribution to their members' time problems. Rather than adding to the burdens already imposed upon members by society, they can—like Jesus—place upon them a yoke which is easy and a burden which is light, one that will give rest to their souls (Matt. 11:29–30). But churches should not only seek to lighten the time-load of others. They should also seek to enhance their use of time. Meetings of the church and other Christian gatherings provide an excellent opportunity for this. They could become a model, or at least a stimulus, for changes in all kinds of other meetings that we attend. In a modified way, some of the principles and character of a genuinely communal church life can be translated into the most secular settings and institutions.[11] Local churches and para-church groups can also give their members a more integrated sense of time. They can do this by creating a greater sense of continuity between past and present in the life of their church or organisation. To write a brief history of a local church or group, or encourage older members to tell stories about the past, is important. When this is done, today's conservative church officers sometimes turn out to be yesterday's experimenters or radicals. This enables different generations to view one another in a new light.

We all have much to learn in these and in other areas. It will take time for us to do so. At points the difficulties will seem all too overwhelming and progress frustratingly slow. But the results are worth the effort and those who come after us will appreciate what we have done. Some of us may hear the call to start experimenting now, on the borders of mainline church life, where the going is easier. But we can all begin somewhere, and we can all begin now.

Footnotes

1. K. Barth, *op.cit.*, pp. 557–558.
2. H. Thielicke, *The Trouble with the Church* (Grand Rapids: Baker, 1965) pp. 81–83.
3. On this, see the earlier remarks by C. Hummel, *op.cit.*, p. 5.
4. Cf. D. and V. Mace, *op.cit.*, pp. 61–71.
5. For a thoughtful discussion of the possibilities see L.O. Richards, *A New Face for the Church* (Grand Rapids: Zondervan, 1970) and C. Olsen, *The Base Church: Creating Community Through Multiple Forms* (Atlanta: Forum House, 1973). Relevant too is the phenomenon of base communities in the Catholic church. See, for example, the report on *Basic Communities in the Church*, Pro Mundi Vita Bulletin, 62 (September, 1976).
6. I have discussed the way in which the contribution of house churches would benefit the local church in R. Banks, 'Small is Beautiful: The Relevance of Paul's Idea of Community to Local Church Life Today', *Zadok Paper* (Series 2), No. T18 (1983).
7. Cf. J. McInnes, *op.cit.*, p. 25.
8. J. Moltmann, *Theology and Joy*, p. 85. A fuller discussion of Moltmann's view of the church may be found in his booklet *The Open Church* (London: SCM, 1979) or, more fully still, in his book *The Church in the Power of the Spirit* (London: SCM, 1979).
9. Cf. J. Vanier, *Community and Growth* (Sydney: St. Paul, 1979) pp. 237–249.
10. H. Thielicke, *op.cit.*, p. 83.
11. Further to this see R. Banks, 'The Early Church as a Caring Community and Some Implications for Social Work Today', *Interchange* 30 (1982) pp. 32–46.

24

A More Relaxed Attitude to Work and Leisure

We need to make greater attempts to bring work and leisure rhythms into harmony with the inner tempo of our personal lives. Those who have a say in the physical settings we live in and temporal schedules we live by at work and in our leisure should consider our inner rhythms.

> An architect who treats his own bodily needs and emotional responses as an annoying impediment to the rapid completion of his task is unlikely to design a building that is pleasurable to live in. The same may be said of planners, executives, technologists, teachers, parents and so on.[1]

Such people should be aware of people's varying rhythms (rhythms differ between men and women, between different ethnic groups, between people of different ages). Significant people in the community need to take these variations into account in their planning, employing, inventing and teaching. Perhaps the most important contribution they can make to the work situation is to loosen our rigid time patterns and give people more timing choices. Individuals should be given more opportunity to create their own time orders, orders suited to their constitutions, temperaments and situations.[2] Community leaders can also help to improve the leisure situation. They should aim to stimulate more grass-roots participation in various leisure activities and seek to encourage larger social celebrations to take place. But all of us have a responsibility to press for changes in our time at work and leisure.

Diversifying work patterns

Flexi-time, permanent part-time work and slightly reduced working hours have already partially loosened our work-time patterns. While the flexi-time does not increase the quantity of time a person has at his or her disposal, it does improve the quality of both work and free time. If more flexi-time could be accumulated and taken as time away from work, its value would increase. Part-time work increases the quantity and quality of free time. It is the most significant social change relating to work since women began to enter the labour force in large numbers. A modest lowering of working hours, especially for women raising families, has occurred in a few places. If a general reduction in working hours is introduced abruptly without accompanying alterations in attitudes to free time, it may not improve the quality of leisure but only increase the amount of time spent in consumption and household production.[3]

There is room for greater flexibility than these innovations provide. Why not a variable working day and week? We could stagger working hours in different occupations, or offer workers more choice in arranging their working habits. There could be more permanent part-time work and job-sharing. The introduction of a general shortened working day and week would suit people with families, and employees could be allowed greater freedom to choose the days they would like to work. Studies in places where some of these reforms have been tested show that they are appreciated only if introduced on a large scale; otherwise there are insufficient opportunities for socialising when not at work to make the gains in flexibility and free time worthwhile.[4] There could also be a more varied approach to how and when annual holidays are taken, both for workers and students.[5] Making long-service available to all workers would open the way to periodic mini-sabbaticals for all. We could do with more flexible arrangements for entering the workforce, much as tertiary institutions do not insist on an immediate transition from school to further study. Graduated retirement would be welcomed by many just as early retirement schemes have been eagerly seized by some. Flexible life scheduling would also enable men and women to alternate periods at work, at home and in continuing education.[6] At present too many people still follow the fixed single career or set sex-role patterns.

More flexible transport routes and schedules are needed. We should consider mini-bus runs with routes and timings worked out according to 'phone-in requests; alternative types of transport, with varying speeds to fit different travel needs; timetabling to take account of bodily rhythms and needs, with more regular halts on long-distance journeys. Some of these recommendations are already in operation in various parts of the world.[7] But most helpful of all would be a decentralisation programme giving rise to a large number of small cities. This would cut down the amount of time spent commuting and allow for more flexible timing arrangements. Even a more equitable spread of work opportunities in our present over-sized cities would alleviate some transport problems.

All these proposals seek to free people from needless restrictions and allow them to shape their own lives. None by itself is a panacea. Those in positions of responsibility should proceed on several fronts at once, after careful consideration of the alternatives and their short-term and long-term repercussions.[8] But they need to beware of the inadequacies that purely managerial or bureaucratic schemes possess. The most realistic new timing patterns will arise out of experiments conducted by small groups.[9] It would be nice to see Christian individuals in executive and senior management positions or small firms with a predominantly Christian workforce providing a lead.

Having said all this, we have to remember that such changes will be largely cosmetic unless a fundamental shift in values takes place. If we do not lower our materialistic expectations and adopt a less addictive, self-justificatory attitude to work, changes in work and commuting patterns will merely improve distribution of the time at our disposal; they will not help us generate the extra time we so desperately need. In the area of values and priorities,

Christians could play an influential role, not only by defining them but by setting an example to others. Widespread changes in social attitudes often arise from the practice of committed minority groups.

Jobs would take on a more natural tempo if people's responsibilities were better fitted to their capacities, if complementary activities were linked, if tasks were carried out in a logical sequence, and if enough time of the right kind was allocated to each undertaking. In many work situations there is room for self-pacing by individuals and groups. Ninety-minute work patterns which harmonise with people's internal rhythms could be introduced by allowing more breaks in the working day or rotating tasks on a ninety-minute basis. Following up the benefits derived from the introduction of summer-time, seasonal variations in the number of hours worked (more in winter, less in summer) could be made available. And why should we judge work by time spent rather than by results achieved? We could allow the person who has accomplished his day's work by lunchtime to take the remainder of the day off.

Relevant also are the practical guidelines laid down by time-management consultants. We should analyse where our time goes, set goals and priorities, understand the primacy of function over tasks. We can frame action plans, guidelines and schedules. We ought to delegate work, where possible, fulfil important demands rather than urgent ones, deal with time-wasting activities, and follow-up and evaluate all that has been accomplished.[10] To these suggestions we can add whatever lessons we have learned by experience. For example, we need to come to terms with the fact that things always take longer than we expect and that unexpected intrusions will always happen. Translated into practical terms this means that tasks will generally take one-and-a-half to two times longer than we initially reckon.

Fitting our capacities to our responsibilities may mean drastic change. I may decide that, rather than reaching the top of my field or going high up the promotional ladder, I prefer to stop at a particular level. This allows me to continue to use my real gifts rather than taking on more and more administrative burdens. It also prevents me entering into an ever busier, more mobile work routine which jeopardises my home life and leisure. People in senior positions may choose to demote themselves—as has already happened in some universities—or they may transfer to lower status, lower-paid positions in order to find time for other things. Those who elect to stay where they are, and those who have no choice in the matter, often have a real time struggle on their hands. They may feel constrained, for instance, to work longer hours than are strictly required, generally without benefit of overtime or time off in lieu. If such people insist on working only the statutory hours, this may lower their standing in the eyes of their colleagues; it may even cost them their jobs. If they do not, working longer hours will gradually become the norm. Unless a few begin to take a stand somewhere we will no longer have to cope with individual workaholics but a compulsory institutional workaholism. Employees in the service of totalitarian regimes often seek to preserve their moral integrity, even at the cost of losing their jobs or being imprisoned; similarly, people facing totalitarian demands from employers or work structures must seek to preserve their personal freedom.

Because of these pressures, some people choose to take up what Ivan Illich calls 'the right to useful unemployment'.[11] They decide to relinquish their full-time jobs and search out alternative activities which are more personally, socially and spiritually edifying. Sometimes this involves the creation of a job de novo which sustains them financially at a modest level. Sometimes unpaid activity may be combined with part-time, occasional or intermittent paid employment. Sometimes it takes the form of working with a voluntary organisation for meagre rewards. Such a step should not be taken lightly. We need to be certain that we are doing the right thing in God's eyes. In most cases such a decision means opting for simpler, low-cost housing, food and transport. Many people shy away from making such a decision because of the financial insecurity involved. Yet it is feasible even in our inflation-ridden societies; most of us could live comfortably on a good deal less than we presently earn. And the gains in time are inestimable.

Enriching leisure activities

We need to learn to celebrate our leisure. Unfortunately we are not very good at celebrating at all in our individualistic Western societies. Even the biggest and best of our festivals have something artificial about them. Unlike the participants in Latin-American carnivals and Mediterranean feast days, we tend to remain passive. Such celebrations have never really developed on Australian or English soil. Americans do better, as do ethnic or coloured groups in all three countries. But we should want to celebrate time, not simply organise it.

In previous societies, social and religious rituals provided one of the main bridges between past and present, as well as opportunities for 'a really good time'. Nowadays, once you take away the struggling City Festival or Easter Show, which have little historical content anyway, such rituals are largely non-existent and affect only a proportion of the population. Religious rituals certainly continue but, like the persistence of the Harvest Festival, link us up only with a pre-industrial not our own more recent past, and do so in a less than exhilarating way. But we all need special happenings, which contain a shared, vivid present enlarged by group expectations and memories. Important national and city events in which *all* can take part, and not only look on, are important. So are suburban, street and neighbourhood gatherings. We should have observances to mark the change of the seasons, eg, the coming of spring and the onset of autumn. And we should give special attention to important life stages: birth, attainment of adulthood, marriage, residential moves, retirement, and death.[12]

We need to be developing new social rituals and revivifying existing ones, not simply resurrecting old rituals which are no longer appropriate to our way of life. The church can make a significant contribution here. In churches people are already meeting together and acting in accord with one another; this can provide a basis for rediscovering the social-ritual dimension to living as well as for engaging in more specifically religious celebrations. In both whole church and house church meetings we should look for opportunities to do this. Special times in the year, special moments in the lives of individuals, and special events in the life of the group, can all become the occasion for the development of natural, contemporary rituals.

Our regular periods of recreation should include meditation, prayer, appreciation of God's world, culture, creative activities (individual and group) and participatory, non-competitive games. Given the hectic pace most people experience during the week, there is much to be said for the Jewish and Seventh Day Adventist custom of keeping one day a week completely free from our ordinary activities. While I do not see any purely theological, New Testament justification for this practice, there are practical reasons in favour of it. It involves a complete break from the rhythms of the work-a-day world and gives our bodies, nerves and spirits 'breathing space' from it. Those who have practised this for some time know how much delight it brings and can testify to its restorative value.[13] During recreation periods, friendship and good company enrich our hearts, minds, emotions and spirits.

There is value, too, in sheer idleness—however difficult we may find it at first to just 'do nothing'. Anyone who has a problem here should remember the advice of the Chinese philosopher Lin Yutang who said 'it is amazing how people are conscious of the importance of lying in bed' or turn to G.K. Chesterton's delightful little essay on the subject. Chesterton speaks of lying-in as a 'beautiful experiment' and a 'great art' which is wrongly condemned by the majority as 'hypocritical and unhealthy'. He feels sure that 'it was from persons in this position that all the original inspiration came for covering the ceilings of palaces and cathedrals'. Chesterton says lying in bed can be a sure indicator of a person who has strong ideals and is able to be flexible in minor matters. 'I dare say', he reflects, 'that when I get out of this bed I shall do some deed of an almost terrible virtue.' He concludes: '[T]here is one emphatic caution to be added ... if you do lie in bed, be sure you do it without any reason or justification at all'.[14]

That is the paradox. As we yield ourselves up to moments of genuine idleness or leisurely, carefree play, intellectual, moral and spiritual vigour are infused. Karl Jaspers rightly described freedom to do nothing as 'the source of everything essential'.[15] To be able to 'take time' for this purpose is actually one of our great cultural

Meet me in the sun-shine   Meet me in the rain.
heard the Father call-ing as He reached down from above

Come and share my laugh-ter   Come and heal my pain. And
You need no great a-chievements to earn my precious love. So

when the day is   end-ed   and time has slipped away   I'll
when my life is   ov-er   and my time is finally thru'   In

still find breath to praise you and I'll still have time to pray.
everything I want to say I   did it Lord   for you.

Time to say I   love you   Time to know you're there.

Time to vis-it   neighbours and show them that I care

Time to find the   answers   Time to write the   songs

Time to get to know myself and see where I   belong.   2. I've
                                                          1.
Verse 2 modulating to E   J. Vincent

achievements, quite apart from whether anything profitable comes out of it.[16] It demonstrates that we are not bound to the necessity of labour, nor tied to the demands of our own organism. It is a sign that we are not made for work but that work is made for us. Thomas Merton saw this very clearly:

> What is serious to man is often very trivial in the sight of God. What in God might appear to us as 'play' is perhaps what he himself takes most seriously ... the Lord plays and diverts himself in the garden of his creation, and ... we are invited to forget ourselves on purpose, cast our awful solemnity to the winds and join in ...[17]

If only we could join in we would enjoy a foretaste of that wonderful, playful, love-full, time-full world to come—a world where distinctions between work and leisure, effort and relaxation, activity and meditation will be finally overcome.

Conclusion

In the meantime we continue to live in a provisional world. Everything is not as we would like and at times there is not a great deal we can do about it. We cannot all find the work we would like. Improving our working conditions is not always a possibility. Taking radical steps to create alternative employment may not be an option, at least for the time being. Other factors intrude—personal and institutional—and circumscribe our actions. Life is a struggle and there does not seem any foreseeable end to it. In such a situation, we can only make the most of our situation, work for change in whatever quiet or modest way is open to us, and take heart from the fact that those who come after us may not have it so difficult. Times of leisure then become even more important. Instead of using them merely to compensate for the drabness or regulation of our working hours, we should seek to preserve some time for more creative, challenging and fulfilling activities. And allow time for idleness, just 'messing around' and quiet reflection.

In any case, and this may stand over all we have said in these closing chapters, no matter how far we free ourselves from the tyranny of time and redirect ourselves towards the things that matter most, no matter how much we appreciate the world about us and the ordinary events of which each day is made up, no matter how far we enter into the lives of others and into the heart of God himself, our experience of these things is temporary and partial. If we are fortunate we may have 'three score years and ten', but that is scarcely enough time in which to realise all that we would like to do and to savour all that we would like to enjoy. Increasingly, as life wears on, the expectation of death dims our hopes and discourages our efforts. No matter how well we deal with time pressures, eventually time runs out for us.[18] There is something lacking in even the most satisfying of our achievements on God's behalf, and in the most fulfilling of our experiences. Such achievements and experiences give us a sense of a different kind of time, but they are always incomplete and never quite long enough to grant us what we desire.[19] These limitations on our best earthly times remind us how precious life is, and how thankfully and wisely we should chart our way through it. Also how provisional our present existence is, and how genuinely and longingly we should look forward to the life beyond. In the new world of God's making we will at last experience the completion and rest which we long for in this life but glimpse only now and then.

Footnotes

1. Philip Slater, quoted in K. Lynch, op.cit., p. 35. In his book Lynch gives many examples of the sorts of things city councils, town planners and private developers could do to bring this about.
2. So H. Allenspach, Flexible Working Hours (Geneva: International Labor Organisation, 1975). On this particular subject see further S.J. Baum and W. McEwan Young, A Practical Guide to Flexible Working Hours (London: Kogan Page, 1973).
3. See J.D. Owen, op.cit., pp. 123–134.
4. A.A. Evans, Hours of Work in Industrial Countries (Geneva: International Labor Organisation, 1975) pp. 35–88.
5. See the Final Report of the International Conference on New Patterns of Working Time (Paris: OECD, 1972).

6. J. de Chalendar, *Lifelong Allocation of Time* (Paris: OECD, 1976) pp. 1–41. Cf. A.A. Evans, *op.cit.*, pp. 15–34, 89–109.

7. Cf. T. Bendixson, *Instead of Cars* (London: Temple Smith, 1974) pp. 127–140.

8. See further D. Maric, *Adapting Hours to Modern Needs: The Time Factor in the New Approach to Working Conditions* (Geneva: International Labor Organisation, 1977).

9. K. Lynch, *op.cit.*, p. 76.

10. See further J.D. Ferner, *Successful Time-Management* (New York: Wiley, 1979). Other books on the subject are cited in the footnotes to chapter 4. One of the most helpful, and accessible, is by a world-renowned figure in the time-management field who also happens to be a Christian: R.A. Mackenzie, *The Time Trap: How to Get More Done in Less Time* (New York: McGraw Hill, 1972).

11. I. Illich, *The Right to Useful Unemployment and Its Professional Enemies* (London: Marion Boyars, 1978). See also, though less radically, some of the suggestions in E.F. Schumacher, *Good Work* (London: Sphere, 1980).

12. K. Lynch, *op.cit.*, p. 88.

13. See on this S. Bacchiochi, *Divine Rest and Human Restlessness* (Rome: Gregorian University, 1980).

14. G.K. Chesterton, 'On Lying in Bed', *Eight Essayists*, ed. D. Cairncross (London: Macmillan, 1940) pp. 209–213.

15. K. Jaspers, in his philosophical autobiography, translated from the 1977 German edition, p. 63.

16. H.M. Barth, *Fulfilment* (London: SCM, 1980) pp. 95–96.

17. Thomas Merton, *Seeds of Contemplation* (Norfolk: New Directions, 1949) p. 230.

18. Cf. R. McAfee Brown, 'Making friends with time is for those who want a fuller life', *Canadian Churchman* (September, 1981) p. 5.

19. This feeling is beautifully and movingly captured in S. Vanauken, *A Severe Mercy* (London: Hodder and Stoughton, 1977) esp. p. 198 ff. For a theological discussion on human temporality, see K. Barth, *Church Dogmatics: Vol. III, 2—The Doctrine of Creation* (Edinburgh: T. & T. Clark, 1960) pp. 511–572.

Epilogue

The time has come for judgment to
begin with the household of God.
1 Pet. 4:17

We hear a good deal about shortages of one kind or another these days, even in the affluent West. There is no longer enough work for everyone and unemployment has become a fact of life. Energy shortages have also become a regular occurrence. Disruptions in the supply of foods and raw materials are common. And with the steady urban drift in almost every country, lack of space in cities is a critical problem. These are the shortages everyone is talking about. The newspapers are full of them day after day.

Yet none of these shortages compares with the desperate scarcity of *time* in Western societies. The consequences of this shortage affect every aspect of life. Most of us have so conditioned ourselves to the ravages of our way of life that we exhibit resigned acceptance rather than vigorous rejection. We are losing the capacity to diagnose the problem, let alone prescribe a solution. Some symptoms of our malaise are too intrusive to be overlooked, but we have become so accustomed to others that we do not even realise we have them. Like someone who has been in poor health for as long as they can remember, we scarcely know what we are lacking; we see our state as normal. Even when we do recognise the symptoms, we tend to attribute them to the wrong causes. We regard our problems as an intrinsic part of modern life about which nothing can be done, or we frantically treat the symptoms: in other words we either wince and bear it or run around in circles getting nowhere!

As Christians we are unwilling to face up to the fact that our way of looking at time and our everyday use of it are virtually identical with the attitudes and behaviour of those about us. Any differences are superficial and tend to intensify the problem rather than alleviate it. Christians have uncritically absorbed the spirit of the age. We have allowed the world to squeeze us into its mould. We have betrayed our vocation to be different. We have failed to provide a genuine alternative to the stifling pressures of modern society.

This is why 'the time has come for judgment to begin with the household of God'. Unless we start to change now, there will come a time when it will be too late to do so. Too late because our way of life will have become habitual. Too late because others will have already suffered too much as a result of our obsessive regulation and haste. Too late because God will have given us up to our own desires.

More poignantly than anywhere else in modern literature, we are brought face to face with our dilemma in Thornton Wilder's beautifully crafted play *Our Town*. Though set in rural America at the turn of the century it hauntingly captures the time problems we all have, especially in our relationships. It is a story about an ordinary couple—their youth, marriage and its aftermath. Towards the close of the play Emily, the 'heroine' of the story, dies in childbirth at a young age but is given the opportunity to return in wraith-like form to her previous body and home. Given a choice of times to 'relive', she fastens on one of her happiest moments, her twelfth birthday. At first she is enchanted with the appearance of the town of her youth. Then she is torn by the disparity between the youth of her parents and her knowledge of their future ageing. And she feels anguish that the precious moments of interaction between herself and her parents were then treated casually. 'Oh, Mama', she cries out, while her mother is chattering, 'just look at me one minute as though you really saw me just for a moment now we're all together. Mama, just for a moment we're happy. *Let's look at one another.*' Her mother cannot hear her plea and moves on to attend to something else. The pattern continues, with exchanges between the two taking place but her mother not really giving Emily her genuine attention. A little later Emily bursts out: 'I can't. I can't go on. It goes so fast we don't have time to look at one another.' She breaks down sobbing. On stage the lights dim. 'I didn't realise', Emily cries to herself. 'So all that was going on and we never noticed.' Further on again she asks: 'Do any human beings ever realise life while they live it?—every, every minute?' And when she returns to the graveyard, another resident bitingly cries: 'Yes, now you know. Now you know! That's what it was to be alive. To move about in a cloud of ignorance; to go up and down trampling on the feelings ... of those about you. To spend and waste time as though you had a million years.' Though his remarks are partly qualified by some of the others, Emily nevertheless finally asks a neighbour: 'They don't understand, do they?', and receives the reply: 'No, dear ... they don't understand'.[1]

If they didn't understand then, in that leisurely day and place, how much less do we understand now in our more regulated, accelerated world? It is not too late yet, but something needs to be done. Now, of all times, it is time to do something about time.

Footnote
1. T. Wilder, *Our Town and Other Plays* (Harmondsworth: Penguin, 1962) pp. 88–90.